Rethinking Media Research for Changing Societies

This agenda-setting volume brings together leading scholars of media and public life to grapple with how media research can make sense of the massive changes rocking politics and the media world. Each author identifies a "most pressing" question for scholars working at the intersection of journalism, politics, advocacy, and technology. The authors then suggest different research approaches designed to highlight real-world stakes and offer a path toward responsive, productive action. Chapters explore our "datafied" lives, journalism's deep responsibilities and daunting challenges, media's inclusions (and non-inclusions), the riddle of digital engagement, and the obligations scholars must attempt to meet in an era of networked information. The result is a rich forum that addresses how media transformations carry serious implications for public life. Original, provocative, and generative, this book is international in its orientation and makes a compelling case for public scholarship.

Matthew Powers is Associate Professor of Communication and Co-Director of the Center for Journalism, Media and Democracy at the University of Washington. He is the author of *NGOs as Newsmakers* (2018). Currently, he is working with Sandra Vera-Zambrano on a book entitled *What Journalists Are For*.

Adrienne Russell is Mary Laird Wood Professor and Co-Director of the Center for Journalism, Media and Democracy at the University of Washington. She is the author of *Networked* (2011) and *Journalism as Activism* (2016), and a co-editor of *Journalism and the NSA Revelations* (2017) and *International Blogging: Identity, Politics and Networked Publics* (2009).

T0371320

Communication, Society and Politics

Editor
W. Lance Bennett, University of Washington

Founding Co-Editor, Emeritus
Robert M. Entman, The George Washington University

Politics and relations among individuals in societies across the world are being transformed by new technologies for targeting individuals and sophisticated methods for shaping personalized messages. The new technologies challenge boundaries of many kinds – between news, information, entertainment, and advertising; between media, with the arrival of the World Wide Web; and even between nations. Communication, Society and Politics probes the political and social impacts of these new communication systems in national, comparative, and global perspective.

Other Books in the Series

Erik Albæk, Arjen van Dalen, Nael Jebril, and Claes de Vreese, *Political Journalism in Comparative Perspective*

Eva Anduiza, Michael James Jensen, and Laia Jorba, eds., *Digital Media and Political Engagement Worldwide: A Comparative Study*

C. Edwin Baker, *Media Concentration and Democracy: Why Ownership Matters*

C. Edwin Baker, *Media, Markets, and Democracy*

W. Lance Bennett and Robert M. Entman, eds., *Mediated Politics: Communication in the Future of Democracy*

Rodney Benson, *Shaping Immigration News: A French-American Comparison*

Bruce Bimber, *Information and American Democracy: Technology in the Evolution of Political Power*

Bruce Bimber, Andrew Flanagin, and Cynthia Stohl, *Collective Action in Organizations: Interaction and Engagement in an Era of Technological Change*

Clifford G. Christians *Media Ethics and Global Justice in the Digital Age*

Lynn S. Clark and Regina Marchi, *Young People and the Future of News*

Peter Dahlgren, *Media and Political Engagement, Citizens, Communication and Democracy*

Murray Edelman, *The Politics of Misinformation*

Frank Esser and Barbara Pfetsch, eds., *Comparing Political Communication: Theories, Cases, and Challenges*

Myra Marx Ferree, William Anthony Gamson, Jürgen Gerhards, and Dieter Rucht, *Shaping Abortion Discourse: Democracy and the Public Sphere in Germany and the United States*

Hernan Galperin, *New Television, Old Politics: The Transition to Digital TV in the United States and Britain*

Tim Groeling, *When Politicians Attack: Party Cohesion in the Media*

(continued at the end of the book)

Rethinking Media Research for Changing Societies

Edited by

MATTHEW POWERS

University of Washington

ADRIENNE RUSSELL

University of Washington

CAMBRIDGE UNIVERSITY PRESS

CAMBRIDGE
UNIVERSITY PRESS

University Printing House, Cambridge CB2 8BS, United Kingdom

One Liberty Plaza, 20th Floor, New York, NY 10006, USA

477 Williamstown Road, Port Melbourne, VIC 3207, Australia

314–321, 3rd Floor, Plot 3, Splendor Forum, Jasola District Centre,
New Delhi – 110025, India

79 Anson Road, #06–04/06, Singapore 079906

Cambridge University Press is part of the University of Cambridge.

It furthers the University's mission by disseminating knowledge in the pursuit of
education, learning, and research at the highest international levels of excellence.

www.cambridge.org
Information on this title: www.cambridge.org/9781108840514
DOI: 10.1017/9781108886260

First published 2020

A catalogue record for this publication is available from the British Library.

Library of Congress Cataloging-in-Publication Data
NAMES: Powers, Matthew, editor. | Russell, Adrienne, editor. | Cambridge University
Press.
TITLE: Rethinking media research for changing societies / edited by Matthew Powers,
University of Washington, Adrienne Russell, University of Washington.
OTHER TITLES: Communication, society, and politics.
DESCRIPTION: First Edition. | New York : Cambridge University Press, 2020. | Series:
Communication, society and politics
IDENTIFIERS: LCCN 2020025145 | ISBN 9781108840514 (Hardback) | ISBN
9781108886260 (eBook)
SUBJECTS: LCSH: Communication in politics. | Mass media – Political aspects. | Mass
media – Social aspects. | Social media – Political aspects. | Mass media – Influence.
CLASSIFICATION: LCC JA85 .R466 2020 | DDC 320.01/4–dc23
LC record available at https://lccn.loc.gov/2020025145

ISBN 978-1-108-84051-4 Hardback
ISBN 978-1-108-81418-8 Paperback

Contents

Figure

Contributors

Melissa Aronczyk Associate Professor of Media Studies, Rutgers University

Rodney Benson Departmental Chair and Professor in the Department of Media, Culture, and Communication, New York University

Lynn Schofield Clark Chair of the Department of Media, Film and Journalism Studies and Director of Estlow International Center for Journalism and New Media, University of Denver

Stephanie Craft Professor and Head of the Department of Journalism, University of Illinois at Urbana-Champaign

Nick Couldry Professor of Media, Communications and Social Theory, London School of Economics and Political Science

Nabil Echchaibi Associate Professor and Chair of Media Studies and Associate Director of the Center for Media, Religion and Culture, University of Colorado Boulder

Daniel C. Hallin Distinguished Professor in the Department of Communication, University of California at San Diego

Seth C. Lewis Professor and Shirley Papé Chair in Emerging Media, School of Journalism and Communication, University of Oregon

Morten Stinus Kristensen PhD candidate at the Institute of Communications Research, University of Illinois at Urbana-Champaign

Charlton McIlwain Professor of Media, Culture, and Communication and Vice Provost for Faculty Engagement and Development, New York University

Matthew Powers Associate Professor in the Department of Communication and Co-Director of the Center for Journalism, Media and Democracy, University of Washington

Adrienne Russell Mary Laird Wood Professor in the Department of Communication and Co-Director of the Center for Journalism, Media and Democracy, University of Washington

Sandra Vera-Zambrano Académico de tiempo in the Department of Communication, Universidad Iberoamericana, Mexico City

Silvio Waisbord Director and Professor in the School of Media and Public Affairs, George Washington University

Hartmut Wessler Professor of Media and Communication Studies, University of Mannheim

Guobin Yang Grace Lee Boggs Professor of Communication and Sociology, University of Pennsylvania

Bilge Yesil Associate Professor of Media Culture at the College of Staten Island and Doctoral Faculty of Middle Eastern Studies at the Graduate Center, City University of New York

Acknowledgments

This book came together through conversations first sparked at the Shifting Landscape of Public Communication Symposium held at the University of Washington in October 2018. The event was made possible through the generous financial and logistical support from the University of Washington's Simpson Center for the Humanities and the Department of Communication. An enormous thanks to all of the symposium participants, who are also the contributors to this volume. Thanks all of you for bringing your ideas, research, energy, time, critical feedback, and good humor to the project. We would also like to express our appreciation to Rian Wanstreet for her careful and skillful work organizing the symposium and performing edits of the book in its early stages. Thanks also to Luyue Ma and Kyle Kubler for their logistical support during the conference and to Megan Jeffrey and Jasmine Wang for making sure it all went off without a hitch. And thanks to the symposium "mini-seminar" students for their lively engagement and thoughtful commentaries on core themes and issues in advance of the conference. We would also like to express appreciation to the Helen Riaboff Whiteley Center for providing us with an incredibly beautiful and quiet space in which to work.

Many University of Washington colleagues served as commentators on the papers presented in this volume. For their engaging questions and thoughtful feedback, we thank Michael Blake, David Domke, Kirsten Foot, Stephen Groening, Christine Harold, Benjamin Mako Hill, Divya McMillin, Margaret O'Mara, Katy Pearce, Sarah Quinn, Kate Starbird, Doug Underwood, and Ekin Yasin.

At Cambridge University Press, we would like to thank Lance Bennett for his help in focusing the project, especially in the early stages, Sara Doskow for shepherding the book through the editorial process, and Anjana Karikal Cholan for careful copy-editing. Two anonymous reviewers provided insightful commentaries during this period, and the book is better because of them.

And thanks finally to Ekin Yasin and John Tomasic, the high-spirited taskmasters and ideas generators who helped us with all of it.

I

Introduction

Matthew Powers and Adrienne Russell

The great changes rocking media in the networked era come with profound implications for public life that give new urgency and relevance to the work of media scholars. The evolving practices, platforms, and algorithms that shape digital communication; the dawn of simultaneously massive and precise data-sweeping and -sorting technologies; and the rise of new infrastructures raise questions about how public attention is being steered and toward what ends. Shifts in media industries like journalism, public relations, and marketing give new force to old questions about who produces news and information and for whom. The expanded range of voices seeking to influence public life, overtly and covertly, creates novel forms of potentially liberating and empowering engagement while also thinning the force of established sources of authority, including the news media, scientific research, and political parties. At the same time, growing levels of social polarization, increasing economic inequality, rising authoritarianism, and declining trust in major institutions of public life cast doubt on the potential for media to meaningfully engage individuals across various lines of social difference. In this roiling landscape, to what extent has the work of scholars of media and public life changed? To what extent should it?

There has been no shortage of scholars calling for communication research that does more to make sense of – and engage in debates about – these transformations. Lance Bennett and Barbara Pfetsch have argued that real-world changes in media and public life necessitate a "fundamental rethinking" (2018: 245) of core concepts in the field, rather than the continuation of research on long-studied topics using well-established research methods. Sonia Livingstone has written that the "nature of media power is shifting substantially, along with deeper geopolitical changes," and warns that these developments leave "critical scholarship scrambling to keep up" (2019: 174). Rasmus Nielsen has observed that communication scholars are often "irrelevant" in public debates about issues pertaining to media and public life, and suggests that they do more to engage in "the 'rough process' of public discussion" (2018: 149).

The purpose of this book is to explore how scholars working at the intersections of journalism, politics, and activism make sense of and relate to some of the most pressing issues concerning contemporary developments in media and public life. Each contributor to this volume was asked to identify what they saw as the most pressing issue for scholars of media and public life to engage. By starting from the basis of asking questions, we hope to bring to the fore issues and topics worth knowing, rather than what extant theories, concepts, or methods enable one to know. In doing so, we aim to demonstrate some of the ways that real-world concerns can be translated into scholarly research topics. While the contributors are disparate in their theoretical, empirical, and normative orientations, they agree on the importance of revisiting issues of long-standing concern while also engaging in themes and topics brought into focus by contemporary developments in politics, technology, and culture. Together, the contributors offer a diversity of perspectives on the role scholars can, do, and ought to play in making sense of current developments and demonstrate the strength of strong theoretical frameworks in shaping how scholars perceive and position themselves in relation to research questions.

I.I RECURRENT QUESTIONS ABOUT MEDIA
AND PUBLIC LIFE

Scholars have of course long studied the role media play in public life by considering what media do to people, and what people in turn do with media. As Silvio Waisbord points out in the epilogue to this volume, that work is typically built on normative assumptions about the nexus between media and a well-functioning society. Such assessments are further spurred by perceived crises in public communication that stem from political turmoil, economic crisis, and media transformations. What media? For what public life? Indeed, asking questions about the role of media and public life has always been central to the work of communication scholars. Implicit in these questions is the idea that scholars have something distinctive to add to contemporary discussions of media and public life.

Consider the inaugural issue of *Public Opinion Quarterly*, which in 1937 brought together leading thinkers from across the social sciences, including Harold Lasswell, Paul Lazarsfeld, Robert Merton, and Margaret Mead, and asked them to examine threats and opportunities created by shifts in the media environment. The editorial introduction – penned amid growing concerns about the rise of fascism in Europe – sounded themes not entirely dissimilar from those articulated by many scholars of media and public life today. The editors wrote that the "miraculous improvement of the means of communication" (p. 3) opened up "new dimensions" and "new intensities" that influence how political and economic power are wielded. They noted the growing prevalence of opinion polling conducted by private firms and the implications of such developments for democratic governance: "Private polls are taken on public issues. The fate of representative government grows uncertain" (p. 3). They underscored the growing use of propaganda by governments, even as the rise of "new agencies of mass impression" (radio, motion pictures) created "difficult problems of private editorship and government control" (p. 4). Finally, they highlighted the development of advertising as both "a science and art" as well as the need for businesses to retain public relations support. To the editors, the shifts appeared fundamental and thoroughgoing; their "surging impact upon events become the characteristic of the current age" (p. 3). Then, as now, the question was whether transformations in media served to benefit or to damage public life.

Amid the transformations of their era, the editors emphasized the need to refine concepts, revisit questions, and define the terms of their scholarly engagements. Most obviously, given the journal's title, they sought to refine their understanding of public opinion. "Under these conditions the clearest possible understanding of what public opinion is, how it generates, and how it acts becomes a vital need touching both public and private interest" (*Public Opinion Quarterly*, 1937: 4). But they also sought to revisit core questions about public opinion posed by earlier generations of scholars. With nods to Alexis de Tocqueville and Ferdinand Tönnies, among others, they dedicated themselves to using recent developments to test prior hypotheses and introduce "greater precision of thought and treatment" in their analyses (p. 3). They also articulated a clear position in relation to their objects of analysis. While acknowledging that their research might inform politicians, civic groups, business leaders, and others, they tasked themselves not with "evaluating these proffered causes or of discovering new ones" (p. 4). Rather, they endeavored to strictly maintain a "wholly objective and scientific point of view."

Of course, *Public Opinion Quarterly* and the people around it represented merely one way – and hardly a uniform one at that – of approaching these transformations. The contrast with thinkers associated with the Frankfurt School, a term first used in 1937, is instructive (Horkheimer, 1972). Max Horkheimer and Theodor Adorno (1944), writing as exiles living in North America, sought to explain the "barbarism" wrought in World War II by linking it to long-term historical developments in capitalism and Enlightenment ideals of progress, and more. For them, the chief development in media and public life – though their explanation for the ascent of fascism was broader – was the rise of the "culture industry," and its primary effect was to produce docile and passive citizens rather than engaged and informed citizens. They criticized efforts among scholars to identify invariant universal laws based on cumulative knowledge, which was precisely the sort of knowledge that many of their colleagues at *Public Opinion Quarterly* sought to develop. In its place, they introduced new concepts (culture industry) that could serve as a basis for developing a critical (rather than affirmative) stance vis-à-vis contemporary social arrangements (Horkheimer, 1972). These concepts could help to answer important questions – such as how culture may have influenced the rise of fascism – that built on long-running debates, including those found in the works of Marx, Weber, and Freud. The Frankfurt School also articulated a different sense of engagement than their peers at *Public Opinion Quarterly*. Horkheimer and Adorno were relatively cut off from social movements and offered largely theoretical arguments rather than detailed empirical engagements. At the same time, they argued that emancipation is found in concrete historical circumstances and that part of the role of the scholar was to identify possible steps on the road to liberty.

Questions surrounding how to think about and relate to transformations in media and public life are thus basic to media scholarship, and the answers given are as varied and complex as the scholars who propose them. The examples in preceding paragraphs, however, suggest several more general points regarding scholarly engagement with media and public life that are reflected in this volume. First, engaged scholarship does not stand in binary opposition to disengaged or detached scholarship. As Norbert Elias (1956) once argued, some degree of both involvement and detachment is required for scholarly engagement with any research object. On the one hand, time and distance from the objects they study create the potential for scholars to produce knowledge rather than merely express their opinions. It affords the perspective necessary to theorize a problem, challenge or integrate extant views on that problem, and design and develop research that enables a systematic exploration of the issue. On the other hand, some degree of involvement is needed to identify, conceptualize, and operationalize the topic that one will or does research. Knowing where to look, and what to examine, depends in no small part on the everyday engagements and experiences of scholars living in the world. Focusing singularly on either involvement or detachment can easily become problematic (i.e., complete involvement raises questions about what makes scholarship distinctive vis-à-vis other perspectives on media and public life; total detachment runs the risk of ignoring the very realities that one claims to study). While our contributors vary in the degree to which they see their research as more or less engaged, they all generally navigate the tension between involvement and detachment.

Second, and relatedly, stances that scholars adopt can calcify over time, moving from highly involved to problematically detached. Whatever their other differences, the individuals associated with both the inaugural issue of *Public Opinion Quarterly* and the Frankfurt School understood themselves to be intimately engaged with making sense of their own most pressing contemporary problems. They studied the effects of media on public opinion and the rise of the culture industries, for example, because doing so provided insights into important forms of social power, which could only be challenged or altered to the degree that such power was understood. Yet the very success of these research agendas sometimes leads to inertia, as later generations of scholars adopt the agenda separated from the context – the historical and scholarly realities – that prompted its initial development. This is what Bennett and Pfetsch (2018) perceive and criticize when characterizing political communication as a field that "increasingly studies itself" – that is, that seeks to develop knowledge within a preexisting framework while paying less attention to whether real-world social transformations expose that framework as obsolete or in need of substantial revision. The more general question this poses, and which our contributors address, concerns how and in what ways scholars engage with prior research paradigms. Should they revisit core concepts with the aim of refining them for the current era, or should they seek to develop new tools that might be better adapted to the contemporary moment?

Third, these debates raise a range of questions about the standpoint of scholarship. Then and especially now, academic researchers are asked to make their work relevant to a number of stakeholders (e.g., project funders, community groups, state bureaucracies, business organizations), which brings to the fore issues regarding whose interests and perspectives are represented in the research, as well as academics' capacity to act as counterweights to the worldview defended by those holding substantial amounts of power in a particular time and place. Put simply, how well can scholars of media and public life act as critics of extant social arrangements when, in many cases, the capacity to collect and analyze data is held by large, for-profit companies with an interest in promoting their own interests? This can be connected more broadly with the question of whose standpoint ought to be represented in scholarly research of media and public life. Should scholars adopt the view of particular – typically subaltern – groups, or should they instead seek to construct a space in which sense can be made of the varying forms of collaboration and competition across a range of groups? The debate is long-running and familiar, especially to feminist scholars, who have for decades debated the relative merits of adopting the standpoint of women in order to challenge dominant conceptions of gender, family, and society more broadly. But the issue touches on nearly every domain of scholarship, including scholars studying media and public life, and can be seen in the different ways our contributors position themselves in relation to their chosen research problems.

1.2 MEDIA AND PUBLIC LIFE TODAY: PREVIEW OF CHAPTERS

Authors included in this volume came together in the fall of 2018 for a symposium at the University of Washington. Prior to the symposium, each person was asked to write an essay detailing what they saw as the most pressing question with which scholars of media and public ought to grapple. At the symposium, the first drafts of these essays were discussed collectively and in detail; invited faculty from a wide range of departments and disciplines at the University of Washington, including communication, philosophy, sociology, history, information sciences, and human-centered design and engineering, served as discussants, probing the issues raised from their theoretical and disciplinary vantage points. Each author then revised and expanded their contributions for the current collection, integrating the cross-disciplinary perspectives on their work articulated at the symposium. The different perspectives taken up by the authors result in part from the varied ways they each relate to their object of research. Moreover, the heterogeneity of the concerns included in the collection hints at the great diversity of approaches that scholars can and do assume regarding complex topics surrounding media and public life.

The book is organized into five parts based on themes that emerged as core areas of concern throughout our conversations. These themes hardly exhaust the range of issues that might be explored; however, we do hope that they collectively suggest ways that scholars might do similar work regarding different problems. They are: living in a datafied world; journalism in times of change; media and problems of inclusion; engagement with and through media; and the role of media scholars. In the parts that follow, we briefly introduce the core issues discussed under each of these themes, while also highlighting points of agreement and disagreement across our contributors. The volume concludes with an epilogue written by Silvio Waisbord that extends the scope of discussion by addressing what changes in media and public life might mean to communication as a field more broadly.

1.2.1 Living in a Datafied World

Chapters in Part I address the ways new communication tools and infrastructures fuel the collection and analysis of unprecedented amounts of personal data. In this "datafied" environment, digital platforms play host to a widening array of political, commercial, professional, and social interactions, producing digital footprints that are the object of pervasive corporate and government collection and surveillance. While data have long been a byproduct of political, economic, and social activities, their volume and value have vastly increased due to the advancement in technologies that manage so-called big data, or large data sets that can be manipulated to reveal the patterns and associations of our concerns and behavior, and to make predictions about what we will be concerned about and how we will behave in the future. A growing number of scholars therefore argue that big data not only measure but also shape reality (Hintz et al., 2018; Turow, 2012; Zuboff, 2019).

These developments can be viewed on a number of discrete fronts. Industries use data obtained from our digital lives to better understand and target customer preferences. Banks and insurance companies use data to predict customer risk profiles. Police use such information to predict crime. So-called smart cities gather data through sensors to improve the efficiency and sustainability of urban spaces by measuring traffic patterns, air quality variations, public transportation efficiencies, and the behavior of its publics. Data activists use data to make visible social problems that are being ignored or denied. For example, the group Freedom for Immigrants[1] maintains data on the US immigration detention system gathered from government offices, a national call hotline, and a network of volunteer detention-center visitors.

While technology developers, digital rights groups, and surveillance experts have long been concerned with the implications of mass corporate and government surveillance, it was not until whistleblower Edward Snowden exposed the surveillance activities of US and UK intelligence agencies in 2013 that pervasive collection of personal data became a prominent issue of public concern (Hintz et al., 2018). The Cambridge Analytica scandal, which revealed that the company harvested the personal Facebook data of 87 million users in an effort to manipulate how they vote, marked another high point of attention around the issue (Cadwalladr, 2018). The story revealed the ways data collection and sorting practices have transformed election campaigns and other political communication strategies through the use of psychometric data to micro-target advertisements, amounting to covert and deceitful messaging, including massive efforts to dissuade people from voting (Howard and Bradshaw, 2017).

The chapters included here focus on the ways personal data is used as a source of profit as well as a proxy for public opinion. In his chapter, "The Corporate Reconfiguration of the Social World," Nick Couldry explores the challenges for scholars approaching the contours of a social

[1] See www.freedomforimmigrants.org.

world in which every layer, as he puts it, has been "reconfigured... so that it becomes 'naturally' extractable for profit." Couldry argues we are living less through a new phase of capitalism and more through a new phase of colonialism. Rather than appropriating land or bodies, the new colonists appropriate data. He argues that data collection is so pervasive that it has become a basic "condition of human life."

As a central point, Couldry considers the normative values that ought to drive communication researchers engaged with corporations. He suggests scholars recognize Facebook's response to the Cambridge Analytica scandal, for example, as an unabashed attempt to camouflage continued and concerted antidemocratic practices that serve to bolster economic and social trends that benefit the company. CEO Mark Zuckerberg publicly apologized for his company's involvement with Cambridge Analytica on CNN, calling it an "issue," a "mistake," and a "breach of trust." But the extended use of personal data is not a departure from but rather the foundation of Facebook's business model. That is, Facebook is not a victim of but rather an accomplice to Cambridge Analytica crimes. Couldry encourages media scholars to be at the forefront of the effort to break down the contradictions between what networked-era data companies say and what they do.

Melissa Aronczyk's chapter, "Public Communication in a Promotional Culture," also explores the implications of a datafied life. By illustrating the gap between the principles and practices of corporate data mining, Aronczyk takes up what Couldry (2015) has elsewhere called "the myth of us," or the belief that our exchanges on social media platforms are a natural form of social connection rather than a manufactured arrangement for the creation of economic value. Her critique of datafication focuses less on the fact of its existence, or on how data are deployed in the service of promotional culture, and more on what we assume we can know about public opinion through data. She argues that the data collected by private media companies are often relevant only to specific behaviors carried out in a predetermined context. It reflects behaviors shaped less by user interests, concerns, or habits than by the way the system is engineered to maximize attention and profit and to adhere to security and privacy regulations. These factors, Aronczyk argues, create data sets that are highly specific to conditions of their collection and that cannot – and indeed should not – stand in for any more general public opinion. She suggests that personal data is "a tool but not a condition of public life." By examining how the United Nations uses data sets donated by private companies to address their agenda for climate mitigation, for example, she questions the reliability of that data for making inferences about human behavior. More broadly, Aronczyk interrogates the wisdom of taking our cues from corporations by adopting the same assumption they make about what their data mean. "As media and communication scholars increasingly turn their attention to the inequities of our digital platforms," she writes, "we need to devote more energy to investigating the disparities between the affordances of these platforms and the actual social and cultural truths of the people using them."

1.2.2 Journalism in Times of Change

Authors in Part II turn their attention to the challenges and opportunities for journalism in the contemporary era. On this front, few would dispute that journalists confront major challenges. Nearly every news organization is undergoing some form of restructuring. This is discussed most prominently among "legacy" news media, which employ the majority of professional journalists, and for whom traditional revenue sources are declining or threatened, as is the case for many public service media (Nielsen and Selva, 2019). Yet even so-called new (e.g., online) or what we might think of as "newish" (e.g., cable) media outlets find themselves undergoing restructuring of one sort or another. In January 2019, for example, three prominent US-based digital start-ups – Buzzfeed, Vice, and Huffington Post – laid off hundreds of journalists in an effort to reduce costs (Peiser, 2019). While the empirical specifics vary across organizations and national contexts, uncertainty is a core feature of contemporary journalism, both with respect to the work that journalists ought to be doing and the types of organizational and political economic structures that might realistically support such work.

To be sure, these challenges come with a number of possible upsides. Technology-enabled collaboration among journalists – as seen in the Panama Papers, for example – allows for the creation of reporting that would otherwise be too costly for a single organization to pursue on its own (Sambrook, 2018). New publishing ventures, moreover, have the potential to expand the range of voices and viewpoints in the news, in part by cultivating relationships with civil society actors or historically underrepresented groups (Russell, 2016). Civic engagement is also in some ways being deepened, with members of the public, at least in some circumstances, using digital tools to create, circulate, and interact with news to a much greater degree than previously possible (Bennett and Segerberg, 2013).

Yet risks also clearly abound. A small number of platform companies now function as the primary gateway for journalists to reach their audiences (Hindman, 2018). The attention economies these companies produce are marked by deep asymmetries between the limited few outlets or individuals that capture attention and the vast majority that do not. This is a problem not only for the journalists and news organizations that fail to capture such attention (and thus end up receiving small or diminishing audience shares); it also increases the tendency of each subsequent development in journalism to orient itself to whatever provides the best chances of capturing attention in such an economy. In other cases, the risk is that economically weakened news organizations will find themselves "captured" by political or business power-holders (Schiffrin, 2017). Beyond business models, the same tools that might deepen civic engagement can also be used to spread propaganda and "disinformation" (Phillips, 2018).

The challenges that confront journalism also interact with some of the already-mentioned broader social transformations. Deepening political polarization in many countries dovetails with partisan attacks on the news media, as does rising authoritarianism (Mason, 2018; Yesil, 2016). This polarization interacts with rising inequality – in terms of income as well as educational attainment – as members of the public self-select news that affirms their views or, in some cases, ignore the news altogether (Clarke, 2014; Stroud, 2011). Reduced trust in government, combined with sustained political efforts by some to see markets as arbiters of social worth, also overshadow the view that journalism is a public good in some national contexts (Pickard, 2017).

The contributors to this part situate their pressing questions in relation to these transformations. In his chapter, "Press Freedom and Its Context," Daniel Hallin notes that the concept of press freedom seems especially salient in a range of contemporary contexts, with political leaders in multiple countries openly rejecting it as a worthwhile principle, and the spread of online propaganda everywhere raising questions about what press freedom ought to mean in practice. Yet the concept, as he points it, "has never been the subject of a particularly well-developed body of either theory or empirical research" among communication scholars (p. 54). Drawing in part on his own engagements as an advisor producing press freedom ratings for the Americas for Freedom House, he explores the history of the concept, its measurement, and discusses some problems associated with using a standardized measure to capture diverse empirical realities. Rather than provide an essential definition, Hallin's chapter offers guidance on how to think about the concept in ways that take seriously the empirical details of particular contexts while also remaining aware of the concept's necessary limitations.

Matthew Powers and Sandra Vera-Zambrano use the challenges facing journalism to revisit an old question concerning journalists' purposes in their chapter: "What Are Journalists for Today?" Rather than provide a normative answer to the question, they draw on their comparative research of journalists in France and the United States to argue that what journalists are for depends on the position one occupies in the field. Some tell stories as a way to inform publics, hold elites accountable, and cultivate empathy, while others focus on accurately reporting the facts and engaging their audiences. They argue that these are not merely individual choices but instead reflect differences in social origins, professional trajectories, and national contexts. In calling attention to the hierarchical nature of journalists' purposes, they argue that, while contemporary journalists might face similar pressures, those pressures do not impact everyone in the same way, and that the diversity of these responses and the particular kind of varied approaches to the work they reveal are in part what helps reproduce a class-based social order.

In their chapter, "Noise and the Values of News," Stephanie Craft and Morten Stinus Kristensen pose the question of whether news values – that is, journalistic judgments regarding the merits of a given piece of information – can serve a contemporary media environment that is chaotic, crowded, and noisy. Drawing on examples from the 2016 American presidential campaign, they argue that values like impact, conflict, and novelty are increasingly incompatible with a media environment that demands and rewards sharing news incrementally and repeatedly, treating every new piece of information with "breaking news" intensity. These mismatched values are further fueled by commercial pressures that favor such values, as well as by "bad faith" actors who seek to game these values to steer coverage in ways that promote their causes or muddy public understanding of core issues. Rather than advocating for a return to a romanticized "simpler" time of journalistic gatekeeping power and professional authority over news, Craft and Kristensen argue that journalists and journalism educators alike need to rethink some of the basic premises of journalistic norms and practices, with the aim of developing news values that are better able to provide the public with the information necessary for political life to function.

1.2.3 Media and Problems of Inclusion

The chapters in Part III take on the problems of creating and sustaining inclusive media content and, more broadly, media environments. They stem from the observation that the legitimacy of contemporary societies, especially those which are or profess to be democratic, rests in important ways on their claim to being inclusive. It is "the people" as citizens – rather than subjects of someone's rule – that are said to possess the decisive voice in organizing such systems. The very idea of who counts as a citizen is thus both a recurrent issue and the object of ongoing struggles (Gaxie, 1993). Media have long played a contradictory role in such struggles. On the one hand, by providing publics with information they need as well as a forum that exposes those publics to a range of viewpoints, they can and sometimes do serve as a vehicle for greater inclusion and integration across multiple lines of social difference (Habermas, 1989). On the other hand, media are also regularly found to exclude and marginalize individuals and groups, contributing to, rather than diminishing, exclusionary social tendencies (Clarke, 2014).

The advent of the World Wide Web and the spread of digital communication led many scholars to imagine that such tools, as well as the practices associated with them, might serve as forces for inclusion and integration. Across a wide range of empirical settings, scholars documented ways that new technological-enabled social action appeared more egalitarian than prior modes of social organization (Benkler, 2006; Bimber et al., 2012). Related lines of research suggested that such tools might also offer individuals and groups novel ways of redressing exclusion, in part by bypassing or strategically interacting with media that might otherwise exclude their messages (Castells, 2009; Jackson, Bailey and Foucault Welles, 2020). Taken together, this and related lines of scholarship helped chart the course for research that evaluates the degree to which such tools did indeed foster greater inclusion or deeper forms of engagement.

Today, enthusiasm about the inclusive nature of contemporary media appears in some ways to be overstated. Many now worry about the various ways in which the media remain exclusionary and indeed sometimes exacerbate various forms of exclusion across multiple lines of social difference (Sunstein, 2017). One particular concern pertains to exclusion from production and consumption of media. Scholars note that journalists are increasingly well-educated (Hanitzsch et al., 2019) and that the makers of digital tools are comprised disproportionately of men (Noble, 2018). The products they create, therefore, tend to reflect the standpoints from which they see the world, which often occlude perspectives and experiences of those occupying other positions in class, gender, racial, or other social hierarchies. Such exclusion is pernicious in part because it is misrecognized as the result of things deserved rather than of the unequal distribution of opportunities.

Current discussions have also seen a revival of long-standing concerns about whether media can strengthen voice – thus acting as a force for inclusion – without also subjecting those voices to manipulation. Scholars note that many members of the public have good reasons for feeling dissatisfied and excluded from contemporary public life. Globalized capitalism not only contributes to rising inequalities; it also threatens the sense of status enjoyed by some members of the public and their sense of belonging to a larger community (Horschild, 2016). Yet these sentiments are also manipulated to serve a range of ulterior motives, which in the process contribute to exclusion rather than inclusion.

The authors in this part take up distinct aspects of these problems. Rodney Benson, in "Journalism and Inclusion," asks whether news organizations, in their search for sustainable business models, are acting increasingly as a force for exclusion. In some cases, he writes, the exclusion is economic, as happens when subscriptions are too expensive for audience members who might otherwise consume such news. In other cases, the exclusion is cultural, which can be seen in publications freely available to all but that in fact only attract the interest of those with proportionally larger volumes of economic and cultural resources than the average member of the public. He calls for scholars to see exclusion as socially organized and to aid in the search for solutions to the problem of "civic" inclusion, which he imagines will include media literacy initiatives, newsroom recruitment to ensure better representation of people from diverse backgrounds, government policies to support independent media, and a range of other initiatives.

Charlton McIlwain in "*Afrotechtopolis*: How Computing Technology Maintains Racial Order" examines the way digital technologies reinforce racialized social hierarchies. He argues that cultural histories of the Internet typically exclude black history and that such an oversight makes it difficult to grasp how racial representations and institutional structures have long shaped computing systems. Sketching a history that extends back at least to the 1960s, he shows that governments and corporations have long sought to develop technologies that would thwart any attempts at challenging racialized hierarchies and that such efforts can be seen today, as in the revelation that IBM used New York Police Department surveillance footage to develop technology that uses skin color to search for criminal suspects. He argues that any effort to challenge racialized social hierarchies has to consider the technological grounds on which their struggles are waged. While acknowledging that digital tools have been immensely useful for recent movements like Black Lives Matter, he argues that any effort to address technologically enabled racialized hierarchies, which he terms *Afrotechtopolis*, must develop its own technologies.

In her chapter, "Exploiting Subalternity in the Name of Counter-Hegemonic Communication: Turkey's Global Media Outreach Initiatives," Bilge Yesil asks how scholars should grapple with the communication initiatives that advocate for inclusion on some issues while remaining antidemocratic and highly exclusionary in other key respects. Taking the case of Turkey's governing party, she explores a wide-ranging media ecology – a state-financed public broadcaster and news agency, government-aligned English-language dailies, NGO digital efforts – that purports to speak on behalf of subaltern groups (Muslim refugees, African Americans, Palestinians) in the global public sphere. She argues that such efforts cannot be read as simply antihegemonic; rather, they must be understood as instrumental uses of "subaltern" discourses (while abandoning the principles historically associated with it). Yesil's analysis demonstrates why scholarship examining authoritarian and populist communication needs to look beyond simply the ways such actors speak and polarize publics, and instead grasp how these efforts aim to legitimate themselves while neutralizing their critics. In doing so, she calls attention to the way inclusion–exclusion dynamics are not merely single-nation stories but rather are constructed in part through transnational relations among nation-states.

1.2.4 Engagement with and through Media

The chapters in Part IV take on issues related to how people engage with media and one another through media. They are based on the assumption that democracies are not sustainable unless they foster informed and engaged publics. And just as early forms of the web were celebrated for their potential for inclusion, the widespread adoption of digital communication at the turn of the century prompted scholars concerned with public life to celebrate the way they imagined digital tools would strengthen democratic communication and the robustness of the public sphere. Yochai Benkler (2006), for example, argued networked publics could engender a shift away from commercial media and centrally organized knowledge production toward "nonmarket" and distributed production. Similarly, Henry Jenkins (2006) described a more socially distributed intelligence, which he saw growing in the activities of, for example, spoiler groups watching the reality television show *Survivor*. The information environment created through networked engagement, he said, extended beyond entertainment writing: "By pooling information and tapping grassroots expertise, by debating evidence and scrutinizing all available information, and perhaps most powerfully, by challenging one another's assumptions, the blogging community is spoiling the American government" (332). Like discourses surrounding inclusion, today optimistic analyses of engagement have given way to more measured assessments, as the stark realities of antidemocratic uses of digital platforms have come to light. The consequences of digitization, as well as previously mentioned challenges to journalism and new conditions for inclusion, set the stage for new avenues through which to engage with one another, with media, and with governing institutions, as well as new ways for such engagement to be manipulated.

Indeed, the rise of commercial platforms has led to what Frank Pasquale (2017) calls the "automated public sphere," in which platforms like Facebook and Google have come to control the type and quality of content, turning engagement into data points, and ordering content based on market considerations rather than public interest. Those who focused on the engagement potential of the Internet did, however, give prominence to a more nuanced understanding of public engagement that challenges traditional notions of participation in the public sphere.

Indeed, while the notion of the public sphere – Jürgen Habermas's theoretical communication space located between state and private spheres – has been central to conceptualizing democratic engagement, it is also regularly criticized for, among other things, its emphasis on rationality as the dominant arbitrator of any issue. In what has been called the "emotional turn" in media studies that began in the early 2000s, affect is seen not as the opposite of reason but rather as an essential and complementary ingredient in the creation of political subjectivities (Papacharissi, 2015; Wahl-Jorgensen, 2019). Making emotions visible and gauging their impact on political decision-making is therefore key to understanding how people engage and to what effect. Zizi Papacharissi (2017) finds, for example, that while affective publics can be distracting and misinformed, they can also make positive contributions to public discourse by disrupting dominant narratives. Affect, of course, has also been weaponized in political campaigns, exploited by ratings-hungry media companies, and leveraged by attention-seeking technology platforms that sort users into affective categories and shape content and feeds to fuel more emotional engagement for political or commercial gain.

Chapters in this part address engagement not as an ideal or flawed side effect of the current networked media environment, but rather as a fluid process in which human agency remains central. Hartmut Wessler, in his chapter "Constructive Engagement across Deep Divides: What It Entails and How It Changes Our Role as Communication Scholars," focuses on what constructive engagement might look like, rather than on the polarization and echo chambers and other conditions that stack the deck against constructive engagement. Wessler identifies three ways current scholarship can be shifted to better address the topic: first, to move from research that emphasizes voice to the practices associated with listening; second, to turn from disruptive conflict toward identifying the potential for integrative conflict; and third, by moving from modes of argumentation to research that examines the "self-transcendent emotions" that fuel constructive interaction with individuals across social divides. The chapter suggests that focusing on constructive engagement can link long-standing concerns articulated by theorists like Habermas focused on rational-critical deliberation with efforts made by social theorists like Georg Simmel, Lewis Coser, and Helmut Dubiel to highlight the integrative and constructive potential of robust but contained conflicts.

Lynn Clark explores youth engagement in her chapter, "Fostering Engagement in an Era of Dissipating Publics," pointing out that youth engagement is less about issues of public concern and more about how youth publics coalesce and dissipate around particular events and issues. She argues that through practices of curation made possible with mobile phones and social media platform feeds, young people create anchoring narratives that can serve as reminders for themselves and for others of past engagements with news and with current events. These anchors or artifacts of individual and collective engagement with current events and issues can be generative in ways that hold potential for the coalescing of future publics. She asks: "How can the phenomena that we have known as journalism work to better trigger and support those processes of coalescing youthful publics in the face of constant dissipation?" In order to better understand coalescing and dissipating youth publics, she suggests we need to direct our concerns away from worries about apathetic and misinformed young people and toward concerns about fixing the systems that seem incapable of listening and responding to their lived experiences. Young people may be news consumers, but our responsibilities to them extend beyond hoping that they will one day replace today's reading, listening, or viewing news audiences. She argues that scholars need to know more about how news and information can contribute to developing their critical consciousness and sense of political efficacy, which may be related to how and when they engage in sharing, inserting themselves into, and creating news.

1.2.5 The Role of Scholars

The authors in Part V of the book assert that the need for scholarly engagement in public life has reached new levels of urgency. Public intellectuals are often celebrated as a bridge spanning the distance between the academy and society, but scholarly public engagement can take many forms, including participating in collaborative popular- or public-culture projects, creating alternative ways of communicating research findings, and focusing work on topics of direct relevance in the world beyond the academy. Engagement in many of its various forms is an idea that scholars support, and there are recurrent efforts across the social sciences and humanities to define and promote the notion that researchers have a responsibility to narrow the distance between themselves and the public and contribute to solving social problems.

Authors in this final part consider scholars' relationships to contemporary publics, challenging media researchers to make their work more relevant and collaborative and suggesting concrete ways to do so. Seth Lewis takes on what he calls the conundrum of the field's double-sided struggle for relevance: how media studies gets lost among academic disciplines, on one side, and how it fails to connect with publics, on the other. In his chapter entitled "What Is Communication Research For?

Wrestling with the Relevance of What We Do," Lewis scrutinizes the disconnect between the field of media studies and people's deeply mediated lived experience. He approaches the topic in three ways: first, conceptually, considering what questions scholars are asking and not asking as a way to explore the assumptions, worldviews, and theories driving the research that does and does not get done; second, methodologically, delving into how scholars ask questions, to which groups of people, and gathering what kinds of data; third, communicatively, asking for whom scholars undertake their work, looking particularly at how research is being communicated to multiple audiences and with what normative aims. Lewis highlights sources of disconnection by exploring well-researched media topics of central concern to publics – media bias, information inequality, and religious faith. He demonstrates the field's failure to provide the public with satisfactory responses.

In "Communication as Translation: Notes toward a New Conceptualization of Communication," Guobin Yang argues that scholars need to transform their approaches to knowledge and knowledge production. He suggests that taking a view of communication as translation, as opposed to transmission, community, or ritual, makes central a recognition of difference. Drawing on Walter Benjamin (1968), he argues that, like translators, communication researchers can never overemphasize the ethos of openness and receptiveness to difference inherent to the work and the centrality to media scholarship of pedagogies on listening, learning, and attunement. The role of the communication scholar, he argues, is not just to translate the experiences of those we study, but also to learn from those experiences. "We should cultivate methodological orientations and sensibilities that let human subjects teach us about their experiences, rather than explaining to them in academic jargon about their own experiences."

In "What Are We Fighting For? Academia or the Humility of Knowledge," Nabil Echchaibi challenges the conviction of Edward Said and others that intellectuals comprise an elite class that alone possess a unique capacity to raise difficult questions and challenge the status quo. These thinkers, he argues, "remain acutely silent about whether the public can talk back to intellectuals, to inform, question, and improve their knowledge and practice." Drawing on his own collaborative work with scholars and artists on the questions of immigration, borders, and frontiers, Echchaibi suggests that scholarship is enriched when subjects are invited in as collaborators. He invites scholars to collectively reimagine our research as a collaboration across a diverse set of expertise and genres, work that embraces the obliqueness of knowledge with the hope of producing an "other" form of knowledge that goes beyond the intellectual boundaries and epistemic and linguistic limitations that shape media scholarship. Rather than making our work more accessible to the public, he argues, we should be working with publics in order to transform our work to be more relevant and therefore more readily heard to publics beyond academia.

1.2.6 Media Research and Mediated Shifts and Crises

In his epilogue to the book, Silvio Waisbord extends the discussion of how media scholarship might best engage publics and how it might best intervene in shaping media and public life. Given the scope and scale of current change in the communication landscape, Waisbord calls on media scholars to revisit the analytical scaffolding and normative arguments that form the basis of the field. He calls on scholars to acknowledge and work to better understand the reality of fragmented media ecologies, heterogeneous forms of public engagement, and fractured public knowledge as we work to find "viable courses of action to build more democratic and just societies."

Like the authors in the final part on public scholarship, Waisbord argues that media scholars face unique challenges today and that they carry an ethical obligation to engage with their research objects in order to help meet those challenges on behalf of the public. To be sure, the authors in this volume differ in their assessment of the nature of these challenges. Indeed, when they came together in person to share their essays, they came to no consensus on how to label, much less meet, the challenges facing contemporary mediated societies. Some suggested that the "shifting landscape of public communication" – the banner under which we initially met – would be more accurately replaced by one that described the foundations of media and public life as "crumbling beneath our feet." They said we were living through a crisis and that our efforts as scholars to make sense of and engage in the crisis should address it as such. "But a crisis compared to what?" others asked, pointing to societies that have long endured authoritarianism, propaganda, economic instability, mass surveillance, and political and economic graft. They argued that recognizing a crisis requires context – that is, some background understanding of what constitutes normal and for whom such normalcy exists. Authors in the volume, therefore, describe very different approaches to negotiating the relationship between scholarly engagement and detachment and how they relate to the groups they study. One area of consensus, however, seemed to form around the idea that social transformations, whether characterized via the language of "crisis" or "shift," demand scholars move beyond existing frameworks – that research paradigms and core concepts that shaped our understanding of media and public life in the past must also be refined to better serve research and analysis of the contemporary moment. This book is thus the product of deep concern, thoughtful deliberation, and sometimes heated debate. The editors hope it helps move the field in a productive way towards better understanding the massive challenges that confront media and public life today.

References

Benjamin, Walter (1968). *Illuminations*. New York: Schocken Books.

Benkler, Yochai (2006). *The Wealth of Networks*. New Haven, CT: Yale University Press.

Bennett, Lance and Barbara Pfetsch (2018). "Rethinking Political Communication in a Time of Disrupted Public Spheres." *Journal of Communication*, 68(2), 243–253.

Bennett, Lance and Alexandra Segerberg (2013). *The Logic of Connective Action*. New York: Cambridge University Press.

Bimber, Bruce, Andrew Flanagin, and Cynthia Stohl (2012). *Collective Action in Organizations*. New York: Cambridge University Press.

Cadwalladr, Carole (2018, March 18). "The Cambridge Analytica Files." *The Guardian*.

Castells, Manuel (2009). *Communication Power*. New York: Oxford University Press.

Clarke, Debra M. (2014). *Journalism and Political Exclusion*. Montreal: McGill-Queen's University Press.

Elias, Nobert (1956). "Some Problems of Involvement and Detachment." *British Journal of Sociology*, 7(3), 226–252.

Gaxie, Daniel (1993). *La Démocratie Représentative*. Paris: Montchrestien.

Habermas, Jürgen (1989). *The Structural Transformation of the Public Sphere*. New York: Polity.

Hanitzsch, Thomas, Folker Hanusch, Thomas Ramaprasad, and Arnold S. de Beer (eds.) (2019). *Worlds of Journalism: Journalistic Cultures Around the Globe*. New York: Columbia University Press.

Hindman, Matthew (2018). *The Internet Trap*. Princeton, NJ: Princeton University Press.

Horkheimer, Max (1972). *Critical Theory: Selected Essays*. New York: Continuum Press.

Horkheimer, Max and Theodor Adorno (1944). *The Dialectic of Enlightenment*. Palo Alto: Stanford University Press.

Horschild, Arlie (2016). *Strangers in their Own Land*. New York: New Press.

Jackson, Sarah H., Moya Bailey and Brooke Foucault Welles (2020). *#HashtagActivism: Networks of Race and Gender Justice*. Cambridge, MA: MIT Press.

Livingstone, Sonia (2019). "Audiences in an Age of Datafication: Critical Questions for Media Research." *Television and New Media*, 20(2), 170–183.

Peiser, Jaclyn (2019, January 25). "BuzzFeed's First Round of Layoffs Puts an End to Its National News Desk." *New York Times*.

Philips, Whitney (2018). *The Oxygen of Amplification*. New York: Data and Society.

Pickard, Victor (2017). "The Big Picture: The Misinformation Society." *Public Books*. Retrieved from www.publicbooks.org/the-big-picture-misinformation-society/

Public Opinion Quarterly. (1937). "Foreword." 1(1), 3–5.

Mason, Liliana (2018). *Uncivil Agreement*. Chicago: University of Chicago Press.

Nielsen, Rasmus Kleis (2018). "No One Cares What We Know: Three Responses to the Irrelevance of Political Communication Research." *Political Communication*, 35(1), 145–149.

Nielsen, Rasmus Kleis and Meera Selva (2019). "More Important but Less Robust? Five Things Everyone Needs to Know About the Future of Journalism." Oxford: Reuters Institute for the Study of Journalism. Retrieved from https://reutersinstitute.politics.ox.ac.uk/sites/default/files/2019-01/Nielsen_and_Selva_FINAL_0.pdf

Noble, Safiya Umoja (2018). *Algorithms of Oppression: How Search Engines Reinforce Racism*. New York: New York University Press.

Papacharissi, Zizi (2015). *Affective Publics: Sentiment, Technology, and Politics*. New York: Oxford University Press.

Pasquale, Frank A (2017). "The Automated Public Sphere." University of Maryland Legal Studies Research Paper No. 2017-31. Retrieved from https://ssrn.com/abstract=3067552

Russell, Adrienne (2016). *Journalism as Activism*. Cambridge: Polity.

Sambrook, Richard (2018). "Global Teamwork: The Rise of Collaboration in Investigative Journalism." Oxford: Reuters Institute for the Study of Journalism. Retrieved from https://reutersinstitute.politics.ox.ac.uk/sites/default/files/2018-03/sambrook_e-ISBN_1802.pdf

Schiffrin, Anya (2018). "Introduction to Special Issue on Media Capture." *Journalism*, 19(8), 1033–1042.

Stroud, Natalia (2011). *Niche News*. New York: Oxford University Press.

Sunstein, Cass (2017). *#Republic: Divided Democracy in the Age of Social Media.* Princeton, NJ: Princeton University Press.

Wahl-Jorgensen, Karen (2019). *Emotions, Media and Politics.* Cambridge: Polity.

Varnelis, Kazys (ed.) (2007). *Networked Publics.* Cambridge, MA: MIT Press.

Yesil, Bilge (2016). *Media in New Turkey.* Champaign, IL: University of Illinois Press.

PART I

LIVING IN A DATAFIED WORLD

2

The Corporate Reconfiguration of the Social World

Nick Couldry

Wherever we look, there are interconnecting questions that make more complex our debates about media's contribution to the public world: areas such as ethics, journalism's business models, audience practices, political uses of media, and modalities of regulation. The radical expansion of media's presence in daily life itself poses challenges that are often both practical and interpretative: how, for example, to understand the new forms of power in large-scale artificial intelligence (AI)-driven "private use" systems with public domain implications, such as Amazon Echo (Crawford and Joler, 2018)? Those are already enough topics for a whole suite of essays.

The question, however, that I want to discuss is a more remote combination of the practical and the interpretative. It is a question of imagination. In my view, the most pressing question today for commentators on media and the public world lies not in particular scandals, such as fake news or platform power. It is something deeper: the question of how we can even get in view the force that drives much of the corporate world today, within but also far beyond the domain of media and in both the "West" and China and the zones in between. Let me be more specific.

Thanks to the editors and attendees at the University of Washington symposium, particularly my respondent Kate Starbird, for very useful comments on an earlier draft.

How can we grasp for analysis, let alone critique, the corporate dream and highly practical project of *reconfiguring every layer and element of the social world, so that it becomes "naturally" extractable for profit?*

The medium for this dream is familiar to us from many daily encounters with its symptoms: data. But what we do not encounter daily is the sheer boldness of the unspoken corporate ambition that connects all of our specific data relations: the ambition to remake social processes so that they are fused indissolubly and irreversibly with processes of *profitable data extraction*, which in turn are based on *continuously tracking* human subjects with a view to *continuously influencing* them and nudging them ever more securely into circuits of extraction. And how do we live intellectually with our new destiny, as human subjects who will become continuously "trackable and tractable" (Fourcade and Healy, 2017: 19)?

You might reply that capitalism has always wanted to dominate social life, to saturate it with commercial messages and manage the desires of consumers, while capitalist labor relations take up most of people's productive energies. But even Marx's remarkably broad understanding of capitalism, at least as normally understood, falls short of grasping the vast corporate ambition we are confronting here. In the book I have recently published with Ulises Mejias of SUNY Oswego we develop a framework for grasping this new corporate ambition as a genuinely new phase not so much of capitalism as of colonialism – *data colonialism* – and so of colonialism's ongoing relations with capitalism. This new colonialism is likely to pave the way for a new and more integrated stage of capitalism that, as yet, we are unable fully to map.

Rather than present here the full argument of that new book,[1] for it is not the exact nature of the possible answers to my question that I am concerned with here, I want in this chapter to reflect on some specific challenges which *flow from* reading the digital world in terms of such a question.[2] These challenges are important, *whether or not* Ulises and I are right in the details of our analysis of data practices. They are

---

[1] See Couldry and Mejias (2018 and 2019).
[2] I started getting interested in this question around six years ago (see Couldry, 2014). But the first time I formulated it clearly was in a talk I gave in Helsinki in March 2016 when I was beginning work on my book with Ulises Mejias (Couldry and Mejias, 2019) and just emerging from completing my preceding book with Andreas Hepp (Couldry and Hepp, 2016). I mention this because at the heart of the question I am interested in here is the theoretical issue that connects the two books, the changing nature of *social order* in an age of deep mediatization. I fully recognize, however, that others were far ahead of me in recognizing the general corporate transformation at work here, for example, Mark Andrejevic, Julie Cohen, and Shoshana Zuboff.

challenges for how we conduct communications research today and connect with the meta-concerns that I suspect underlay the call that brought
this book together: How should we be thinking about media and the
public domain, and how therefore should we be orienting our lives as
critical academics working in the field of communications at this time?

First, however, I must give at least a sketch of Ulises' and my argument,
so that readers have some context for my later discussion of where the
transformations that we analyze leave communications research.

2.1 A COLONIAL PERSPECTIVE ON WHAT'S GOING ON WITH DATA

What's happening today in digital societies, where data harvesting seems
such a natural, such a basic feature of everyday life, is not just
a development, or even a new phase, of capitalism, as many writers have
claimed.[3] It is arguably something even bigger: a genuinely new phase of
colonialism that will, in time, provide the fuel for a later stage of capitalism, whose full shape we cannot predict yet. This is what we start to see if
we shift the timescale from the past thirty to forty years, in which, for sure,
capitalism has become embedded into ever more sectors of daily life, to the
past 500 years, over which time the relations of capitalism to colonialism
have played out.

Ulises Mejias and I are thinking about colonialism here in terms of its
fundamental historical function: as the appropriation of resources on
a vast scale. In 1500 and for the next 450 years it was territory that was
acquired, it was the resources of the land, and of course the bodies, for
a long time those of slaves, needed to extract value from those resources.
Today, the resource being appropriated is *us*: human life in all its depth,
extracted as value through the medium of data. This possibility that we
are entering a genuinely new phase of colonialism where human beings are
the target is, as the cliché goes, the bad news. But there's also some good
news: first, that this cycle of colonialism is only just starting (by "just"
I mean in the past twenty years); second, that today we have a memory of
what historic colonialism did and how over centuries it fueled industrial
capitalism, and in the West we would do well to listen to those whose
memory of colonialism's impact is sharper than ours. The third piece of
good news is that we certainly know what capitalism is, having lived much

---

[3] See, for example, Zuboff (2015).

or all of our lives under it. The initial victims of historic colonialism did not have those last two advantages.

To give a sense of what we might gain by interpreting our present relations with data on this longer timescale, think back to a key moment in the gradual public realization that something big is going on with data: the Facebook/Cambridge Analytica scandal, which broke in mid-March 2018. This scandal prompted many to check what data was being routinely collected from and about them via platforms such as Facebook, via search engines such as Google. Many were shocked, though they already knew this. As the scandal heightened, the Edward Snowden of this moment, Christophe Wylie, a former employee of Cambridge Analytica, commented on Twitter on Cambridge Analytica's plans for expanding its operations to India: "this is what modern colonialism looks like."

But, you might say, that's too easy! Yes, the legacy of older colonialism lives on, as we all know, in the geography of global capitalism, in the dominant power to this day of American culture, in the racial divides in the United States, Brazil, and many other countries, in the dynamics of migration. Almost *every* form of power imbalance today can, in some way, be related back to the legacy of *historic* colonialism, and so has been called "neocolonial" by one critic or other. And the sort of power that Facebook has sought to exercise in Africa through its Facebook Free Basics platform is surely best understood as a neocolonial move, benefiting from the historic asymmetry between Africa and the US capital. But surely that, of itself, doesn't mean what is going on with data today is a *new type* of colonialism.

And you would be right: it *is* too easy to use the word "colonialism" as a metaphor, including in relation to all things digital. But, when we talk about data colonialism, we do not mean it as a metaphor. We are claiming instead that what is going on with data today represents potentially *as* far-reaching an appropriation of resources as the conquest of gold and territory in historic colonialism, a land grab in digital territory the implications of which are likely to be *as* far-reaching as those of historic colonialism: a colonial reality, not a metaphor, to which we need to wake up.

Think of the terms of service to which we sign up every time we install an app, every time we join a platform. In normal times (so in times when a major global scandal has *not* made such terms and conditions headline news), no one reads them. We just click "accept," because we want to get on and use the app or the platform. Sometimes our acceptance is just assumed, no questions asked, though the General Data Protection Regulation (GDPR) has tried to disrupt that assumption. Sometimes our employer encourages us to use a Fitbit to monitor our health (which requires us to accept Fitbit's terms and conditions, whether we like them or not), or we may be required to accept terms and conditions of data extraction by an insurer or by the supplier of a "smart" appliance in our home. But by that act of acceptance (actual or implied) we enter into a whole set of "data relations"[4] that unfold in ways we understand only very partially.

It sometimes seems a mystery how we can accept so much with so little resistance, but it makes more sense if we think historically, through a colonial lens. Think back to a document used in the early days of the Spanish conquest of Latin America, called the *Requerimiento* or demand. Almost exactly 500 years ago (the document was drafted in 1513 at the Spanish court), conquistadors would ride up to within a mile or so of a village whose gold they wanted and read out this document in the middle of the night, in Spanish (a language they knew the locals did not understand). Here is a little of it:

if you do not [submit], I certify to you that, with the help of God, we shall powerfully enter into your country, and shall make war against you in all ways and manners that we can, and shall subject you to the yoke and obedience of the Church and of their Highnesses; ... we shall take away your goods, and shall do you all the mischief and damage that we can ....

The next morning, they would ride into the village and take the gold they wanted, using whatever violence they needed to do so, and more.

You'll notice, immediately, a difference: that we really do click accept, and so no violence is needed to take our "gold" as we use the platform or app whose terms appeared to us. I'll come back to why in a moment, but first let's try to map, more precisely, the key features of historic colonialism onto data colonialism today.

The fundamental moves and historic function of original colonialism can be understood in terms of four levels: the appropriation of resource, the creation of new social relations to stabilize that appropriation, the extreme concentration of wealth that flowed from that appropriation, and finally the ideologies that were used to tell a different story of what was going on, most notoriously, the ideology of "civilization."

We see these same four levels at work with data colonialism. First, there is the appropriation of resources: human life itself, human experience and action, becomes a direct input to capital. The outcome of this is often told

---

[4] See chapter 1 in Couldry and Meijas (2019).

us as cliché, the idea that data is just worthless human "exhaust" that is taken, and anyway just naturally there for the taking, which conveniently forgets the mechanisms that are needed to gather, format, extract, and process this supposedly "natural" resource. Second, social relations are being colonized by data processes, as *all* social relations increasingly take the form of "data relations" that maximize data extraction for value. Third, the economic value that's extracted is hugely concentrated in the vast wealth of new colonial corporations, what Ulises and I call "the social quantification sector" (Facebook, Google, Alibaba, Tencent, and so on). And finally, there are new colonial ideologies that seek to disguise what is going on: not the idea of "civilization" yet exactly, but the idea that we must always stay connected, that everything must be put into data form, so that, for example, we can get more *personalized* messages and products, and the idea that all of this, including the tracking, is somehow inevitable.

We can therefore see all four dimensions of historic colonialism at work in our life with data today, but there is one crucial difference. Unlike in 1500, when colonialism emerged *without* the background of two or three centuries of capitalism, today's new colonialism builds *on top of* the already existing social order of capitalism, which is why it does *not* generally need violence to be effective. How should we think about this emerging social order? Karl Marx showed that industrial capitalism's social order was based on labor relations and our deep relations to commodities which make our labor relations seem natural. But Marx was such a remarkable social theorist that, if we interpret him right, we can see that he allowed for another possibility, that capitalism's social order might at some time in the future be built on *other* forms of abstraction than labor relations – perhaps those same *data* relations that, as I just noted, we already enter into every day of our lives, a habit that is becoming so natural that it doesn't seem like appropriation much of the time, just convenience.

You might object that corporations and, long before them, states have been gathering information about consumers and citizens for decades, even centuries, and indeed they have. But that is very different from what is underway with data today. In terms of scale, today's computer-based infrastructures of connection ensure not only that data is collected every time we are online but that ever more aspects of life can be *continuously* mediated via infrastructures of connection that ensure entry into data relations, for example, processes of self-tracking (in the personal realm) or just-in-time logistics (in the corporate domain). Data collection is no longer a discrete, bounded process, but more like a *condition* of human life, at least until we start to resist this.

And that is not all. The all-encompassing nature of today's data collection makes possible a larger shift: indeed, the transformation of social knowledge itself. There is much more I could say here.[5] But the two core points are these. First that, when we compare the dynamics of Big Data with an earlier transformation of social knowledge – the birth of social statistics in the nineteenth and early twentieth centuries – it is striking that today's knowledge is, for the most part, privately collected processes, owned, used, and debated, whereas earlier statistics were public in all those respects. This transformation changes the relations of "social knowledge" to society's institutional structures: today, in many societies, governments are more likely to be buying Big Data from corporations, not producing it. Second, this shift in how states and markets relate to the production of social knowledge is no accident but flows from an even more striking change. Until the current era, the sources of knowledge and the sources of economic value were always, in principle, separate. Of course, knowledge could, and often did, come to have economic value, but that did not alter the fact that its sources were in principle separate from the sources of economic value. But today, to the extent that the datafication of the economy proceeds, the boundary between knowledge and economic value is loosened. Data are at the same time *both* the stuff of knowledge *and* the stuff of economic value. That changes, potentially quite radically, how we think about whatever becomes social knowledge. Claims to corral economic benefit can easily be disguised as claims to expand knowledge. The Wild West of data colonialism is sometimes housed inside universities themselves.

Without doubt these are large changes. It is hard to get this all into view. So, by way of summary of this section, let me be very direct. Perhaps the most important thing going on with data today, the heart of data colonialism, is so large that it almost escapes us. It is the new corporate strategy and dream that underlies most of the details of datafication, the dream of *annexing* to capital every point in space and time, *cloning* social relations on digital platforms and elsewhere so that this annexation to capital seems just natural, and, through this, *building* a social order that capitalizes human life without limit. This annexation of human life to the forces of capital would be a land grab without precedent in human history, but one that, to be effective, does not need the violence that prised

---

[5] See chapter 4 in Couldry and Mejias (2019).

the gold from Latin America, because a vast and all-encompassing network of social relations is already in place, on the foundations of which new forms of data relation can be built, provided we go on agreeing to enter into those relations. We are used to the idea that there is no alternative to capitalism in general, but that is not the question that needs asking: the question, instead, is whether there is an alternative to capitalism of *this datafied sort*. That is the context, I suggest, for the challenges that face communications research today.

2.2 WHAT FOLLOWS FOR WIDER COMMUNICATION RESEARCH?

Considering these profound changes, the most urgent question for communications researchers today is not to address specific problems such as so-called fake news or the often terrifying spread of gossip on social platforms but instead to see more clearly the wider transformation in how corporations view the social world. If so, some important challenges follow for how we do communications research.

By challenges, I do not mean the investigative challenges of pursuing the consequences of data colonialism, for example, the extraordinary likely concentration of corporate wealth in a few hands, or the new geopolitics of the battle between the United States and China to dominate big data, AI, and so on, or the shifting pattern of political and commercial influence over the public domain. I mean instead challenges in how we *think* about human beings' relations to corporate life and corporate life's relations to public values.

First, there is the challenge of taking corporations seriously when their thinking seems rather like social theory. We are used to being told that industry has the best technical resources for data processing, or even for social interpretation (Savage and Burrows, 2007). But what if corporations are becoming an important site for social theory too, insofar as corporations are increasingly focused on reengineering the social world? Should universities challenge this? This seeming intellectual scandal will continue until we get better at developing theories of how corporations *themselves "theorize" the social*, how they succeed in embedding and installing theories of the social world in their design of platforms, apps, and so on (Rieder, 2012).

Second, there is the challenge for social sciences' own theory of taking seriously corporations' practical ambitions to *build* a different social reality. We can go on, if we like, describing the social world in terms of the historic ontologies for social description – classes, families, groups, institutions, networks – but perhaps the most interesting objects in social ontology today are the platform and the app: the platform as the software-enabled domain where a convincing new "social" is produced for capital; the app as the portable window onto the domain of the platform. Some excellent new work is coming out that tries to build a bridge between this new language and older languages of social description,[6] but lurking here are very difficult questions about how much weight we should give in our social ontology to the working ontology of the corporations that build and, by default naturalize, the work of platforms and apps.[7]

Third, there is the challenge of taking sufficiently seriously this new corporate "social theory" and "social construction" when it comes not just from "the West" but from institutions and locations not influenced by Western liberalism, in particular, China. We are all now free to read English translations of the People's Republic of China's policies on the Internet, AI, and, most notoriously, "social credit." The issue is much more than taking China itself seriously: that at least has been standard in the West's intellectual debate for three or more decades. The issue is to take seriously the emergence in "our" time, and "under Western eyes," of a world whose dynamics of change may be *better understood* through the institutions and values of China than through those of the West. What if China's policy documents are more honest, indeed accurate, as framings of what is going on with data, platforms, and AI today, than the familiar but bland rhetoric of Facebook?

Consider the Chinese government's statement in its Social Credit System policy document that AI provides "a market improvement of social and economic order" (State Council of the People's Republic of China, 2014). What if it is much more accurate, when thinking about the Internet of Things or the expansion of AI projects across almost every area of public policy, to put the emphasis, as this phrase does, on not market "freedoms" but market's role in improving the achievement of social and economic *order*, in other words on governance *and rule*? What if it is marketers' language of "personalization" and Big Data evangelists' language of collective "empowerment" that are more ideological and obfuscatory?[8] If so, then we have to consider an even more disturbing possibility, that the "Western" values of freedom, and the like, which for

---

[6] For example, Bucher (2018) and Van Dijck, Poell, and De Waal (2018).
[7] For an attempt to open up this question, see Couldry and Kallinikos (2017).
[8] For example, Kelly (2016).

two centuries have been assumed to underpin, indeed legitimate, the West's domination of where history is heading, are *no longer useful for explaining* what is going on around us. Could values such as freedom and autonomy be useful now less as norms on which we can rely to sense the direction of history and more as a "counter-statement" against the growing prevalence of authoritarian norms in politics and social life (Burke, 1968)?

If this third challenge is real, then it implies another: to stop reading corporate attempts, such as Facebook's, to respond to criticism of the damage they are causing to the democratic fabric as well-meaning attempts to preserve Western values under pressure, and to read them instead as camouflage for the damage that will likely be done by data colonialism. Rather than seeing Zuckerberg as an overweening but well-meaning liberal, why not take seriously his avowed interest in the first Roman emperor Augustus. Zuckerberg is on record as admiring Augustus for his role in establishing two centuries of peace, even if, as he put it, "he had to do certain things" (Osnos, 2018). Augustus certainly moved fast and broke things! But Augustus, after whom Zuckerberg named his daughter, was also notorious for the ambiguities on which his steady acquisition of absolute power relied. What if the era of data colonialism is precisely one where we are less able to distinguish between societies that are formally democratic and societies that are formally authoritarian?

Finally, if there is any substance to these challenges posed by the new corporate dream of reconfiguring social reality, it is worth asking what do they mean for those working in, or through, the institutional matrix of higher education? For multiple reasons, some good, some definitely bad, academics are told today to "engage" with industry, that is, to discount their traditional academic independence. Could this be exactly the wrong move today, when what is needed is to get ever greater distance from official corporate narratives and to defend our counter-values? To be, in short, uncompromisingly more normative and less pragmatic?

This last point is important, so let me explore it in a little more detail. I am not, of course, arguing against contact with the corporations of the social quantification sector. On the contrary, it is vital that as wide a possible civic and social debate is had about the issues raised by data colonialism, which must of course include those most active in promoting it. Even more important, there have been plenty of signs of internal dissent at Google, Facebook, Uber, and other corporations in the past few years which signal that it is exactly within those corporations that more debate could be productive. For sure, data colonialism is not what most young data engineers and coders signed up to advance through their work.

There are dangers, for sure, in such dialogue, not least because it will require us to be open to those corporations about our critical positions, which could bring risks for researchers that need data flows from those very same companies precisely *because* of their increasingly dominant role in staging the social world. What matters, however, is how that dialogue is staged. Confrontation might initially be unhelpful. Data colonialism, after all, is not a conspiracy but the emergent outcome of a massive transformation of contemporary economies, governance, and societies. It results from an attempt to "fix" new sources of economic value that turns out to have massive and unwelcome side-effects for the value of freedom, very possibly against the intentions of many of those directly involved. In short, data colonialism is an ecological problem for humanity and, where dialogue emerges with the social quantification sector and those who work within it, should be framed as such. It is in that context that I propose academics should be more normative and less (narrowly) pragmatic. This is the only way that academics can contribute anything of value to whatever counter-movement can build against data colonialism.

2.3 CONCLUSION

I have listed a number of serious challenges which flow from taking seriously the implications of the question which for me is today paramount in communications research, indeed the social sciences: How to get the measure of living in a social world which, for the first time, corporations, and only secondarily governments, claim the right to redesign and reshape without constraint to their own ends?

While I disagree with other things in popular historian Yuval Harari's recent account of Big Data, his sense of the scale of the question and the struggle it requires is apt. He writes: "a crucial examination of Dataist dogma is likely to be not only the greatest scientific challenge of the 21st century, but also the most urgent political and economic project" (2017: 459). Communications research is surely central to both challenge and project. The continuing public relevance of communications research depends, I suspect, on how far it takes up that role.

References

Bucher, Taina (2018). *If … Then: Algorithmic Power and Politics*. New York: Oxford University Press.

Burke, Kenneth (1968). *Counter-Statement*. Berkeley: University of California Press.

Crawford, Kate and Vladan Joler (2018). The Anatomy of an AI System: The Amazon Echo as an Anatomical Map of Human Labor, Data, and Planetary Resources. AI Now Institute and Share Lab, online article, September 7.https://anatomyof.ai/

Couldry, Nick (2014). "A Necessary Disenchantment: Myth, Agency and Injustice in the Digital World." *Sociological Review*, 62(4), 880–897.

Couldry, Nick and Andreas Hepp (2016). *The Mediated Construction of Reality*. Cambridge: Polity Press.

Couldry, Nick and Jannis Kallinikos (2017). "Ontology." In J. Burgess, A. Marwick and T. Poell (eds.), *Sage Handbook of Social Media* (pp. 146–159). London: Sage Press.

Couldry, Nick and Ulises Mejias (2018). "Data Colonialism: Rethinking Big Data's Relation to the Contemporary Subject." *Television and New Media*, 20(4), 336–349.

Couldry, Nick and Ulises Mejias (2019). *The Costs of Connection: How Data Is Colonizing Human Life and Appropriating It for Capitalism*. Stanford, CA: Stanford University Press.

Fourcade, Marion and Kieran Healy (2017). "Seeing Like a Market." *Socio-Economic Review*, 15(1), 9–29.

Harari, Yuval Noah (2017). *Homo Deus: A Brief History of Tomorrow*. London: Vintage Press.

Kelly, K. (2016). *The Inevitable: The 12 Technological Forces That Will Shape Our Future*. New York: Penguin Press.

Osnos, Evan (2018, September 17). "Can Mark Zuckerberg Fix Facebook before It Breaks Democracy?" *The New Yorker*. www.newyorker.com/magazine/2018/09/17/can-mark-zuckerberg-fix-facebook-before-it-breaks-democracy

Rieder, Bernhard (2012). "What Is in PageRank? A Historical and Conceptual Investigation of Recursive Status Index." *Computational Culture a Journal of Software Studies*, 2, 1–28.

Savage, Mike and Roger Burrows (2007). "The Coming Crisis of Empirical Sociology." *Sociology*, 41(5), 885–899.

State Council of the People's Republic of China (2014). *Planning Outline for the Construction of a Social Credit System (2014–2020)*. Beijing: State Council of the People's Republic of China. https://chinacopyrightandmedia.wordpress.com/2014/06/14/planning-outline-for-the-construction-of-a-social-credit-system-2014-2020/

Van Dijck, José, Thomas Poell, and Martijn De Waal (2018). *The Platform Society*. New York: Oxford University Press.

Zuboff, Shoshana (2015). "Big Other: Surveillance Capitalism and the Prospects of an Information Civilization." *Journal of Information Technology*, 30(1), 75–89.

3

Public Communication in a Promotional Culture

Melissa Aronczyk

One of the most pressing questions we face as media scholars is how to reckon with the ways private media companies take users' personal data as a proxy for public life, and with what consequences for public knowledge.

To start wrestling with this issue, we need first to understand how the proliferation of behavioral data as a proprietary asset has allowed several kinds of companies to get into the business of media. The sports apparel company Nike is a classic case. In 2006, Nike introduced an iPod kit. It included a tiny transmitter that fitted into a Nike running shoe, allowing runners to keep track of their time, distance, and pace. The data receiver was located in an Apple iPod Nano. When the iPod was connected to a computer, it transferred runners' data to their profile on the Nike website. Runners' related habits (listening to music, monitoring progress, connecting with other runners for motivation and community building) were now mediated via an integrated series of Nike-branded products – an accelerometer, a GPS app, application programming interfaces (APIs) on

Facebook and Twitter – and those of its business partner, Apple. For Nike, this integrated system constituted "an 'owned' media channel for runners" (Wacksman and Stutzman, 2014: 83), one that incentivized a shift for the company toward the development of digital services over sports products.

This phenomenon, since exploited by Google, Amazon, and many other corporate behemoths, is what business leaders like to call an "ecosystem." Firms seek to expand the grounds for value creation by finding ways to mine aspects of the social and cultural environment in which they operate. Companies mediate their users' online activities to achieve "functional integration" (Wacksman and Stutzman, 2014), a form of expansion deemed superior to horizontal or vertical integration because of its ability to incorporate public communication and everyday (nonconsumer) habits into its value chain. Nike's brand value is predicated on both this capacity for ongoing expansion into public life and a concurrent inflexibility: runners' access to this community is conditional upon the regular purchase of Nike products and the steady provision of personal data.

When companies bank on the commodification of personal data instead of the production of goods, one consequence is the loss of advertising revenue for "traditional" media institutions. As Nike and its peers focus on data, they reduce their advertising budgets for mass media outlets, since their publicity is ensured not through TV or newspaper ads but by "building relationships with loyal groups of consumers who become participants and evangelists for the entire interconnected ecosystem of products and services" (Wacksman and Stutzman, 2014: 73).

A second consequence is the transformation of the advertising business itself, with further implications for media production. The so-called platform economy allows several kinds of organizations to perform many of the creative and media-buying functions of ad agencies, even as the creative storytelling of advertising and its placement are seen as less and less relevant against the economic imperatives of data analytics. Public relations consultancies have decreased their source-building with major news outlets and instead tweet, blog, or create podcasts for clients. Legacy news organizations like the *New York Times* replace retiring journalists with copywriters and art directors to create branded content for organizational customers (Auletta, 2018).

These contexts create new patterns of legitimacy in the public sphere. Numbers of followers or likes, rankings, and other reputational metrics appear to evaluate their owners' trustworthiness and reliability, even as they work to transform the practices in which their owners engage (Espeland and Sauder, 2007; Petre, 2015). Industries of promotional intermediation (e.g., marketing, public relations, management consulting, lobbying) are now supplemented by a secondary industry that mediates online content through analytics, directories, and management software (with a tertiary "shadow industry" of bots, troll account operators, and "black hat" PR strategists promoting what some scholars call "networked disinformation") (Ong and Cabañes, 2018).

Perhaps the most problematic implication of these transformations is the mounting perception that the personal data on which private media companies increasingly run constitutes the sum of who we are as public people; and that decisions about public policies should be decided on that basis. This perception relies on at least two discordant principles: first, that the data we provide as individuals in one context is transferable to another and, second, that the data we provide is reflective of actual demographics, politics, and priorities.

In this chapter, I want to illustrate the gap between the principles and the practice of personal data mining by private companies and begin to undo the increasingly pervasive "myth of 'us'" (Couldry, 2015) that behavioral data fosters among media producers and analysts. I will do this in three moves. First, I want to review some of the logics by which companies collect user data, in order to reveal the partial, fragmented, and incomplete nature of this data. While it is true, as Lisa Gitelman (2013: 2) writes, that "'raw data' is an oxymoron," it is also the case that most user data is not representative of the human behavior its owners claim to have captured. Data is captured by media companies in contexts of competition for market share, pressure to reduce costs, and anxieties over regulatory compliance. These logics force companies to isolate, hoard, and obfuscate their data relations in an attempt to maintain their value.

Second, I wish to draw on some of my ongoing empirical research to describe a recent attempt by a group of private companies to manipulate user data to address issues of sustainable development. This example demonstrates how personal data, as partial as it is, is nevertheless being actively used to make policy-related decisions with lasting public consequences.

Third, I will consider some of the implications of this state of affairs for our role as media scholars and bearers of knowledge about the ins and outs of the media professions. In the shadow of the "data turn," where media companies have reoriented their business models around the steady collection and management of user data, how should our research, teaching, and mentorship address the future of the industries?

3.1 THE DEATH OF MAD MEN

In a number of ways, the advertising business is an ideal model to demonstrate how media companies have been transformed by the quest for data as a primary source of value. Advertising is rarely recognized by media scholars as a media industry in its own right. It is more often characterized as a support system for news organizations and more "legitimate" cultural industries such as music, film, or publishing; and evaluated as either a necessary evil, in terms of its role as funder of these legitimate sources of mediated content, or a liability, in terms of its constant potential to downgrade the quality of public communication (Pickard, 2015).

The dual role of the ad business as both media industry and primary support to other media, however, makes it a doubly relevant exemplar to illustrate the transformation of media companies. As the currency of personal online data gains in value, the traditional ad business – like every other media business – has been upended; and its role as the source of financial support to many other cultural industries means that its shape-shifting risks have even greater consequences for media systems.

The failure of the traditional advertising industry initially appears counterintuitive. Digital advertising is characterized as "the lifeblood of the internet, the source of funding for just about everything you read, watch and hear online" (Manjoo, 2018).

But digital advertising is entirely unlike its legacy form. It is predicated not on building images, brands, or relationships. Neither does its value accrue through storytelling, entertainment, or education. Instead, its value is derived from creating and owning digital territory (including online territory and digital devices in the physical world, per "the internet of things") to attract consumers and then finding ways to monitor, measure, and eventually monetize whatever activities the consumers engage in while on that territory, all the while directing them to engage in further activities on or annexed to that territory. To this end, the ad industry is undergoing (at least) three changes.

3.1.1 Control and Fragmentation of Consumer Information

Until recently, advertising agencies served an intermediating function across industry sectors. It was standard for a single agency or group of agencies within an advertising holding company to work for diverse clients in sectors such as healthcare, financial services, fashion, tourism, and automotive. Agency expertise was sought after in part for its ability to deploy knowledge gleaned from such cross-sectoral engagement. An insight from a focus group on patient care in a health services organization may help the agency develop a campaign for a clothing brand.

With digital advertising, marketing "insights" are developed through the analysis of consumer data. In principle, the more data points a company can collect about a user, the more valuable the data becomes. But no small to medium-sized company, and certainly no news organization or publishing company, can generate user data to compete with the internet technology giants Alphabet (Google), Facebook, and Amazon. Instead, companies attempt to harness data that is distinctive to their business and unique within their sector, and to protect this data from being accessed by the internet behemoths.

In this context, companies have increasingly moved to create in-house advertising capacity and to end their relationships with legacy advertising firms. The intermediating function of ad agencies, once a marker of status for a firm, now poses an increasing liability for companies that wish to hoard potential insights that can be used for distinctive, targeted marketing to their clients.

The consequence of this is that many companies' consumer data is increasingly insular and less broadly applicable. The competitive nature of the data implies that within a single market each company may seek to obtain different data and not to share it. This data is typically only relevant to highly specific behaviors in a predetermined context.

3.1.2 Automation and Algorithms

The 2016 US presidential election offered a stage for the dramatic presentation of Facebook's structural model for algorithmic advertising and its implications (Tufekci, 2018). Along with other technology platform companies, Facebook has automated many of the functions formerly performed by advertising agencies, such as media buying, ad production, and audience monitoring. Companies not only save money by replacing their ad agencies with Facebook's services; they also capitalize on Facebook's massive storehouse of user data to select customer characteristics, plan for increased business with "lookalike" audiences (Facebook, 2019), and closely monitor the progress of their consumers toward engaging with (i.e., making a purchase from) the company.

If Facebook's role in the presidential election revealed the capacity of our platforms to monitor us, it also revealed the capacity of the platforms to get things wrong. Researchers have shown that the various persuasion models used by social media sites like Facebook or YouTube to encourage users to stay on the site or invite more friends to join are not necessarily representative of individuals' ordinary or "natural" behavior (Ugander et al., 2011, quoted in Salganik, 2018: 35). The network structures of social media sites are at least partly performative for this reason (Healy, 2015, quoted in Salganik, 2018: 36). The Facebook data on which companies rely to build and target audiences are therefore what Salganik (2018) calls "algorithmically confounded": that is, the data are shaped less by user behavior than by the engineering goals of the systems.

Of course, traditional advertising agencies also regularly got things wrong. The old model of advertising was predicated not on accuracy but rather on a series of intimacies: relationship-building with clients; creating personable, relatable brands; and storytelling (in thirty seconds) to yoke social values to economic value. Despite their modern trappings, professional associations, and cool interior design, most ad agencies owed their power to nineteenth-century invocations of "magic" (Williams, 1980) conjured to give meaning to consumers' lives through the benefits of buying. And advertising expertise was modeled through quasi-occult prescience: the charismatic personalities of advertising "gurus" were looked to as masters of persuasion and creativity.

The magic of *Mad Men*-era advertising was all the more necessary because of the inherent difficulties in measuring advertising effectiveness, captured in the common refrain where the client says, "I know half my budget spent on advertising is working. I just don't know which half."

The difference between the questionable effectiveness of pre-internet advertising and that in the digital era lies primarily in the companies' attitudes toward data collection, which can be summed up as a disturbing fealty to data as a form of knowledge production, and a conviction that our online behaviors say more about us than we could ever say about ourselves (Davies, 2015).

3.1.3 Transformations in Marketing Expertise

Management and professional service consultancies, previously hired for their expertise in accountancy, tax, insurance, and business risk, are developing advertising services, further contributing to the decline in market share for traditional advertising agencies. Companies such as Deloitte, Accenture, PricewaterhouseCoopers LLC, KPMG, and McKinsey have restyled themselves as digital ad agencies, proposing to integrate marketing with their strategic business and technological acumen (Abboud, 2017; Morais, 2018).

These companies are well versed in international regulations and laws around corporate activity and have prior relationships with state governments, in addition to their ability to build technological platforms. They offer consulting in cybersecurity, privacy, intellectual property, and other data-related problems. Online, this know-how can serve a valuable marketing and advertising function; and it can be applied to much earlier phases of their clients' product research and development.

Knowledge of regulatory issues is especially relevant in the context of growing public and political concerns over data protection. The European Union's (EU) General Data Protection Regulation (GDPR), for instance, which took effect on May 25, 2018, had a chilling impact on companies that do business in the EU. In the wake of increasing government efforts at data protection, professional consultancies propose extensive control strategies ("privacy by design") for companies to maintain compliance while continuing to harvest and protect their valuable data (PricewaterhouseCoopers, 2019).

3.2 WE ARE NOT OUR DATA

Private media companies' data is a competitive asset. As the abovementioned examples show, this means that the value of the data is predicated on its users' adherence to its companies' products. Its value is also built on its inelasticity (Wacksman and Stutzman, 2014: 78), meaning the data is unique to its corporate owner. Both these value attributes limit the data's utility for public knowledge. No one dataset, not even a combination of datasets, could be expected to stand in for the public life of an entire jurisdiction, neighborhood, or nation. We are not our data. And yet arguments that we are in fact our data are informing social and technical choices.

In our ongoing research on the uses of big data for action around climate change, for example, Maria Espinoza and I discovered that transnational organizations like the United Nations are appealing to private companies to "donate" their user data for the "public good" (Kirkpatrick, 2011, 2013). Such "data philanthropy" is presented to business leaders as a form of corporate social responsibility and environmental sustainability, benefiting society as well as the brand. In 2017, UN Global Pulse, in partnership with data storage company Western Digital and the Skoll Foundation, issued a "Data for Climate Action Challenge": researchers submitted proposals to use anonymized datasets donated by private companies to address the United Nations' 2030 Agenda for Sustainable Development, with a focus on climate change mitigation. Participating companies included Waze (a traffic and navigation application), Orange (a French telecommunications company), BBVA (a Spanish financial retailer), Crimson Hexagon (a US-based social media analytics company), and the Nielsen market research firm (providing data on EnergyStar-labeled product purchases).[1]

As a representative from UN Global Pulse told us about his organization's mission: "This is really about looking at how we can use digital evidence of human behavior to make reliable inferences about what's happening offline at the household level" (Manjoo, 2018).

But how reliable? And at what price, the gap between the inferences and actual lived experience? The data collected for brand value does not hold the same value for goals of public welfare. At the same time, what these outcomes suggest is the "brandification" of public life such that there is less and less difference between how brand value is assessed and how public concerns are valued.

The elision of brand value and social value redirects our attention toward what seem to me more dubious goals: effectiveness, interpreted as measurable results for social impact, and risk management. To the extent that social values are wrapped up with a brand's competitive positioning, as articulated in the business guru Michael Porter's popular concept of shared value (Porter and Kramer, 2011), the social values that are privileged are those that do not test the operating principles or profits of the firm (Aakhus and Bzdak, 2012).

3.3 MEDIA RESEARCH IN THE DATA BREACH

As media and communications scholars increasingly turn their attention to the inequities of our digital platforms, we need to devote more of our

---

[1] Information available at www.dataforclimateaction.org/.

energy to investigating the disparities between the affordances of these platforms and the actual social and cultural truths of the people using them. We are not our data. Though faced with constant reminders of this fact, our own tendency to take data as a proxy for social or political behavior risks inserting the same blind spots into our research findings. It is not simply the multiplication of anxieties around fake social media user accounts that is not being reflected in our research agendas. When we use Twitter feeds as barometers of public sentiment (to take only one example of academic appropriation of commercial data) we elide the strategic, promotional, or incidental registers that characterize our actual digital media habits.

These conditions challenge scholars to rethink their categories of ana-lysis. Concepts such as public opinion, already problematic in terms of constitution, access, and equal voice, are further scrambled by various proxies for publicity that undermine arguments about democratic parti-cipation and deliberation. The task for critical scholars is to develop philosophical, theoretical, and methodological principles to deal head-on with these patterns rather than see them as outliers or anomalies to a more legitimate system of representation.

As a researcher committed to investigating the tenets and practices that make up our promotional culture, I'm struck by the speed and ease with which individuals and institutions adopt corporate marketing methods into their everyday habits. But I am equally struck by the nature of critiques against it. At the heart of our headshaking over the Instagram habits of twelve-year-olds (Lorenz, 2018), the self-branding techniques offered by career counselors on university campuses, and the rabid irredentism of Facebook, I often detect a pained nostalgia for an ideal of public life and democratic deliberation, as though pointing out the smallness of our media selves will lead us to our better angels. But it is not always clear what is meant by these ideals, or how we might realize them.

Calls for deliberation, transparency, or social justice are not in them-selves sufficient, if only because private companies have themselves adopted this terminology to describe their own actions (e.g., PayPal's social mission is "financial inclusion" and Facebook's is "participation"). Neither are critiques leveled on the basis of media companies' "fake news," as recent events have demonstrated. The suggestion of fakery or lying as a fetter on public knowledge is especially problematic because it portends its opposite: that stripping away the fake or untrue will reveal the more accurate realities beneath.

Instead of focusing on whether commercial media companies are transparent enough, on the artificiality of contemporary political discourse, or on the pathologies of public opinion, what if we attended to the multifariousness of public lives and the possibilities of media to respond to them? I believe this is what Bruno Latour (2004) means when he invokes the contrast between matters of fact and matters of concern. If the importance of the long-standing and well-established critique of matters of fact was to push over totems, pull back the curtain on the constructivism of hallowed traditions, and question power in precedents, can we recognize a new kind of power in our critical potential, one that seeks to reconcile media and public life by showing how publics want and need them?

Latour (2004: 232) asks, "Can we devise another powerful descriptive tool that deals this time with matters of concern and whose import then will no longer be to debunk but to protect and to care?" To begin with the premise that *what seems real to people matters,* and take it from there? Is it possible to make a new category, one of public care rather than public opinion, which is not summed up by the collection of data but is manifested through what is experienced?

Maybe this is how we can begin to push back against the encroachment of corporate media and the promotional register onto our everyday habits of knowledge: not by opposing it to a realer or more pure existence but by recognizing it as one among many resources, a tool but not a condition of public life.

References

Aakhus, Mark and Michael Bzdak (2012). "Revisiting the Role of 'Shared Value' in the Business–Society Relationship." *Business & Professional Ethics Journal,* 31(2), 231–246.

Abboud, Leila (2017, May 8). "A Bunch of Nerds Are Laying Siege to Madison Avenue." *Bloomberg.* www.bloomberg.com/opinion/articles/2017-05-08/a-bu nch-of-nerds-are-laying-siege-to-madison-avenue

Auletta, Ken (2018). *Frenemies: The Epic Disruption of the Ad Business (and Everything Else).* New York: Penguin.

Couldry, Nick (2015). "The Myth of 'Us': Digital Networks, Political Change, and the Production of Collectivity." *Information, Communication & Society,* 18(6), 608–626.

Davies, William (2015). *The Happiness Industry: How the Government and Big Business Sold Us Well-being.* London: Verso Press.

Espeland, Wendy Nelson and Michael Sauder (2007). "Rankings and Reactivity: How Public Measures Recreate Social Worlds." *American Journal of Sociology,* 113(1), 1–40.

Facebook Business (2018, August 15). "About Lookalike Audiences." April 19, 2019. www.facebook.com/business/help/164749007013531

Gitelman, Lisa (ed.) (2013). *"Raw Data" is an Oxymoron*. Cambridge, MA: MIT Press.

Healy, Kieran (2015). "The Performativity of Networks." *European Journal of Sociology*, 56(2), 175–205.

Kirkpatrick, Robert (2013). "A New Type of Philanthropy: Donating Data." *Harvard Business Review*, March 21. https://hbr.org/2013/03/a-new-type-of-philanthropy-don

Kirkpatrick, Robert (2011). "Data Philanthropy Is Good for Business." *Forbes*, September 20.www.forbes.com/sites/oreillymedia/2011/09/20/data-philanthropy-is-good-for-business/#66793d1d5f70

Latour, Bruno (2004). "Why Has Critique Run Out of Steam? From Matters of Fact to Matters of Concern." *Critical Inquiry*, 30(Winter), 225–248.

Lorenz, Taylor (2018, August 22). "Posting Instagram Sponsored Content is the New Summer Job." *The Atlantic*. www.theatlantic.com/technology/archive/2018/08/posting-instagram-sponsored-content-is-the-new-summer-job/568108/

Manjoo, Farhad (2018, January 31). "Tackling the Internet's Central Villain: The Advertising Business." *The New York Times*. www.nytimes.com/2018/01/31/technology/internet-advertising-business.html

Morais, Richard (2018, September 9). "Big Deal: How Brian Whipple Transformed Accenture Interactive into a Marketing Leader for the Digital Age." *AdWeek*, 59(23), 14–17.

Ong, Jonathan Corpus and Jason Vincent A. Cabañes (2018). "Architects of Networked Disinformation: Behind the Scenes of Troll Accounts and Fake News Production in the Philippines." The Newton Tech4Dev Network, February 5. http://newtontechfordev.com/newton-tech4dev-research-identifies-ad-pr-executives-chief-architects-fake-news-production-social-media-trolling/

Petre, Caitlin (2015, May 7). *The Traffic Factories: Metrics at Chartbeat, Gawker Media, and the New York Times*. New York: Tow Center for Digital Journalism. www.cjr.org/tow_center_reports/the_traffic_factories_metrics_at_chartbeat_gawker_media_and_the_new_york_times.php

Pickard, Victor (2015). *America's Battle for Media Democracy: The Triumph of Corporate Libertarianism and the Future of Media Reform*. New York: Cambridge University Press.

Porter, Michael E. and Mark R. Kramer (2011). "Creating Shared Value." *Harvard Business Review*. January–February, 62–77. https://hbr.org/2011/01/the-big-idea-creating-shared-value

PricewaterhouseCoopers LLC (2019). General Data Protection Regulation (GDPR), February 4. www.pwc.com/us/en/services/consulting/cybersecurity/general-data-protection-regulation.html

Salganik, Matthew J. (2018). *Bit by Bit: Social Research in the Digital Age*. Princeton, NJ: Princeton University Press.

Tufekci, Zeynep (2018, March 19). "Facebook's Surveillance Machine." *The New York Times*. www.nytimes.com/2018/03/19/opinion/facebook-cambridge-analytica.html

Ugander, Johan, Brian Karrer, Lars Backstrom, et al. (2011, November). "The Anatomy of the Facebook Social Graph." https://arxiv.org/abs/1111.4503

Wacksman, Barry and Chris Stutzman (2014). *Connected by Design*. San Francisco: Jossey-Bass.

Williams, Raymond (1980). *Base and Superstructure in Marxist Cultural Theory. Problems in Materialism and Culture*. London: Verso Press.

PART II

JOURNALISM IN TIMES OF CHANGE

4

Press Freedom and Its Context

Daniel C. Hallin

"Press freedom" is one of the central concepts of media studies. It is also, in ways that might have seemed surprising fifteen years ago, an increasingly fraught issue in contemporary politics. Here in the United States, for the first time in our history, we have a president who openly rejects the principle of press freedom. His views of the press are closely parallel to those of many other – unfortunately – more skilled and effective leaders in various forms of "electoral authoritarian" systems, like Viktor Orban in Hungary, Recep Tayyip Erdogan in Turkey, or Vladimir Putin in Russia. In China, political control of the media has been consolidated in recent years, and the Chinese model seems likely to grow in influence as the United States and other Western countries decline in global prestige. At the same time, the spread of propaganda on social networks and the new centrality of platforms and tech companies as gatekeepers have provoked new kinds of debates about what media freedom means in practice. The rise of social media was accompanied originally by a utopian vision according to which technology and engineering could accomplish what the social institutions of the media never quite could, extending press freedom to everyone (Volokh, 1996). Now this libertarian vision looks deeply problematic, with new forms of mass manipulation and new kinds of power structures appearing, and we are back to a debate reminiscent of the one the Hutchins Commission (Leigh, 1947) famously addressed in the 1940s, about what we need to do to make media freedom compatible with democracy and a culture of truth and reason.

As central as it is, however, both to public discussion and to scholarship in media studies and social science more generally, the concept of media freedom has never been the subject of a particularly well-developed body of either theory or empirical research. That probably needs to change, given the issues that currently face us. I have been thinking about this subject in recent years, in part because I have been serving as a "ratings advisor" for Freedom House, helping to produce press freedom ratings for the Americas. In the process of producing those ratings we have had a lot of interesting debates that have provoked me to think about different understandings of what press freedom is, about the limitations of the concept, and about its relationship with other concepts, such as democracy, pluralism, openness, or truth. In this chapter I will outline some of those issues and illustrate them by elaborating on some of the Latin American cases, which are the focus of my current research. My focus here is not on press freedom as a purely normative concept, though clearly normative implications are central, but on press freedom as an empirical concept, which we might use in understanding media systems and their consequences for political life.

4.1 HISTORY AND MEASUREMENT OF THE CONCEPT OF PRESS FREEDOM

The dominant core conception of press freedom, rooted in liberal ideology, defines it, to take the formulation used by Kellem and Stein (2016: 43) in an analysis of press freedom in Latin America, as "an environment in which journalists can report independently of government and with minimal regulation or state intervention." This traditional understanding of media freedom was consolidated in the early days of contemporary social science. The first press freedom index classfied media systems on a scale ranging from "Free press system; normally no major government controls" to "Authoritarian press system" (Nixon, 1960). The consolidation of this conception of press freedom came in the context of U.S. global hegemony in the Cold War period and clearly reflected the perspective of the U.S. liberal model of media system. By the 1970s, however, more complex views of press freedom were beginning to develop. In 1974, for example, David Weaver identified three components of press freedom:

absence of governmental constraints, absence of nongovernmental constraints, and structures that aided the dissemination of ideas to large
audiences.[1] The debates in the 1970s and early 1980s over the global
flow of information and the "New World Information and
Communication Order" accelerated the critique of the traditional liberal
conception of press freedom and led to the development of "radical"
conceptions rooted often in critical political economy traditions of scholarship and social democratic policy traditions, which gave more attention
to nongovernmental constraints and to the positive role of the state policy,
as, for example, in the case of public service broadcasting.

One way to think about the range of perspectives on press freedom is to
consider the question of who is the *subject* of press freedom. The earliest
press freedom ratings (Nixon, 1960) were produced by the International
Press Institute and Inter American Press Association, which essentially
represent commercial media *owners*, for whom freedom from state regulation is the central concern. This view is still deeply rooted in the
dominant core concept of press freedom. Another conception of press
freedom centers around the journalist as its subject. Merrill (1989), for
example, distinguishes between "press freedom" in the traditional sense
and "journalistic freedom." Much of the discussion of press freedom
today is driven by this journalist-centered perspective, which not only
relies heavily on the traditional conception but also broadens it. Reporters
Without Borders, which produces one of the main indices, is of course an
organization that advocates for journalists; and within Freedom House,
I would say that the most central participants in the process were people
associated with similar organizations that advocate for press freedom on
behalf of journalists. From this point of view, government intervention is
often a threat to press freedom; but so, potentially, are ownership concentration, political intervention by owners, and poor labor market conditions for journalists. A very heavy focus for the main organizations that
do press freedom ratings is violence against journalists, which is carried
out by a mix of governmental and nongovernmental actors.

Finally, much discussion of press freedom conceives of the *public* as the
main "subject" of press freedom, in the sense that we assume that press
freedom is ultimately important because it affects the access members of
the public have to information and debate, and their ability to have their
voices heard and their concerns addressed. One report on Press Freedom
and Pluralism in Europe carried out by researchers from the European

---

[1] Weaver's 1974 paper at the ICA is cited in Martin, Abbas, and Martins (2016: 95).

Communication Research and Education Association (Czepek, Hellwig, and Nowak, 2009: 37) makes the point that "in the context of consolidating and enhancing democratic processes, freedom of the press is seen as the opportunity for every citizen or societal group to be informed and have their voices heard and views reflected in public debate." This view is often referred to as "positive" press freedom, and it is of course much more open to arguments that government regulation or intervention of the right kind may enhance press freedom, as well as to arguments that media themselves may not always be good guarantors of it. In the case of Latin America, this perspective on media policy is often connected with the concept of a "right of information," which entered into political and scholarly discourse during the 1970s and remains important today (Rodriguéz Arechavaleta, 2011). Civil society organizations inspired by this conception in Latin America sometimes share much of the agenda of more traditional press freedom organizations, and sometimes diverge from it. The Mexican Association for the Right of Information[2] advocates not only on issues clearly associated with press freedom, like violence against journalists or access to government information, but also, for example, in favor of a provision in a new broadcast law that establishes rights of the audience (the Mexican constitution includes both a right of free expression and a right of information). One of the key issues in the controversy over this policy has to do with regulating the separation of news content and political advertising. Paid political content is highly lucrative for the two companies that dominate Mexican television. These companies have enormous power to shape media policy – "regulatory capture" by the media industry is typical in Latin America – and neither has a history of championing democracy or free expression.

Both public discussion and scholarly research on press freedom have been heavily shaped by the indices produced by Freedom House and Reporters Without Borders (RSF, using its French acronym). It is clearly ironic that scholars have relied so heavily on these indices, since they are produced by activist organizations, and their methodology is not based in any systematic way on social science theory. I recall raising questions in Freedom House discussions and being told "that sounds like a good question for a social scientist" – a bit of boundary work intended to get us on to the task at hand. These indices have been criticized for the lack of a systematic basis for the methodology and also for bias both toward liberal notions of press freedom and toward countries more aligned with

---

[2] See www.amedi.org.mx/.

the United States politically, in the case of Freedom House (Becker, Vlad, and Nusser, 2007; Burgess, 2010; Bush, 2017; Martin, Abbas, and Martins, 2016).

These agencies have been responsive to critiques over the years (Freedom House announced a major revision of their methodology but never completed it and has now discontinued press freedom ratings); and I would say that the rating process is done with a lot of integrity, by people with strong knowledge of (most of) the countries covered. They do definitely give greater weight both to government restrictions on or control of media and to violence against journalists than to other factors; as mentioned previously, they tend to take the perspective of the journalist as subject of press freedom, more than that of the public as subject. But they do incorporate all three conceptions. The Freedom House methodology, for example, included 5 points out of 100 for scoring "diversity" in media – perhaps not as well-defined as it could have been – and also included scoring for ownership concentration and transparency, editorial bias, corruption, and journalistic self-censorship, which can have various origins. Ownership concentration and political instrumentalization by owners were always significant factors in our discussions of Latin American media freedom, and we also were concerned with things such as the ability of community broadcasters to obtain licenses. Another less-known index (done only for parts of the world, not including Latin America), the IREX "Media Sustainability Index," includes more extensive coding for journalistic professionalization than Freedom House or RSF. Any index that is intended to measure social phenomena across such a wide range of contexts is likely to create many questions about validity in specific contexts and likely to leave out a lot that we would want to know about the role of media in different systems. And our discussions in Freedom House certainly raised many interesting questions about what media freedom actually is, how we distinguish it from other characteristics of media or of democracy, and how we think about its social effects. Let me turn to some examples from contemporary Latin America.

4.2 PRESS FREEDOM, DEMOCRACY, AND LATIN AMERICAN POPULISM

The abstract of Kellem and Stein's article (2016), which presents data showing that press freedom declines in Latin America under populist governments of the left, begins, "The media hold democratically elected leaders accountable by exposing corruption and policy failures." This is a normative statement – presumably – but also, I would say, an implicit assumption about media system context that generally underlies the concept of media freedom. As Kellem and Stein acknowledge, the media in Latin America very often do not play this role: the level of professionalism is typically low; media are often "captured" by elites with particular interests and are collusive with or dependent upon political actors (Guerrero and Márquez Ramírez, 2014); and they are often political actors themselves, with considerable power to shape policy and political life. For these reasons, "press freedom" is a more contested concept in Latin America than in the United States or Europe, and is often seen as an ideological weapon wielded by commercial media owners (most media in Latin America are commercial) to block any kind of public policy that would damage their interests and power.

Kellem and Stein's main finding is that press freedom declines in Latin America when leftist presidents come to power in landslide elections, which has happened in a number of countries in the region, part of a populist wave sometimes referred to as the "pink tide." In these situations, they note, there are normally weak levels of political competition due to the collapse of an existing party system, and populist presidents see the media, which has historically been aligned with traditional elites, as their most viable opposition, attack them "to sustain their base," and hence become a "threat to press freedom" (66). Their findings, though, that press freedom ratings go down when leftist populist leaders come to power and enter into conflict with traditional elites and media, could be interpreted as supporting critiques of press freedom ratings themselves as ideologically biased. Kellem and Stein also present data showing that between 1993 and 2013, Freedom House ratings for the region showed the levels of press freedom moved in the *opposite direction* from those for democracy – which would be consistent with a common view in Latin America of many critics of the concept, that "press freedom" is basically about protection of established power relations between media, business and political elites, and is negatively related to democracy.

The reality of the changes in the region in recent decades is complicated, in fact; and it was precisely the kinds of cases that Kellem and Stein discuss that provoked the most extensive discussions that I recall within Freedom House and motivated me to think about the limitations of our conceptualization of the concept of press freedom. Four cases in Latin America illustrate these issues particularly well. In Argentina, Ecuador, Venezuela, and Bolivia, populist governments of the left came to power and eventually entered into conflict with established commercial media, often producing what are known in Latin America as "*guerras mediaticas*," media wars in which media are divided into highly partisan opposing camps. In all of these countries, issues related to media and democracy predated the rise to power of populist presidents, and "media accountability movements" (Soledad Segura and Waisbord, 2016) existed which focused on issues like ownership concentration, expansion of community media, representation of ethnic minorities, and more generally access and openness in the public sphere. Typically, populist leaders allied with these media accountability movements to carry out measures that were presented as moves to democratize media and attacked by the opposition as attacks on press freedom.

In Argentina, an important law on media concentration was passed under the government of Cristina Fernández de Kirchner, the main effect of which would have been to break up the powerful Grupo Clarín media conglomerate, and conflict between Kirchner's Peronists and Grupo Clarín was intense. Clarín was able to delay implementation of the law, and when conservative president Mauricio Macrí was elected in 2015, he immediately abrogated it by decree. There was no question that the Kirchner government intended to use the law, and other measures, to attack a political enemy. There were also, however, good arguments to be made that media accountability advocates were right in calling for legislation to deconcentrate Argentine media markets. Did media freedom go down in Argentina during the Kirchner years? It's hard to give a definitive answer. There were strong government attacks on media; there was also a high level of pluralism in the media system, with the most dominant commercial media strongly and loudly in opposition to the government. Did press freedom go up when Macrí came to power? Conflict between media and the state declined, but many saw a return to old patterns of collusion between media and the state, with the majority of media shifting to progovernment stances.

In Ecuador, under President Rafael Correia, a much broader media law was passed, which included not only regulation of market concentration but forms of content regulation. This law, contrary to the visions of media accountability organizations that pushed for it, was implemented with regulatory bodies that had little political independence, and was much more problematic than the Argentine law from a press freedom point of view. There is no question that, as Waisbord (2011) argues, Latin American populism typically understands the elected leader as embodying the will of the people and sees independent institutions that might check the leader's power as undemocratic, including not only media but civil society organizations and independent regulatory bodies. In Ecuador, like

Argentina, the populist leader eventually lost power, and the "guerra mediatica," for better or worse, gave way to more traditional, collusive relations between the president and the media. The Ecuadorian case is complicated too, however, and it is not entirely clear how to evaluate the effect of the rise and fall of the populist leader on the Ecuadorian media and public sphere. In interviews my PhD student, Manel Palos-Pons, has done with journalists in Ecuador, some say that the media law passed under Correia had the effect of forcing journalists – whose level of professionalization is historically very low – to be more professional, checking the accuracy of information. I also remember noticing while reading newspapers on a research trip there that there were a significant number of stories about events organized by community groups based in indigenous and Afro-Ecuadorean communities – not the kind of thing one usually expects to find in a Latin American newspaper. People explained that this was the newspaper's way of fulfilling a provision of the law that required 10 percent "multicultural content."

Venezuela was, of course, the most dramatic case of conflict between the established media and a populist leader. Kellem and Stein wrote that "presidents without viable electoral opponents vilify opposition media to portray them as their political opponent" (41). But commercial media really were central to the opposition to Hugo Chávez in Venezuela and were involved in a coup attempt against him in 2002; it is important to keep in mind that we are not talking about the kinds of nonpartisan media with high levels of journalistic autonomy that prevail in North America or Northern Europe. In the case of Venezuela, unlike the other cases mentioned here, the populist leader eventually won the *guerra mediatica* and media freedom in any meaningful sense clearly did decline – and of course much more dramatically so under his successor, when the regime lost popular support and degenerated into simple authoritarianism. But the Chávez regime, more strongly than those in Ecuador and Argentina, was a mobilizing regime that brought previously marginalized lower-class sectors of the population into political life. So in some sense, at least before the later years of the regime, the Venezuelan public sphere, as conflictive as it was, clearly became more open and pluralistic. One element of this had to do with the expansion of community media, which the state supported under Chávez. Opponents of the regime saw this simply as a move by Chávez to create state-supported media as a weapon to fight the political wars. But the people who ran those media, as recounted in an ethnography by Naomi Schiller (2013, 2018), saw this as an opportunity for them, as members of previously excluded populations, to participate in media production, as well as in the state itself, with whose middle-class bureaucrats they aligned, worked, and negotiated, without, in their view, losing their own agency.

Bolivia, under Evo Morales, was also a mobilizing regime under which a dramatic social and political transformation took place, bringing the previously marginalized indigenous population into political power for the first time and initiating a "decolonization" project. In the media sphere, one manifestation of this project was a law on media racism, which, like the other laws discussed here, was the subject of major polemics. It certainly represented an outside intrusion into journalistic practice and had the potential to be used, among other things, to suppress criticism of Evo Morales, the populist leader. But it is also absolutely true that Bolivia's indigenous majority had historically been excluded and denigrated in media content, and the journalists certainly played a major role in this. So far as I know, no one has studied in detail how it actually changed the practice of Bolivian journalism, and how we should evaluate it from the point of view of media freedom – or whether that is the most relevant grounds on which to judge it – is not self-evident. The cases of Venezuela and of Ecuador illustrate a different version of the issue already raised in the text, that of the subject of press freedom. In many parts of the world, press freedom in the traditional sense is seen by large parts of the population as something that has nothing to do with them, as a protection for the middle class and for media institutions that serve them, as Friedman (2011) illustrates using the case of South Africa.

One issue that often occurred to me in thinking about how these cases were reflected in the press freedom ratings was the question of whether the kinds of variation in the ratings Kellem and Stein take as their dependent variable really reflected variations in media freedom, or perhaps were more a measure of political polarization, and hence of the degree of conflict between the media and the state. In most cases – before the later stage of the Chávez regime – state actions against the media became more frequent. But media opposition to the state also remained very high, very likely higher than the levels that prevailed before the populist regimes came to power, though we have no real systematic research on this. Did media freedom really decline, or did media–political relations just become more conflictual? An interesting passage appears in one of the early studies of press freedom (Nixon, 1965: 7): "the country with the largest number of reported infractions of press freedom in the 1960–3 period was France. It nevertheless receives a rating of 2 [the second highest on a 9-point scale] because [raters] should make due allowance for the tensions created in France by the Algeria War." Presumably, the judges were troubled by the idea of giving a developed, Western country like France the rating that would be implied by the number of "infractions" normally used as an indicator. The assumption they introduce, though, that press freedom might need to be understood relative to a political context of polarization, may make some sense.

In 1960–1963, of course, the United States was rated at the highest level in terms of press freedom. But in this period, at the height of the Cold War, the range of opinions in the US media was extremely limited and the journalism often deferential and conventional; it recalls a line from Tocqueville's *Democracy in America* (1969): "I know of no country in which, speaking generally, there is less independence of mind and true freedom of discussion than America" (254–255). "Infractions" of press freedom were rare, but this was in part because political contestation was muted and journalists deferred to the hegemonic views of the time. It may be that the concept of press freedom makes most sense in a context of moderate pluralism and breaks down at both high and low levels of political polarization.

4.3 CONCLUSION

I won't try here to say what press freedom "really is." Press freedom is one of those concepts – there are many – that social scientists use but don't own. It is a concept of ordinary language, and has all of the ambiguity and protean character of such a concept, and we neither can nor should pin it down to some specific definition. It is, however, very much worthwhile in this period when established conceptions and institutions of a "free media" are in many ways in crisis to think about how we can bring clarity to the discussion of what press freedom means and what policies and practices might help to preserve and enhance it.

I would like to conclude with three observations about how to think about media freedom. The first is that we need to think of press freedom not purely as an abstract ideal but as a social and cultural phenomenon, embedded in particular kinds of institutions, and involving particular historically situated actors, interacting within structures of power and interdependence. For me, for example, the kinds of questions we debated about the racism law in Bolivia or the media concentration law in Argentina were ultimately empirical questions, even if we were posing them in relation to normative conceptions. There was no way to say a priori whether these measures "violated" press freedom. We had to look and see how they were implemented and how they affected the practice of journalism, the flow of information, and the voice of social actors.

Second, and closely related, is that context matters. We have to be careful about transferring assumptions about the nature of journalism, the role of media in society, and so on, from familiar contexts into contexts where the reality might be quite different. This is a reason to be skeptical about how much we should rely on standardized measures like press freedom indices (even if, in my view, they do have value). And it is also a reason to think carefully about how media systems everywhere are changing, and how this might affect the way we think about media freedom.

Finally, it's worth thinking about what the boundaries and limitations of the concept of media freedom might be. I've been an advocate for broadening the discussion of press freedom issues to consider a wider perspective – including the perspective that considers the public as its subject. But I will confess that at a certain point you do begin to get into a kind of boundary region where it is reasonable to ask whether press freedom is really the right concept to apply, and whether Giovanni Sartori's (1970) concerns about "conceptual stretching" should be invoked. The ECREA report on Press Freedom and Pluralism in Europe (Czepek, Hellwig, and Nowak, 2009), to take one illustration of this issue, in some places treats pluralism as something separate from media freedom, which might be an *outcome* of it, and sometimes as a *component* of media freedom, which should be included in measures of it. Probably we can think more clearly about media freedom – and all the other criteria by which we might evaluate a media system (pluralism, democracy, truth, the "right of information") – if we don't try to lump them all together, but consider instead the different ways in which they might be interrelated and, perhaps, sometimes come into conflict.

References

Becker, Lee B., Tudor Vlad, and Nancy Nusser (2007). "An Evaluation of Press Freedom Indicators." *The International Communication Gazette*, 69(1), 5–28.
Burgess, John (2010, July). "Evaluating the Evaluators: Media Freedom Indexes and What They Measure." In *Monitoring and Evaluation Report* from the Center for International Media Assistance at the National Endowment for Democracy.
Bush, Sarah Sunn (2017). "The Politics of Rating Freedom: Ideological Affinity, Private Authority, and Freedom in the World Ratings." *Perspectives on Politics*, 15(3), 711–731.

Andrea, Czepek, Melanie Hellwig, and Eva Nowak (eds.) (2009). *Press Freedom and Pluralism in Europe: Concepts and Conditions*. Bristol: Intellect Press.

Friedman, Steven (2011). "Whose Freedom? South Africa's Press, Middle-Class Bias and the Threat of Control." *Ecquid Novi: African Journalism Studies*, 32 (2), 106–121.

Guerrero, Manuel Alejandro and Mireya Márquez Ramiréz (2014). "The 'Captured Liberal' Model of Media Systems in Latin America." In M. Guerrero and M. Márquez-Ramírez (eds.), *Media Systems and Communication Policies in Latin America* (pp. 43–65). London: Palgrave Macmillan.

Kellam, Marisa and Elizabeth A. Stein (2016). "Silencing Critics: Why and How Presidents Restrict Media Freedom in Democracies." *Comparative Political Studies*, 49(1), 36–77.

Leigh, Robert D. (1947). *A Free and Responsible Press*. Chicago, IL: University of Chicago Press.

Martin, Justin D., Dalia Abbas, and Ralph J. Martins (2016). "The Validity of Global Press Ratings." *Journalism Practice*, 10(1), 93–108.

Nixon, Raymond B (1960). "Factors Related to Press Freedom in National Press Systems." *Journalism Quarterly*, 37(1), 13–28.

Nixon, Raymond B (1965). "Freedom in the World's Press: A Fresh Appraisal with New Data." *Journalism Quarterly*, 42(1), 3–14.

Rodriguéz Arechavaleta, Carlos Manuel (2011). "Apuntes sobre el Derecho a la Información en México en los Años 70: Entre el Nuevo Orden Informativo y la Crisis de Legitimidad Interna." *Nuevo Época*, no. 6.

Sartori, Giovanni (1970). "Concept Misformation in Comparative Politics." *American Political Science Review*, 64(4), 1033–1053.

Schiller, Naomi (2013). "Reckoning with Press Freedom: Community Media, Liberalism and the Processual State in Caracas, Venezuela." *American Ethnologist*, 40(3), 540–554.

Schiller, Naomi (2018). *Channeling the State: Community Media and Popular Politics in Venezuela*. Durham, NC: Duke University Press.

Segura, María Soledad and Silvio Waisbord (2016). *Media Movements: Civil Society and Media Policy Reform in Latin America*. London: Zed Books Ltd.

de Tocqueville, Alexis (1969). *Democracy in America*. In J. P. Mayer (ed.), George Lawrence (trans.). Garden City, NY: Anchor Books.

Volokh, Eugene (1996). "Cheap Speech and What It Will Do." *The Communication Review*, 1(3), 261–290.

Waisbord, Silvio (2011). "Between Support and Confrontation: Civic Society, Media Reform and Populism in Latin America." *Communication, Culture & Critique*, 4(1), 97–117.

5

What Are Journalists for Today?

Matthew Powers and Sandra Vera-Zambrano

5.1 THE QUESTION

Seen from one angle, the question of journalists' purposes appears as a pressing problem for journalists. Faced with public distrust, authoritarian politicians, new technologies, and uncertain business models, journalists ask themselves – or are asked by others – how should they respond. Should they pursue the purposes they've sought previously, adapt those purposes to fit new conditions, or embrace new purposes altogether? Even in instances where their purposes seem clear, the conditions for fulfilling them often appear tenuous. A journalist might believe her or his job is to inform citizens, but she or he must still confront the reality that many citizens only consume news that accords with their preexisting beliefs and that some ignore the news altogether (Stroud, 2011). Whatever their specific reactions to these and related circumstances, the question of journalists' purposes appears inescapable.

The same question also presents itself, no less pressingly, to scholars of journalism. For them, journalists' reactions to economic, technological, social, and political changes are not merely interesting; they also offer potential insights into the organization, disruption, and potential reproduction or renewal of a key aspect of contemporary social life. Just as importantly, though less widely recognized, the question of journalists' purposes strikes at the material basis of these scholars' existence. Most work in departments of media and communication, which were formed in part to prepare students for careers in the media, broadly understood (Waisbord, 2019). Insofar as stable enrollments help underwrite their professional activities, scholars need on some level – the salience varies across departments and by rank and specialization within them – to consider the type of training required of students interested in pursuing such careers.

The question of journalists' purposes is thus pressing, though it is hardly novel. Journalists and scholars alike have posed the problem and offered answers to it for at least a century (Lippmann, 1922; Londres, 1929; Siebert, Peterson, and Schramm, 1956; Weber, 1919). Yet however one evaluates the perspicacity of prior perspectives, none can authoritatively claim to be the final word on the issue. As Jay Rosen (1999) notes in his work on the topic, the question of journalists' purposes is one "we need to ask for every age" (1999: 281). And while contemporary developments bring to the fore a range of seemingly novel issues for scholarly analysis, they do not obviate the need to revisit old questions. Indeed, sometimes the most pressing question is also the most basic. What, then, are journalists' purposes today, in this context and under these conditions?

5.2 EXTANT APPROACHES

One approach to answering the question of journalists' purposes is normative. Analysts articulate what a particular society requires of journalists and specify how journalists can go about fulfilling these requirements (Muhlmann, 2010; Schudson, 2008). In Western Europe and North America, these analyses almost inevitably revolve around competing visions of democracy. Journalists' purposes are viewed, variously, as informing the public, holding political and economic elites accountable, cultivating empathy, promoting deliberation, and so forth. Journalists themselves learn these norms through discussions about the sorts of practices and standards that they should and should not engage in. Seemingly every new development – audience engagement, revenue models, industry partnerships – turns at some point into a debate about whether they facilitate or detract from the sorts of things a journalist ought to do. In highlighting such normative considerations, academics and professionals usefully foreground the stakes at the heart of questions concerning journalists' purposes.

Yet asking what journalists ought to be for is not the same as asking what purposes they serve. Normative approaches are certainly useful in assessing the relationship between ideal and actual purposes (e.g., Van Aelst et al., 2017); they are not, strictly speaking, answers to the question of journalists' purposes as such. In fact, such approaches more often than not show the purposes that journalists fail to serve. They are found, for example, to be insufficiently critical of elites and inadequate in their support of reasoned deliberation. Even when analysts do seek to answer the question, they tend to screen out a substantial portion of journalists' lived realities. Political journalism at the national level is overwhelmingly the core reference point. It is an important segment of journalism, but hardly the whole enterprise. Attention to other topics – local news, celebrity gossip, and the like – is justified on the grounds that they have implications for informed citizenship and political engagement, among other things. That all these journalistic forms have normative implications is indisputable. Yet answering the question of journalists' purposes has to explain them as they are, not just how someone would like them to be.

Another approach to answering the question of journalists' purposes – not necessarily opposed to the first – is empirical. Scholars look at what journalists understand their purposes to be and explore how these are crystallized in their beliefs and practices. Using a range of theories and methods, whose vastness we can scarcely adumbrate here, this approach consistently documents a diversity of journalists' purposes. Thomas Hanitzsch and his collaborators (2019), for example, present survey data from sixty-seven countries to show kaleidoscopic variety in the way journalists conceive of their role in society. Coming from the other side of the methodological spectrum, Nikki Usher (2014) draws on detailed field-work research to examine what it means to be a journalist at the *New York Times* during a period of transition to multiplatform publishing. She, too, reveals a range of orientations among journalists with respect to how they conceive of their purposes in the digital age. Taken together, these and related efforts usefully document the diverse realities that normative approaches sometimes screen out.

Surprisingly, the explanations for the observed diversity of purposes generally glaze over the unequal conditions for fulfilling specific purposes. Scholars emphasize the importance of individual motivations, organizational settings, professional norms, national cultures, and media systems, among other things, in explaining why purposes vary so widely. But they tend not to link these diverse purposes to the individual social origins and trajectories – themselves unequally distributed across the journalistic population – that presumably shape them. To take one prominent framework as an example, journalists' purposes are conceived in the Worlds of Journalism Study as occurring in a "discursive space" in which they are constantly "(re)created, (re)interpreted, appropriated, and contested" (Hanitzsch et al., 2019: 18). This approach accurately characterizes the dynamism and diversity surrounding journalists' purposes yet proceeds as if these purposes have no social anchors. Without necessarily intending to do so, the unequal conditions for fulfilling distinct purposes are written out of many empirical answers.

5.3 A BOURDIEUSIAN APPROACH

Can the question of journalists' purposes be answered in a way that reflects their diverse forms while accounting for the unequal opportunities for fulfilling them? A range of theoretical toolkits might be useful in answering this question. We focus here on the approach offered by Pierre Bourdieu, and our aims in doing so are modest: to illustrate what a Bourdieusian approach to the question of journalists' purposes looks like and to suggest some ways such an approach might correct for the blind-spots of extant normative and empirical approaches. We do not claim to definitively answer the question of their purposes.

For Bourdieu (1990), social life could be analyzed in part through the metaphor of a game. He suggested that players – journalists, in our case – engage in a common endeavor to which each is committed. Such engagements are characterized most basically by struggle. Much like sports players, individuals involved in any social game compete against others as well as their own limits. The game they play imposes constraints on them – some moves are permitted, others are forbidden or discouraged – while also demanding constant improvisation to react to the specific circumstances in which individuals find themselves. It is through their participation in such games that players organize, reproduce, and sometimes manage to transform the very games in which they are engaged in playing.

In contemporary societies, Bourdieu (1993) conceived of most games as taking place within social microcosms that he termed "fields." Such fields have their own rules and generate their own stakes, investments, and struggles. As such, they cannot be wholly reduced to forces and interests beyond them. Journalism is one such field, and has been fruitfully analyzed as such by scholars (Benson and Neveu, 2005; Powers and Vera-Zambrano, 2018). Those in the field are committed to and engaged in ongoing struggles over what does and does not count as news, as seen, for example, in debates about whether the details of a politician's private life are newsworthy. They also struggle over the legitimate definitions of journalists' purposes (e.g., how to engage with and report on politicians who seek to discredit journalists as dishonest and untrustworthy). As they struggle over these and related issues, members of the journalistic field also compete for a range of material and symbolic rewards (e.g., career advancement, better salaries, peer recognition).

Several principles govern Bourdieu's analysis of the social games that transpire within social fields; each helpfully sheds light on ways to empirically grasp journalists' purposes. A first is that fields are hierarchically structured. For Bourdieu, fields are always shot through with power relations because individuals within them do not begin from similar starting points, nor do they hold equal amounts of the same resources, whether those resources are money, knowledge, or social networks. The different positions they occupy in the social hierarchy thus reflect this unequal distribution of resources; these positions also shape their orientation to the way the game is played.

One's view of journalists' purposes, therefore, is never neutral nor merely an expression of an abstract ideal. A reporter with limited experience, for example, might see video storytelling as an opportunity to do her job better, while an established reporter might view it as a distraction and thus refuse to use such tools. Taking such positions thus refracts and transforms the specific resources that individual journalists have at their disposal and whose use they improvise to fit the circumstances in which they find themselves.

A second principle is that fields are relational. While individuals within a field engage in a common endeavor, they pursue those ends differently. As such, the plurality of understandings regarding journalists' purposes is a constitutive feature of the journalistic field. If one wants to understand the empirical diversity of purposes that journalists pursue, they must understand how any one purpose fits among the purposes articulated by others in the field, regardless of whether these purposes accord with some normative ideal for journalists' actions. Building on the prior example, one can understand the stances that journalists take with respect to new technologies only by also understanding the positions they hold in the field or the place of the journalistic field vis-a-vis other resource holders in society. This does not deny that specific stances might more or less closely approximate some set of normative aims; rather, it highlights the social relations and resources that underpin one's capacity to take certain actions.

A third principle is that fields are dynamic. In contrast to charges of determinism, Bourdieu recognized that fields are constantly subject to change, and that any change will force individuals to react to the conditions in which they find themselves. In the case of journalism, this dynamism is clearly apparent in the shifting economic fortunes of media organizations, the growing role played by nonjournalistic actors in shaping news content, and the possibilities presented by digital technologies for journalists to produce and distribute news in novel ways (Russell, 2016). Because journalists' purposes are one of the central stakes of struggle in the field, a key question for analysts is to apprehend the way individuals react when the circumstances in which they find themselves change (e.g., some react to shrinking newsrooms by going back to school, others launch new publications, still others leave the profession). This dynamism is embedded in the hierarchical and relational structure of the field itself. Rather than retreat to normative prescriptions regarding journalists' purposes, Bourdieu encourages analysts to identify the social conditions that enable different forms of dynamism to emerge.

Taken together, Bourdieu's approach seeks to highlight the unequal (and thus hierarchical) opportunities to assume diverse (i.e., relational) views that journalists (dynamically) pursue. While Anglophone scholars of journalism have turned to Bourdieu to explore various aspects of journalism, the approach has not explicitly been used to study the question of journalists' purposes. Moreover, their invocations typically rely on specific concepts like field and capital, whereas our effort is to use the epistemological and methodological principles undergirding these concepts to inform our framing of the problem. Given that no problem is more basic or pressing to the study of journalism than the question of journalists' purposes, we turn to it simply to explore what this framework helps us to see.

5.4 AN ILLUSTRATION

In our current work, which we reference here to illustrate our approach, we ask what journalists are for in two cities: Toulouse, France, and Seattle, United States. These cities occupy an intermediate position in their national hierarchies between media capitals like Paris and

New York, which are home to major media companies and journalists with substantial professional prestige, and smaller cities and towns where news media and the journalists they employ typically possess fewer resources. Journalists in both Toulouse and Seattle also face similar economic constraints and technological transformations. Business models for their employers are uncertain, and multiplatform publishing environments present journalists with a range of potentially novel ways to do their work (Powers, Vera-Zambrano, and Baisnée, 2015). Studying journalists in these two cities thus allows us to see the shape that journalists' purposes take in these (intermediate) contexts and under these (similar) conditions.

We used semi-structured interviews to ascertain journalists' purposes. These interviews sampled a cross-section of individuals with varying degrees of professional experiences working across a range of news media. As such, we explicitly sought to include journalists on the "front line" of innovation (e.g., data journalists) as well as those resisting or ignoring such efforts (see Powers and Vera-Zambrano, 2018, for methodological details). Rather than normatively assume their purposes, we asked journalists to discuss work they are proud of, which offers insights into the purposes they see themselves achieving. Furthermore, because we assume that these purposes are relationally constructed, we also asked them to discuss journalists they admire as well as those they dislike. Such answers shed light on the purposes they would and would not like to fulfill. Finally, to explore links between the purposes expressed and the social conditions that enable them, we asked a range of questions designed to elicit information about individual origins (e.g., place of birth, parents' occupations), trajectories (e.g., educational attainment, prior professional experiences), positions (e.g., the news media for which they work), and the fields in which they compete (e.g., how and in what ways they interact with other journalists in the city).

Stating our findings schematically, we find that one set of responses articulate what we might think of as an intellectual orientation toward journalists' purposes. Such respondents conceive of their role as enlightening readers by telling interesting stories that bring broader social problems into view. Talking about a profile of a homeless person that highlighted problems with housing policy, one reporter said: "I love to do those kinds of stories that are able to tell a larger story through one person's life." Respondents also emphasize their grasp on the subject matter and their attention to details when reporting on issues of public interest. "I am the only one who knows all the details about that story," a reporter proudly told us about a report in which he detailed the policy minutiae of a major public infrastructure project. The journalists these respondents most admire tend to be national journalists based in Paris and New York, while the journalists they tend to dislike – and the journalism they espouse – tend to be based in their own cities or emphasize sensational news or infotainment. Talking about bloggers who accept sponsorships, one reporter grimaced: "It is just so far from journalism. It just annoys the hell out of me that they are given any credibility at all."

Another set of respondents express a more practical orientation to their purposes. They convey their pride in telling human-interest stories that absorb audiences while accurately portraying their subject matter. "I think I told the story well," said one journalist when describing a story about a handicapped child from a war-torn country adopted by a local family. They also take satisfaction in their refusal to sensationalize such stories. Discussing his approach to covering crime news, one reporter exclaimed: "I will never tell the sordid details." When discussing the journalists they admire, these respondents mention local as well as nationally recognized reporters. While they also sometimes criticize infotainment and soft news, they emphasize ways such topics can be covered without sacrificing one's principles. As a television reporter put it: "Some people roll their eyes [at soft news]...[but] I want to find somebody who can say something interesting or useful...and give them a voice."

These diverse perspectives on journalists' purposes are rooted in unequal (i.e., hierarchical) social conditions. Those who express an intellectual orientation to journalists' purposes tend to be born in urban settings and raised by parents who work as liberal professionals (e.g., professors, lawyers, journalists). By contrast, respondents who emphasize a practical orientation to their purposes tend to hail from suburban or rural areas. Their parents are more likely to be employees (e.g., government clerks, factory workers, primary school teachers). These different origins shape the distinctive purposes they pursue in their careers. A reporter whose father was a university professor, for example, described journalism as an attractive option because it represented an opportunity to write about social issues that she had been raised to care about. A reporter whose father was a welder, by contrast, described the appeal of journalism as the opportunity "to write and talk with people" every day.

These origins in turn are linked with journalists' trajectories, which also shape how they view their purposes. Those with more education and professional experience are more likely to express intellectual orientations than those with less (see Lafarge and Marchetti, 2017, for a similar point regarding the French case more broadly). Schooling at elite institutions emphasizes the democratic mission of journalism (e.g., informing the public, fostering debate). It also frequently serves as the entry-point to internships and cultivates social networks among prestigious news media organizations. While less elite universities also stress the democratic function of journalists, their recruitment tends to focus more on storytelling. One person told us that she was inspired to go into journalism because a professor told her that she could have a career writing stories. Having been raised on a farm, she said, "it never occurred to me that it [journalism] was a job." The social networks such institutions foster also tend to be linked with less prestigious media (e.g., community newspapers, local television outlets).

Journalists' view of their purposes is further shaped by the position they hold. Beat reporters and editors tend to cluster more closely around intellectual orientations, as do those working for established news media (e.g., major media companies). Such positions afford these individuals the necessary time to produce the in-depth work of which they are proud. After gaining employment at a monthly news magazine that is owned by a major daily newspaper, one reporter remarked: "You have the time to have perspective, to really be sure of weighting every word and to *say something* about our society." By contrast, general assignment reporters more commonly embrace practical orientations, as do those working for less well-known news media (e.g., online news start-ups). As one person at an online news organization put it: "I of course would love to sit around and spend weeks on a…story and spend a lot of time tinkering with it. It's not realistic for my position right now." Such a view does not reject the intellectual orientation to journalists' purposes; rather, it pursues the most attainable version of a shared principle by getting the facts right and writing the story as engagingly as possible.

Finally, journalists' view of their purposes is shaped by the specific field in which journalists interact. In Toulouse, the main media organizations control the lion's share of the market and are thus able to impose their rules of field, which emphasize soft news and *faits divers* (roughly translated as human-interest stories). Journalists can challenge these rules only by seeking out different niches that are not covered by these dominant actors. For example, a group of journalists formed a print magazine dedicated to in-depth reporting after the main newspaper discontinued its own magazine. Those who directly challenge the dominant organizations generally fail, as happened to several online news start-ups that sought to provide public interest news at precisely the moment when the main media companies were moving into the online publishing space.

Hierarchies exist in Seattle but the distribution of power is more dispersed. Journalists working at alternative newsweeklies have for decades challenged dominant news media's neutral approach to covering public affairs. Amid dramatic staffing cutbacks in both alternative and mainstream newsrooms, many journalists have struck out on their own, forming a diverse number of news organizations with distinctive orientations (e.g., covering civic affairs, local sports). In a period of resource scarcity, moreover, journalists working across news media can and sometimes do find opportunities to cooperate while pursuing distinct purposes. Content sharing agreements, for example, have existed between digitally based neighborhood news organizations and legacy news media. Where the former generally emphasize practical information for specific neighborhoods, the latter typically seek to provide middle- and highbrow content for subscribers. While such partnerships foster a diverse range of purposes, the economic conditions for their survival are less certain.

5.5 CONCLUSION

What, then, are journalists for? If we start by answering the question empirically, the response, as numerous other scholars note, is that it is complicated and it depends. While journalists play a shared game that stresses truth-telling and storytelling, the forms their participation take vary. Some tell detailed stories as a way to inform citizens, hold elites accountable, cultivate empathy, and so forth. They express pride in the work they do that fulfills these aims, and they admire other journalists who pursue similar aims. Others recognize the legitimacy of such efforts but focus on pursuing the most attainable version of these purposes. While they may not have the time for investigative reporting or detailed analysis, they can and do try to get the facts right and engage their audiences.

A Bourdieusian lens preserves the complexity of the empirical answer while shedding light on the way journalists' positions in the field, themselves shaped by their origins and trajectories, influence how they understand their purposes. What a journalist stands for is never simply a matter of individual volition, organizational culture, or professional values. It reflects the unequal distribution of resources that begin at birth and constantly shape how any individual plays the game. It also reflects the relations of domination in which journalists find themselves. Journalists with fewer resources, for example, accept as legitimate the sort of work they do not have the time, resources, and training to fully pursue. Extant empirical approaches correctly note the diversity of journalists' purposes and the complexity of their reactions to contemporary transformations. Such purposes must also be understood as hierarchically ordered: Prizes are not awarded to stories that are merely accurate or entertaining. To ignore hierarchy is to ignore reality as journalists experience it.

To say that journalists' purposes are hierarchical and power-laden is not to deny the dynamism that characterizes their pursuit. Those with more resources are not simply gliding friction-free through their careers. They struggle with economic uncertainty, face varying degrees of precarity in their jobs, and make better or worse moves based on the conditions in which the find themselves. Nor are those with fewer resources inherently condemned to occupy the lowest rungs of the journalistic hierarchy. Some do move up in the field and pursue "deviant trajectories" (Bourdieu, 1996). The point is not whether such outliers exist – they do – but rather what conditions and resources make such trajectories possible.

In illustrating a Bourdieusian approach to journalists' purposes, we briefly highlight a limited range of factors that shape the diverse responses. Each of these factors would need to be examined in greater detail than we can address here. Moreover, other factors not explored here – gender, age, and religion, to name a few – are also likely to shape such responses. Finally, structural transformations not examined are crucial for explaining the specific conditions under which journalists' purposes take shape. In both France and the United States, the number of entrants into journalism has grown steadily over the past several decades; their profile has also changed (e.g., they are more educated than in the past and include a greater number of women). Yet the number of available jobs – even when accounting for the new news organizations – has not kept pace. Exploring how these transformations shape the types of purposes that individual journalists pursue is thus crucial for developing a fuller answer to the question of journalists' purposes.

Normative approaches to the question of journalists' purposes usefully articulate what journalism, at its very best, can be. As such, they provide ideals to which journalists can aspire, and that scholars can use to evaluate such efforts. Both among journalists and scholars, debates over what these ideals should entail, moreover, are crucial (e.g., extent to which journalists ought to facilitate deliberation). But such debates also need to be accompanied by the social conditions that make them more or less possible. Calls for journalists to serve democracy by providing hard-hitting investigative reporting sound admirable in the abstract; however, such claims must also confront the uncomfortable reality that such purposes favor some journalists more than others (e.g., those coming from professional families with high levels of education). Failing to face these realities puts scholars at risk of reproducing the meritocratic myth that anyone can do anything regardless of the conditions in which they find themselves.

Conceived as a hierarchical space of unequal possibilities, analyses of journalists' purposes can contribute to a larger question concerning social order. For decades, the question of social order has been basic to scholars working across a range of theoretical perspectives (e.g., Frankfurt School, British Cultural Studies, Gramscian analyses of hegemony). Across their various points of difference, these approaches converge in their effort to explain how the cultural industries, broadly conceived and very much including journalists, maintain social inequalities in part by disguising them. To our eyes, these approaches have in recent years fallen away from the field's center of gravity. They are certainly less utilized in scholarship on journalism today than they were several decades ago. Our use of Bourdieu is one effort to bring such a focus back. It is pressing to do so in part because these approaches shed light on social hierarchies that extant approaches to journalists' purposes do not. More basically, and just as importantly, it is pressing because the hierarchies themselves – and the inequalities they perpetuate – have not, to say the least, disappeared.

References

Benson, Rodney and Erik Neveu (eds.) (2005). *Bourdieu and the Journalistic Field*. Cambridge: Polity.
Bourdieu, Pierre (1990). *In Other Words: Essays Towards a Reflexive Sociology*. Stanford, CA: Stanford University Press.
Bourdieu, Pierre (1993). *The Field of Cultural Production: Essays on Art and Literature*. New York: Columbia University Press.
Bourdieu, Pierre (1996). *The State Nobility: Elite Schools in the Field of Power*. New York, Stanford: Stanford University Press.
Hanitzsch, Thomas, Folker Hanusch, Jyotika Ramaprasad, and Arnold S. de Beer (eds.) (2019). *The Worlds of Journalism: Journalistic Cultures around the Globe*. New York: Columbia University Press.
Lafarge, Gérauld and Dominique Marchetti (2017). "Les Hiérarchies de l'information. Les Légitimités Professionnelles des Étudiants en Journalisme." *Sociétés Contemporaines*, 106(2), 21–44.
Lippmann, Walter (1922). *Public Opinion*. New York: Harcourt, Brace.
Londres, Albert (1929). *Terre d'Ébène*. Paris: Albin Michel.
Muhlmann, Géraldine (2010). *Journalism for Democracy*. Cambridge: Polity.

Powers, Matthew, Sandra Vera-Zambrano, and Olivier Baisnée (2015). "The News Crisis Compared: The Impact of the Journalism Crisis in Toulouse, France and Seattle, Washington." In R. K. Nielson (ed.) *Local Journalism: The Decline of Newspapers and the Rise of Digital Media* (pp. 31–50). London: I.B. Tauris.

Powers, Matthew and Sandra Vera-Zambrano (2016). "Explaining the Formation of Online News Startups in France and the United States: A Field Analysis." *Journal of Communication*, 66(5), 857–877.

Powers, Matthew and Sandra, Vera-Zambrano (2018). "How Journalists Use Social Media in France and the United States: Analyzing Technology Use Across Journalistic Fields." *New Media & Society*, 20(8), 2728–2744.

Rosen, Jay (1999). *What Are Journalists For?* New Haven, CT: Yale University Press.

Russell, Adrienne (2016). *Journalism as Activism: Recoding Media Power.* Cambridge: Polity.

Schudson, Michael (2008). *Why Democracies Need an Unlovable Press.* Cambridge: Polity.

Siebert, Fred, Theodore, Peterson, and Wilbur, Schramm, (1956). *Four Theories of the Press: The Authoritarian, Libertarian, Social Responsibility, and Soviet Concepts of What the Press Should Be and Do.* Urbana: University of Illinois Press.

Stroud, Natalie (2011). *Niche News: The Politics of News Choice.* New York: Oxford.

Usher, Nikki (2014). *Making News at the New York Times.* Ann Arbor: University of Michigan Press.

Van Aelst, Peter, Jesper Strömbäck, Toril Aalberg, Frank Esser, Claes de Vreese et al. (2017). Political Communication in a High-Choice Media Environment: A Challenge for Democracy? *Annals of the International Communication Association*, 41(1), 3–27.

Waisbord, Silvio (2019). *Communication: A Post-Discipline.* Cambridge: Polity.

Weber, Max (1919). Politics as a Vocation. http://anthropos-lab.net/wp/wp-content/uploads/2011/12/Weber-Politics-as-a-Vocation.pdf

6

Noise and the Values of News

Stephanie Craft and Morten Stinus Kristensen

6.1 INTRODUCTION

News' historically unique position, and the role it has played in democratic processes, is increasingly threatened by movements in position and legitimacy of content that, like news, provides information on current events, but does so apart from traditional routines of news production that include the exercise of news values. This not only threatens the status of news as a viable (i.e., profitable) commodity in a largely commercial media system but also challenges the assumption that a citizenry operates with some shared notion of what reality they are living in. Previously, "news" has been trusted (generally, at least) to provide some semblance of facts on what is happening in the world. But as journalist-produced news loses its privileged status, it becomes merely one type of content competing for attention with many others, its distinctiveness lost in a cacophony of media noise. The result is a decentered media landscape in which all media content is roughly equal.

That new entrants increase the volume in the media landscape has been observed before. Forty years ago, the launch of twenty-four-hour cable news networks brought nonstop news and, significantly, nonstop commentary and entertainment values into news, an expansion that blurred the boundaries between news and other kinds of content. What is new about this noisier news environment is the sheer number of sources of (potential) noise, from online news outlets to social media platforms. This multitude of new voices, along with the existing outlets for news, creates a kind of noise pollution – a constant, saturating presence of news that is read, seen, shared, forwarded, retweeted, storified, and posted everywhere. In its ubiquity, content overwhelms news, diluting its distinctiveness and altering its position at the center of information gathering.

Even so, the decentering of the news media landscape is not necessarily a bad thing. And in any case, the outcome seems unavoidable when considering the various developments in, for instance, technology that have helped enable it. Nonetheless, diagnosing the causes of this change may help shed light on what happens to news media's democratic role when media loses its center, when there is no longer a kind of standard or default news available to media consumers. We locate the root causes for this in the very definition of news (values) and the ways in which developments have rendered them obsolete. Amid the swell of content, it is becoming more apparent, we argue, that these reflections of and tools for journalistic control over the current events narrative – shaping what counts as news and thereby obscuring the subjectivity of news selection – were made for a news media landscape that no longer exists.

To untangle news' loss of prominence, we engage Carey's (1989) notion of communication functioning *both* as information transmission and ritual as a lens through which to consider the news values at the heart of news-making practices. These news values have remained remarkably stable since they were first (directly and indirectly) formulated in the early twentieth century and in large part premised on the idea of communication as transmission so dominant at the time (cf. Parks, 2018). But even as the media landscape has undergone a radical transformation that can be characterized at least in part as a shift from this transmission orientation to a more ritual one, news has remained tethered to a relatively static set of news values and, in turn, to the transmission view of communication, designed to affirm its prominence in the media landscape. We consider whether, despite the stability in news values, news has actually "evaporated" (Carey, 1989: 21) as a result of that shift, with the noise we observe one of several byproducts of "news" reaching its end.

6.2 TRANSMISSION AND RITUAL

Carey (1989) outlined two alternative definitions of communication: the transmission view and the ritual view. He defines communication in the transmission view as "a process whereby messages are transmitted and distributed in space for the control of distance and people" (1989: 15). Under the ritual view, communication is "not the act of imparting information but the representation of shared beliefs" (1989: 18). These views represent contrasts between control and representation, linear and networked, and detached and participatory ways of thinking about communication. Key to Carey's argument is that these two views are not mutually exclusive – rituals carry information; information is sent and received in ritual fashion. This is certainly true of news, which simultaneously is constructed as information *and* consumed habitually and ritualistically.

Importantly, Carey situates the period in which the transmission view of communication came to dominate American thinking around the turn of the nineteenth century when newspapers were beginning to grow into their modern form. "Communication," Carey suggests, "was viewed as a process and a technology that would [...] spread, transmit, and disseminate knowledge, ideas, and information farther and faster" (1989: 17). News values were in large part developed around that time, so it is unsurprising that they were closely associated with this idea of communication. As one of the first American journalism textbook authors wrote in 1914, "the role of the press is 'to keep us informed concerning the events that are taking place each day in the world about us'" (Parks, 2018: 12). The transmission view persists in much of journalism today, evident not only in textbooks but also in codes of ethics that highlight accuracy and completeness as essential elements of journalists' ethical obligations as well as discussions among journalists about how new technologies (e.g., algorithms, apps, augmented reality) might improve how they gather and distribute information.

As Jane Singer (2018) notes, the transmission view has similarly dominated scholarship about journalism, such that the focus has largely been "on components of a 'transmission' process identified 50 years ago – the senders and receivers of a message, along with the nature of the message itself" (2018: 215). While it was once relatively straightforward to identify and analyze the element of that process, doing so is "far trickier in a mediated world that has become dramatically less bounded and more interconnected" (2018: 209). If we instead understand journalism as "a fluid, iterative process in which 'messages' are ubiquitous and multidirectional, and the roles of 'senders' and 'receivers' are perpetually reciprocal," then the questions we raise about the effects of journalism or the control of journalists over information and/or the news narrative necessarily change. As Singer asks, "what are the effects of a wholly non-linear media system?" (2018: 220).

One answer to Singer's question is that "news" takes on an entirely new meaning, shaped by a more ritual view of communication. In the ritual view, the notion that one group defines "news" while another group consumes it or, more specifically, that news is distinctive such that only those issues and events selected and shaped according to news values exercised by journalists count as "news" no longer holds water. In Singer's description "the 'media' today constitute a communicative space in which we live constantly rather than a separate thing that we use occasionally" (2018: 216). That description invites us to consider how news exists within and arises from the participants within a space, which aligns with Carey's point that transmission of information is a by-product, not the primary function, of news in the ritual view. Moreover, Singer's notion of media as a space where people live points to the important ritual functions that communication in the form of news can perform in that space. Carey's description of the ritual view sees news as drama, not information: "It does not describe the world but portrays an arena of dramatic forces and action; it exists solely in historical time; and it invites our participation on the basis of our assuming, often vicariously, social roles within it" (Carey, 1989: 21).

Recent technological developments have made ritual a central feature of daily communication practices. From reality television to meme-sharing, the sociality of ritualized communication has become central. This intersects with a broader development within culture where the social aspects of media consumption have come to define and reshape features of media content. But because news values exist in some sense apart from ritualistic functions and thus the potential social role news may play, a tension emerges – not so much because news neglects ritual, but because news neglects to engage *both* transmission and ritual aspects of communication.

So, the challenge to news as a genre of content in this noisier media landscape is not that it cannot be ritualistic. Carey notes that the ritual view does not preclude information transmission but rather "contends that one cannot understand these processes aright except insofar as they are cast within an essentially ritualistic view of communication and social order" (1989: 21). The challenge is that the legitimacy of news is premised on the transmission view, on the accuracy and credibility of information, and on the authority of the information provider. The more shared and participatory construction of news – Carey's description of ritual as portraying and confirming a particular view of the world – poses a threat to journalistic authority grounded in objectivity.

The observation that the public is saturated in news is not an observation, then, about the poor exercise of news judgment per se, so much as an observation about the effects of a shift from a transmission to a ritual orientation. Or, perhaps more to the point, it is an observation that the increasingly noisy news environment is as much a function of continued reliance on outmoded notions of news as it is of the growing number of participants in the news media space. To clarify this point, it's helpful to consider the content and purpose of the news values that have changed little since the professionalization of journalism in the early twentieth century.

6.3 NEWS VALUES AND THE CONTENT TURN

News values are criteria of newsworthiness, "cognitive and normative concepts that refer to what journalists believe should constitute the news" (Strömbäck, Karlsson, and Hopmann, 2012: 719). They represent a way to explain or predict how information, issues, and events are selected for processing and, ultimately, transmission as news. In the research literature, the news values of timeliness, proximity, prominence, novelty or unusualness, conflict, impact, and human interest (though occasionally with different labels) have been observed (see Harcup and O'Neill, 2018; Parks, 2018). News values tend to be more descriptive than prescriptive, more implicit than explicit in journalistic practice. That is, journalists do not generally consult a checklist of values in deciding what to cover; rather, the values are evident in what is selected and how it is presented. News values are part of an "ideational logic" (Parks, 2018: 19) that assists journalists in performing the task of deciding what is news. As Harcup and O'Neill (2018) note in their helpful review of research, journalists typically see themselves as following a "gut feeling" when it comes to news judgment, not engaging in an explicitly articulated process involving the application of specific criteria.

News values are virtually unchanged since the 1900s, but sociocultural context determines how they have been applied, suggesting that they "are neither natural nor inevitable, but rather within journalists' power to change" (Parks, 2018: 1). This durability of news values generally and the ability of journalists to apply them differentially further suggest that these criteria play a role in the construction of journalists' expertise and authority over news. Still, news values are hardly the only factors in selecting news. Indeed, what journalists believe *should* be news and what is actually *selected* as news do not always align (Strömbäck, Karlsson, and Hopmann, 2012).

Attempting to untangle how definitions of news might be implicated in the noisier news environment, we looked back at industry discourse when news organizations began to grapple with how modern technology, in particular the Internet, paved the way for "content" to enter the landscape and pose a challenge to news. In the United States, discourse about "content" and "news" appeared in industry publications such as *American Journalism Review (AJR)*, *Editor & Publisher*, and *Columbia Journalism Review (CJR)*. In those venues, discussions were typically couched, either explicitly or implicitly, in a strong, almost religious, belief in the endurance of news (values) as a commodity. In 1992, for example, an *AJR* article by Roger Fidler, then director of new media at Knight-Ridder, sought to alleviate publishers' fears of new technology by pointing out that "content is what newspaper publishers know best" (Fidler, 1992). In making that assertion, Fidler conflates "content" and "news" and suggests that content produced by news organizations would be easily distinguishable from (and perhaps even superior to) other content. Two years later, Reese Cleghorn, a former president of *AJR*, referenced with implicit endorsement a professor of cognitive psychology who said: "news is unique and it is not just information. It arises from its own methodology and is gathered and conveyed by a group ('call it a cult') that will be clearly identifiable in the future by its methods and underlying values" (Cleghorn, 1994). These passages illustrate not only a belief in the distinctiveness of news with respect to information, the exercise of news judgment as a methodology, but also a potential contradiction in the notion that "news" and "content" are the same thing. (Perhaps in this line of thinking, whatever content journalists produced would be distinctive for journalists having produced it.)

By the 2000s, when it was becoming abundantly clear that technologi-cal transformations presented a major challenge to the news industry's ability to retain its audiences, the unquestioned belief in the prominence and legitimacy of news values remained. "Content" was starting to become synonymous with non-news, something beyond the reach of news values. News and content were seen not merely as different but as each other's opposites, even negations. Journalists expressed concern that the lines between them were blurring and that "issues about what is journalistic content become secondary" (McNamara, 2000). While content was seen as a fluid, catch-all term, news, described in this *CJR* article as "journalistic content," was imagined as distinctive and unchanging. Taken together, this discourse foreshadows how the news industry would seek to differentiate its product from that of the new competition springing up around the Internet. In its emphasis on information, it represents, too, a sort of doubling down on the transmission view of communication in the face of that competition. As Whitney Phillips (2018) has noted, mainstream journalism operates under an "information imperative," a basic impulse to spread newsworthy information. Journalists' impulse to spread news makes them vulnerable to manipulation by bad-faith actors, which in turn creates noise in the news system. The iterative nature of news, Phillips explains, also provides a way for minor stories to gain outsized prominence. Put simply, the norms and practices around news judgment are easily hacked. The consequences of journalism's vulnerability to manipulation extend beyond the stress of the additional noise it creates to the damage it can do to perceptions of press credibility if and when the public is misled.

6.4 THE VALUE OF SPREADING THE NEWS

Even as the industry began raising concerns about the blurring of content and news, researchers observed the emergence of "sociability" (Phillips, 2012) as a pillar of "good" journalism and, related, "shareability" (Harcup and O'Neill, 2017) as a new news value. These represent perhaps the most direct intervention of ritual into an otherwise transmission-oriented model of news. Unlike long-standing news values such as "conflict" or "prominence," which describe the features of an event or issue that make it newsworthy, these new criteria instead anticipate social activity or participation related to the news. That is, they are "preemptive" (Harcup and O'Neill, 2017: 1482) – of other news values and journalistic control. They operate outside the process of deciding what information ought to be processed into news and instead predict the ritual uses to which news might be put.

Of course, there is a much less idealistic way to account for the rise of shareability and sociability: clicks, likes, comments, and shares as metrics of performance. Indeed, as Strömbäck et al. (2012) found, journalists perceive such criteria as contrary to the media's democratic role, with "event properties related to perceived audience interest, production

routines and economic considerations matter[ing] more than they should"
(2012: 726). Noise pollution is a function not only of the number of
outlets for getting news but also of how outlets perceive the nature of
the competition in which they're engaged. If attention is the currency and
attention breeds attention, then the content that consistently captures and
promotes attention – is shared and spread – wins that competition. The
fact that news, like other content, needs to be promoted as well as reported
in such a system further adds to the noise. We are not making any
particular claim about the kind or quality of news saturating the public.
That depends on the networks to which members of the public belong and
the news sources to which they choose to attend. But in this saturated
news environment, notions of proportionality and indicators of importance or impact are hard to come by. So many players are reporting and
commenting on so many aspects of so many events, so frequently, it's easy
for important stories to be overwhelmed, and the public along with them.

The emergence of sociability and shareability, whatever the cause, is
evidence of Parks' (2018) point that news values are not inevitable;
journalists can change them. And the fact that these new values differ
markedly from others – that they are aimed not at the static characteristics
of a potential news event but the potential dynamics of audience interaction with news – lends support to the argument that news as we have
understood it has begun to dissolve (Carey, 1989). Content (unlike news)
does not have to be oriented toward transmission to thrive in the current
system, but it *must* be oriented toward ritual. This is reflected in a media
landscape in which there is content aplenty (including content on current
events) but less news (at least proportionally). News must similarly be
reoriented or redefined to survive.

6.5 CONCLUSION

It is easy to criticize the industry's early impulse to hold fast to a notion of
news as distinctive in the face of the threat posed by the Internet and its
novel content creation and distribution capabilities. Considering that
news organizations had been the predominant, if not the only, mass
distributors of current events content for so long, it is unsurprising that
the conflation of news and content became so ingrained. News as something journalists can and do control – defining it according to certain news
values, gathering and reporting it according to established practices – was
a largely unchallenged notion until, well, technological (and related economic) developments challenged it. We have the benefit of hindsight to see

how news has been overrun by content and how the success of content has begun to reshape the news values journalists employ.

One way to understand how journalism ended up in this predicament is to understand the changes in the media landscape as shifts from a transmission view of communication to a ritual one, as Carey (1989) outlined. And one way to understand the noise we observe across that landscape is as a by-product of that shift. In this chapter we have considered how a definition of news that makes sense in a linear, transmission-oriented media world does not make sense in a networked, ritual-oriented one. Specifically, we have argued that the very stability of the set of news values that has shaped and defined news for over a century renders them suspect in a system where journalists' control is diminished and/or shared. However, a "solution" to this problem, if we want to think of it that way, is not just a simple matter of adapting the news values to fit the present circumstances. Approaching news under the ritual review opens up a path for rethinking the role of journalism in defining the news altogether. Rather than (only) transmitting news to people, essentially operating as importers of information into a system, journalists must also see themselves as full participants in the network through which that news is shared. This would go beyond choosing news based on its anticipated shareability, a practice that has already demonstrated its vulnerability to perverse (with regard to democratic ends) incentives. It would mean asking what is worth sharing and making tough decisions not to share that which is more noise than signal. It would, in danah boyd's (2018) view, require journalists to "own" the subjectivity of news judgment – a difficult task in a transmission-oriented regime in which objectivity is valued but perhaps less onerous in one oriented toward ritual.

We conclude by noting that journalists have employed a consistent set of news values for 100 years for at least one good reason: Those values correspond to how journalists have understood their role in a specific socio-historical context in which few others could undertake the work of informing the public about current events. The historical moment of one-way communication has now passed and in its place a sometimes-cacophonous many-to-many communication system has taken shape. Our argument, then, is not that these were "bad" news values to employ, but that continuing to employ them is not the way to regain the centrality of news or authority of journalism in a noisy, decentered system.

References

boyd, danah (2018). "Media Manipulation, Strategic Amplification, and Responsible Journalism." [blog] *Data & Society Research Institute*, September14. https://points.datasociety.net/media-manipulation-strategic-amplification-and-responsible-journalism-95f4d611f462

Carey, James (1989). "A Cultural Approach to Communication." In *Communication as Culture: Essays on Media and Society* (pp. 13–36). Boston: Unwin Hyman.

Carlson, Matt (2018). "Automating Judgment? Algorithmic Judgment, News Knowledge, and Journalistic Professionalism." *New Media & Society*, 20(5), 1755–1772.

Fidler, Roger (1992, October). "What Are We So Afraid Of?" *American Journalism Review*, https://ajrarchive.org/article.asp?id=1324

Harcup, Tony and Deirdre O'Neill (2017). "What Is News? News Values Revisited (Again)." *Journalism Studies*, 18(12), 1470–1488.

McNamara, Tracy (2000, August). "Defining the Blurry Line between Commerce and Content." *Columbia Journalism Review*, 39(2), 31–32.

Phillips, Angela (2012). "Sociability, Speed and Quality in the Changing News Environment." *Journalism Practice*, 6(5–6), 669–679.

Phillips, Whitney (2018, May 22). *The Oxygen of Amplification: Better Practices for Reporting on Extremists, Antagonists, and Manipulators*. New York: Data & Society Research Institute. https://datasociety.net/output/oxygen-of-amplification/

Parks, Perry (2018). "Textbook News Values: Stable Concepts, Changing Choices." *Journalism & Mass Communication Quarterly*, 96(3), 1–27.

Reese, Cleghorn (1994, April). "Highways and the Nature of Journalism." *American Journalism Review*, http://ajrarchive.org/Article.asp?id=1141

Singer, Jane B. (2018). "Transmission Creep." *Journalism Studies*, 19(2), 209–226.

Strömbäck, Jesper, Michael Karlsson, and David Nicolas Hopmann (2012). "Determinants of News Content." *Journalism Studies*, 13(5–6), 718–728.

PART III

MEDIA AND PROBLEMS OF INCLUSION

7

Journalism and Inclusion

Rodney Benson

Journalism is said to exist to serve the public, the implication being "all the public." This normative vision of journalism's civic purpose is inclusive. And yet all too often, journalism serves as a powerful force for exclusion, for keeping quality information away from those who need it most, and for discouraging anyone but the richest, most educated citizens from participating in the public conversation.[1] Such exclusivity, despite the hype about the democratizing spirit of the digital age, can be found across multiple realms of contemporary cultural reception and production, from

---

[1] From its earliest years, journalism has seesawed back and forth between being a force for exclusion and inclusion. In the seventeenth and eighteenth centuries, the earliest newspapers in England and France provided information about government and finance to a small elite; revolutions in the North American Colonies and France produced a lively partisan press, though again, with a restricted reach. Greater inclusion came with the rise of the commercial "penny press" in the 1830s, but at the price of a more superficial, sensational approach to the news. Radio and television originally reached mass audiences (and still do to a certain extent via public service broadcasting in Europe), but now, along with online media, are increasingly produced for niche, often elite audiences.

blogging and social media to digital activism and documentary television (Deery and Press, 2017; Hindman, 2008; Schradie, 2019).

7.1 EXCLUSION: ECONOMIC AND CULTURAL

Exclusion is produced in at least two major ways: economic and cultural. Some level of economic exclusion is inherent in any profit-maximizing media: so-called free media are funded by advertisers who rarely want to reach everyone, but rather only those members of the public with enough disposable income to buy their products. The meager revenues provided by digital advertising to content producers (i.e., everyone except for Google and Facebook) have led to the rise of paid subscriptions, increasing economic exclusion exponentially.

Cultural exclusion operates when low-income and low-education audiences express little interest in consuming civic-oriented content, even when price is not an issue. To be fair, the reasons for such opting out extend well beyond the strategies of media organizations and include deeply entrenched social inequalities, political alienation, and socialization processes that lead individuals to match their aspirations with their limited options.[2] Nevertheless, media outlets contribute to cultural exclusion when they adopt formats and writing styles that are designed to attract so-called upscale audiences and send an implicit "not welcome" message to everyone else. Because quality media – especially but not only journalism – provide "politically relevant" and "democratically useful" information that are the building blocks of civic life (Williams and Delli Carpini, 2011), we cannot afford to write off such exclusion as the "natural" workings of the market or the "free" choices of consumer-citizens. We need to understand better the extent of exclusion and its causes, as well as solutions that can replace market-driven exclusion with civically focused inclusion.

7.2 PATTERNS AND CONSEQUENCES OF EXCLUSION

Exclusion is nothing new in the media economy. From a purely economic perspective, mid-twentieth-century media were "mass" because they had

---

[2] The classic demonstration of the relationship between cultural consumption/production and class ("social position") is Bourdieu (1984); similar arguments, without systematic empirical data, were also made by Lippmann (1997 [1922]), in his discussion of "social circles." Subsequent sociological studies of social stratification and culture have confirmed, while refining, the general thrust of Bourdieu's findings (see, e.g., Chan, 2010).

not yet figured out an efficient way to reach the "upscale" audiences most coveted by advertisers. With each technological advance in target marketing, media outlets were able to efficiently deliver their advertising clients a closer and closer approximation of likely purchasers. This dynamic was at work during the 1980s and 1990s as metropolitan newspapers increased their revenues by cutting their distribution to low-income neighborhoods (Martin, 2008).

With its supposed drive to make "information free," the Internet was initially heralded as a victory for inclusion, even as its earliest denizens consisted of highly educated elites (Hindman, 2008; Turner, 2006). Even today, it is important to recognize that Internet use is less than universal, even in wealthy post-industrial societies. As of 2015, 84 percent of American adults use the Internet; thus, one in six Americans are excluded. Non-Internet users are much more likely than Internet users to be elderly and to make less than $30,000 per year; they are also much less likely to have a college education and much less likely to make more than $75,000 per year (Perrin and Duggan, 2015).

In the United States, a bifurcated media ecology has been emerging for some time, in which online and print media are increasingly targeted to elite audiences (via subscriptions and donations, supplemented by high-end advertising), while commercial (especially local) television remains the main information source for low-income, low-education audiences (Pew Research Center, 2012; Prior, 2007). The result is a growing gap in the levels of public knowledge and political participation between elites and the rest of the citizenry, far more than exists in northern Europe where taxpayer-supported public media are well-funded, politically autonomous, and trusted by large, inclusive audiences (Curran et al., 2009; Matsa, 2018).

Both economic and cultural exclusion are at work in this splitting of the US public into "news seekers" and "news avoiders." News avoiders, to the extent that they consume news at all, get most of their news from local TV news. Compared to news seekers, news avoiders – half the population – are much less likely than news seekers to have a college degree (17 percent versus 35 percent); much less likely than news seekers to have an income more than $50,000 (15 percent versus 35 percent); and much less likely than news seekers to be registered voters (56 percent versus 82 percent) (Ksiazek et al., 2010).

Data on particular news outlets show a similar overall pattern of exclusion, even as they reveal some differences across types of media, which, I suggest, can be distinguished according to three distinct, but partially overlapping, categories of elite, infotainment, and partisan media (Benson, 2017a).[3] A survey conducted by the Pew Research Center (2012) includes the following outlets: elite (National Public Radio [NPR], *Wall Street Journal*, *New York Times*); infotainment (any local newspaper, *USA Today*, CNN, Network TV, and any local TV); and partisan (MSNBC Rachel Maddow show, Fox News-overall, and Fox Sean Hannity show).

According to Pew (2012), the percentage of college-educated individuals in the audience of elite media are 80 to 100 percent above the national average.[4] Audiences for local newspapers and *USA Today* are 30 to 50 percent above the baseline, but all other infotainment and partisan media are close to the national average. Likewise, audiences for elite media have significantly higher incomes than Americans as a whole. With the exception of the Rachel Maddow show, audiences for infotainment and partisan media hover slightly above or below the national average for income. Finally, we see differences in public affairs knowledge of audiences of various media: Audiences of elite media are 120 to 140 percent above the national average; infotainment media (with the exception of the local newspaper, which is 50 percent over the national average) are in sync with the general population or below (local TV); partisan media consumers, especially of the Maddow Show (more than 150 percent above the average), are better informed than average. My separate analysis of online news media audiences using 2017 Alexa.com data found similar patterns, though the range tended to be narrower and closer to the mean, along with a substantial underrepresentation of African American and other minority audiences and overrepresentation of white audiences.[5]

Thus, we can see that although there are some differences among particular outlets, low-income, low-education, young, and minority audiences tend to be systematically excluded – or exclude themselves – not only from the major national and local print and online news media,

---

[3] The boundaries between these categories are fluid and contested. Many outlets, including network television news, regional newspapers, and digital outlets such as Huffington Post and Vox, try to straddle the infotainment/quality divide. Conservative critics discount claims by the *New York Times* and other "mainstream" media to present themselves as nonpartisan; conversely, Sinclair, the largest local television news chain, seemingly part of the mass infotainment sector, is also highly partisan.

[4] Percentage differences were calculated by the author, comparing outlet audience percentages with national population percentages, as provided by Pew.

[5] Author analysis of March, 2017 Alexa.com audience data by media outlet, with research support from NYU PhD candidate Tim Neff.

especially the elite "mainstream" media, but also some (generally left-leaning) partisan media. The lowest levels of audience education, income, and public knowledge are consistently linked to local TV news, the news source least likely to provide in-depth information on public affairs (Hamilton, 2004).

7.3 HOW SUBSCRIBERS AND DONORS INCREASE EXCLUSION

Two recent tendencies in commercial and noncommercial funding of news outlets seem to be only exacerbating this tendency toward elite siloing of news: digital "paywalls" or subscriptions and nonprofit member financing.

A national survey by the American Press Institute found that newspaper subscribers (combined print and digital) tend to be disproportionately suburban and urban, high or middle income (67 percent versus 57 percent of national population), highly educated (67 percent with college education versus 33 percent of general population), and white (88 percent) (Media Insight Project, 2018).[6]

As one reporter (@RanaForoohar, April, 2018) posted on Twitter: "When I went to the @FT [subscription-only *Financial Times*], a Twitter follower, a steelworker, said: 'That's great for you, but I can't afford to pay to read you anymore.' I think a lot about that every day. I get to do great work. It's only read by the 1%." This is a classic expression of economic exclusion: if not for the high subscription price, this working-class steelworker is saying that he would happily read the quality news coverage provided by the *Financial Times*.

In contrast, philanthropic-supported nonprofit news, created to provide the investigative and other public service news abandoned by many commercial media, is free to all but remains the province of elites. Sadly, given the high hopes it has engendered, nonprofit news demonstrates well the dynamics of cultural exclusion (Benson, 2017b; Konieczna, 2018).

Harvard NiemanLab director Joshua Benton suggests that "paying members of news nonprofits is one of the few media audiences that skews more toward college-educated, upper-middle class, white people

---

[6] In order to compare audience proportions with percentages of the general population, I referred to US government reports: For statistics on US income distribution, see www.statista.com/statistics/203183/percentage-distribution-of-household-income-in-the-us/, and for statistics on US education levels, see www.statista.com/statistics/184260/educational-attainment-in-the-us/.

than daily newspaper subscribers."[7] In principle, however, member donations differ from subscriptions in that "part of what [members] pay for is for others to access" for free.[8] In other words, voluntary contributions are offered in lieu of mandatory subscriptions enforced through paywalls: as a result, some less privileged members of the public *can* make their way to nonprofit news as a result. But how many do? Cultural exclusion is clearly at work. The extant surveys of nonprofit news audiences (including anyone accessing the site, not just members) find elite socio-demographics very similar to those of top-tier commercial media. Forty-three percent of ProPublica's audience has a household income more than $100,000 (compared to 25 percent of the American public); MinnPost's and New Jersey Spotlight's readership surveys likewise have shown that their audiences skew higher income and higher education; Voice of San Diego's "media kit" posted online openly celebrates its affluent audience.[9]

Elite audiences, reinforced by journalists increasingly tending to come from elite backgrounds (Clarke, 2014: 81), produce a commercial media elite-oriented view of the world that systematically underrepresents working class and poor citizens and their perspectives and concerns. A Canadian survey of working-class audiences highlighted the sense of alienation they feel from the kind of news they are presented in most media: 85 percent strongly agree that they are "relatively invisible" in the media. This alienation seems to be at least one factor contributing to the lesser political participation of working-class citizens (Clarke, 2014: 178, 189).

7.4 STEPS TOWARD GREATER INCLUSION

In sum, what is urgently needed, beyond the routine gathering of socio-demographic audience data as part of all news media studies in order to document the extent of exclusion, is a research program addressed to the

---

[7] Josh Benton tweet, April 13, 2018. Benton did not mention specific research.
[8] Carrie Brown (@Brizznyc) tweet, April 14, 2018.
[9] Audience data for these outlets is derived from the following sources: ProPublica, www.propublica.org/article/results-of-our-2017-reader-survey; MinnPost, www.minnpost.com/inside-minnpost/2014/07/survey-finds-our-readers-civically-engaged-and-passionate-about-minnpost-and/; New Jersey Spotlight, https://knightfoundation.org/articles/survey-provides-insight-who-reads-nonprofit-nj-spotlight; Voice of San Diego, www.voiceofsandiego.org/wp-content/uploads/app/pdf/mediakit.pdf

question: what can be done to increase economic and cultural accessibility to high-quality news?

Education is crucial. Starting in primary school, educators need to incorporate media literacy and "free press" appreciation courses as part of a broader civic and critical economic curriculum. Adult education and free access to print and online journalism have long been offered by public libraries: this underappreciated civic institution should be publicly celebrated and strengthened (Klinenberg, 2018). News organization recruitment is also crucial. When and if news organizations that are mostly laying off journalists begin to hire again, it is imperative that they search for journalists with socially or racially disadvantaged backgrounds who can relate to the concerns and interests of non-elite audiences.

For all media, we can demand that they simultaneously achieve civic excellence – watchdog or accountability reporting, diversity of voices and viewpoints, in-depth analysis, historical context – *and* broad public accessibility. However, the means and methods by which these two goals are reconciled will vary by type of media. Let us now consider, each in their turn, the actual and potential steps taken by public, commercial, and nonprofit news media to remove economic and cultural barriers to accessible circulation and consumption of quality news.

7.5 PUBLIC MEDIA

Research has consistently shown that public media, when supported with adequate institutional autonomy and universal citizen funding (which sadly are both lacking in what the United States refers to as "public media," NPR and Public Broadcasting Service [PBS]), offer the most comprehensive and effective means of providing high-quality information to a broad public (Aalberg, 2005; Benson et al., 2017). Universal citizen support of media, through tax revenues or better yet, a dedicated license fee, creates a strong incentive for media to provide a broad range of content in accessible formats for the entire citizenry, even in the age of personalized algorithms (Van Den Bulck and Moe, 2018). In the United States, there is for the moment little hope of increasing national governmental support for public media; there have, however, been some hopeful signs of US "state" governments providing limited funding to keep alive local journalism when the market has abandoned it.[10] PBS and NPR,

---

[10] Rick Rojas, "News from Your Neighborhood Brought to You by the State of New Jersey," *New York Times*, July 30, 2018, www.nytimes.com/2018/07/30/nyregion/nj-

effectively public/nonprofit hybrids, could do more with the resources they have to develop a larger menu of inclusive programming, or to make their existing high-quality news and documentary programming more accessible stylistically and to more aggressively publicize these programs to non-elite audiences. Such a solution would have to be developed in coordination with a foundation sector reoriented toward goals of inclusivity.

7.6 COMMERCIAL MEDIA

While the business model of an increasing number of commercial news outlets has been to attract the highest-income, highest-education audiences in their market (either as subscribers or as desirable targets for advertisers), there do exist some media that still operate according to a mass media model: Buzzfeed, for instance, with its massive but generally younger audience and reliance on native advertising and brand marketing; or local TV news, again, the major news source for lower socioeconomic demographic audiences. The question here is what can be done to inject some level of higher-quality content into a product that relies on sensationalism and clickbait to attract a mass audience. Buzzfeed has added investigative journalism to its website, serious and even prize-winning, but stylistically quite distinct from the kind practiced by the *New York Times*, presumably in order to maintain a bridge to its youthful, irreverent audience (see, for example, a substantial story on abuses by a psychiatric hospital chain headlined "What the Fuck Just Happened?," December 7, 2016[11]). Vice, similarly, joins a youthful style to often quite substantive examination of social problems. Especially strong are its short internationally focused documentaries for HBO; though supported by subscriptions, much of this content is ultimately made available on YouTube for free, suggesting another important way that commercial media can share their quality content with a broad

legislature-community-journalism.html; Christine Schmidt, "How Free Press convinced New Jersey to allocate $2 million for rehabilitating local news," NiemanLab, July 15, 2019, www.niemanlab.org/2019/07/how-free-press-convinced-new-jersey-to-allocate-2 -million-for-rehabilitating-local-news.
[11] See www.buzzfeednews.com/article/rosalindadams/intake. Buzzfeed's financial stability, however, was recently called into question as it was forced to lay off hundreds of journalists. See Janko Roettgers, "Buzzfeed Layoffs Gut National News Desk...", *Variety*, January 25, 2019, https://variety.com/2019/digital/news/buzzfeed-layoffs-national-news-desk-1203118080/.

audience. Efforts underway by the *New York Times* and the *Washington Post* to create Spanish-language online editions offer another potential move toward inclusiveness (to the extent that these editions remain accessible without subscriptions). The question of how much commercial social media platforms like Facebook, Twitter, and YouTube contribute to distribution of professional and amateur media content to a broad, socio-economically diverse audience or alternatively to a narrow, targeted audience ought also to be at the top of our research agenda. A recent study finds that social media tend to diversify rather than narrow users' news diets (Fletcher and Nielsen, 2017).

The British newspaper *The Guardian* and the French newspaper *Le Monde* suggest ways that commercial media can attain civic goals, in both cases involving some willingness to forgo maximum profitability. *The Guardian* is one of the world's biggest news sites, with 155 million monthly unique users; most of its advertising revenues derive from its 10 million regular online readers. This revenue is supplemented by 575,000 "members" who give regular contributions, plus 375,000 "one-off" contributions during the previous 12 months. *The Guardian*'s editor, Katharine Viner, has called the newspaper's approach a "third way [presumably between advertising and subscriptions] to pay for quality journalism." *The Guardian*'s website touts its reliance on voluntary contributions as essential to its "mission to keep independent journalism accessible to everyone, regardless of where they live or what they can afford." This approach has allowed *The Guardian*, owned by the nonprofit Scott Trust, to "break even on an operating basis" by 2019 (Waterson, 2018). It's not clear how much *The Guardian* is actually reaching beyond the "usual suspects" with its free readership – that is, self-selected cultural exclusion may still be at work – but the newspaper has admirably tried hard to eliminate economic exclusion.

Le Monde has adopted a multifaceted approach. The venerable French newspaper has rapidly grown its digital subscriptions to staunch its financial losses, while continuing to offer some free online content. Notable is "The Decoders" (Les Décodeurs), which draws on a fourteen-person team to offer "explainer stories, data visualizations, and debunking of fake news," in short high-quality news written in an "accessible" style for a broad audience. In order to reach young people, *Le Monde* is also posting stories on Snapchat Discovery: the idea is to "repackage our news in a pedagogical/fun way [while] keeping the same rigor" as elsewhere in the newspaper. Finally, *Le Monde* is a partner, along with the news agency Agence France Press, in a government-subsidized association called "Between the Lines" (Entre Les Lignes), which creates media literacy workshops for middle and high schools.

The workshops are designed to help students detect online misinformation and to inform them about professional journalistic ethics and standards (Satariano and Peltier, 2018; Prieur, 2018).[12] *Le Monde*'s approach is exemplary because it addresses cultural exclusion both at the level of production (by consciously "repackaging" its regular content in accessible styles and by recirculating content where its desired audiences will actually discover it, such as on Snapchat) and of reception (raising awareness among marginalized audiences about the importance of quality information and how to know when it is present or absent).

Television is likely to become more rather than less important as an accessible news source in the years to come. As the print and online journalism sectors have suffered massive financial losses and staff cutbacks, television news has enjoyed an economic golden age (Knight Foundation, 2018). Given everything that we know about institutional incentives, we should not be surprised that this financial success has generally not translated into civic service: indeed, in a recent nationwide survey of broadcast journalists, "diminished quality is a rising concern" (Reinardy and Bacon, 2014). Despite the long odds, improving local commercial TV news has to be at the top of any US reform agenda for inclusivity simply because this is where the audience is.

Local television news may still mostly follow the mantra "if it bleeds, it leads," and yet mixed in with all the crime and scandals one can find quality news stories about local government, consumer protection, and policy debates. Some of this higher-quality material may be due to partnerships with nonprofits, as noted in the next section. Other outstanding work may be the result of strategic attempts to win a journalistic prize like a Peabody or Emmy Award, with an eye toward future marketing campaigns.

Research is surprisingly limited, but studies have shown, for instance, that "smaller media group"-owned television channels produced more "local news, more locally produced video, and more use of on-air reporters" than "larger chain-based" broadcasts (Scott et al., 2008); another study (Abdenour, 2018) found no statistically significant difference in "true" investigative reporting between stock market traded and privately held television

[12] All three projects were detailed by Cécile Prieur, *Le Monde* Deputy Editor for Digital Innovation, in an email communication to the author, January 28, 2019, while she was a Knight Fellow at Stanford researching digital accessibility. For information on The Decoders, see www.lemonde.fr/les-decodeurs/article/2018/03/12/ce-que-4-annees-de-de codeurs-nous-ont-appris_5269670_4355770.html; on Snapchat, see www.lemonde.fr/a ctualite-medias/article/2016/09/15/decouvrez-la-premiere-edition-du-monde-sur-snap chat-discover_4997848_3236.html.

stations, but did find a greater amount of investigative reporting in highly competitive markets. Countering the widespread assumption that only low-est-common-denominator content (crime, disasters, and other soft news) will attract audiences, Belt and Just (2008: 194) discovered that "solid reporting on significant issues actually produce better ratings than slapdash or super-ficial tabloid journalism." The challenge in this case is to make sure television editors receive this message: that indeed there sometimes can be a commercial-civic "win-win," but that it requires vision and risk. Scholars should research TV news with an eye toward separating the wheat from the chaff; instead of assuming that all local commercial TV news is "bad," we could search for the exceptions and try to understand better how and why some have broken the mold, even if only occasionally. We should also respect the limitations and potentials of each medium: commercial television news may never be the place to get in-depth information, but it can help make people aware of important issues, sparking interest that will lead to further explorations.

7.7 NONPROFIT MEDIA

Finally, despite its limitations, nonprofit journalism can and must be part of the solution. As noted earlier, the path to financial stability for nonprofits is the same as for high-quality commercial media: toward cultivating and speaking primarily to prosperous elite audiences. One civic path to reaching beyond such circles is partnering with mass commercial media: we see this, for instance, in Voice of San Diego's partnership with a local NBC franchise, to create short segments once a week. The other way is through greater efforts to directly target content and distribution to marginalized audiences. For instance, researchers could examine more closely these and other examples:

- the San Francisco Public Press's sustained four times per year pub-lication of a $1 newspaper (supplementing its website) for circula-tion to readers in poorer neighborhoods that are less likely to have Internet access;[13]
- the St. Louis Beacon's efforts to reach marginalized communities through "accessible" writing and graphics and by holding outreach events in "the most unprivileged section of the city" in order to "hear the voice of an often unheard demographic, the one...market-driven organizations would predominantly ignore" (Ferrucci, 2014: 916); and

---

[13] See https://sfpublicpress.org/where-to-buy-the-newspaper.

- the Chicago news site City Bureau, which has expressly tried to write about and reach underrepresented, especially "black and Hispanic," communities more than its much larger commercial rival, the *Chicago Tribune*, and then has partnered with *The Chicago Reader*, the *Guardian*, and local community papers such as the *Chicago Defender* and the *Chicago Reporter* to help distribute its articles (Nelson, 2018: 208).

Compared to public and commercial media, these nonprofit initiatives are destined to remain small, but they inject needed energy and diversity into the larger media ecology. Working in partnership with commercial or public media, their impact can be further magnified. What is crucial is that the major foundations that underwrite this sector engage in a major rethinking of their vision and purpose. Instead of defining sustainability as the capacity to gain elite donors or impact as measures of influence on policymakers and other elites, they could embrace what they are best equipped to do in the US context: provide long-term, no-strings-attached funds to produce quality news for marginalized audiences ignored by commercial media.

7.8 CONCLUSION

A media system, such as that of the United States, that only reaches half of the population and that reserves "high-quality" news only for a small elite within this half is not adequately serving democracy. As scholars, our responsibility is to learn more about the individuals and organizations who are pursuing a different path, who are aware of the problem of journalistic exclusion, and who are doing what they can to make their quality journalism – both economically and culturally – available to the widest possible audience. In other words: Where is quality and accessibility being joined? Who is working to achieve inclusion, rather than exclusion? What did they do? And how well did they succeed?

References

Aalberg, Toril (2015, December 28). *Report: Does Public Media Enhance Citizen Knowledge?* London: Political Economy Research Centre. www.perc.org.uk/project_posts/perc-paper-13-does-public-media-enhance-citizen-knowledge/
Abdenour, Jesse (2017). "Inspecting the Investigators: An Analysis of Television Investigative Journalism and Factors Leading to Its Production." *Journalism & Mass Communication Quarterly*, 95(4), 1058–1078.

Belt, Todd L. and Marion R. Just (2008). "The Local News Story: Is Quality a Choice?" *Political Communication*, 25(2), 194–215.

Benson, Rodney (2017a). "The New American Media Landscape." In A. Davis (ed.), *The Death of Public Knowledge?* (pp. 69–85). London: Goldsmiths University Press.

Benson, Rodney (2017b). "Can Foundations Solve the Journalism Crisis?" *Journalism*, 19(8), 1059–1077.

Benson, Rodney, Matthew Powers, and Timothy J. Neff (2017). "Public Media Autonomy and Accountability: A Comparative Analysis of Best Policy Practices in 12 Leading Democracies." *International Journal of Communication*, 11, 1–22.

Chan, Tak Wing (ed.) (2010). *Social Status and Cultural Consumption*. Cambridge: Cambridge University Press.

Clarke, Debra M. (2014). *Journalism and Political Exclusion: Social Conditions of News Production and Reception*. Montreal: McGill-Queen's University Press.

Curran, James, Shanto Iyengar, Anker Brink Lund, and Inka Salovaara-Moring (2009). "Media System, Public Knowledge, and Democracy: A Comparative Study." *European Journal of Communication*, 24(1), 5–26.

Deery, June and Andrea Press (eds.) (2017). *Media and Class*. New York: Routledge.

Ferrucci, Patrick (2015). "Public Journalism No More: The Digitally Native News Nonprofit and Public Service Journalism." *Journalism*, 16(7), 904–919.

Fletcher, Richard and Rasmus Kleis Nielsen (2017). "Social Media Appears to Diversify Your News Diet, Not Narrow It." Nieman Lab, June 21. www.niemanlab.org/2017/06/using-social-media-appears-to-diversify-your-news-diet-not-narrow-it/

Hamilton, James (2004). *All the News That's Fit to Sell*. Princeton: Princeton University Press.

Hindman, Matthew (2008). *The Myth of Digital Democracy*. Princeton: Princeton University Press.

Klinenberg, Eric (2018). *Palaces for the People: How Social Infrastructure Can Help Fight Inequality, Polarization, and the Decline of Civic Life*. New York: Penguin Random House.

Knight Foundation (2018, April 5). *Report: Local TV News and the New Media Landscape*. https://knightfoundation.org/reports/local-tv-news-and-the-new-media-landscape

Konieczna, Magda (2018). *Journalism without Profit*. New York: Oxford University Press.

Ksiazek, Thomas B., Edward C. Malhouse, and James G. Webster (2010). "News-seekers and Avoiders: Exploring Patterns of Total News Consumption Across Media and the Relationship to Civic Participation." *Journal of Broadcasting and Electronic Media*, 54(4), 551–568.

Lippmann, Walter (1997) [1922]. *Public Opinion*. New York: Free Press.

Martin, Christopher R. (2008). "'Upscale' News Audiences and the Transformation of Labour News." *Journalism Studies*, 9(2), 178–194.

Matsa, Katerina Eva (2018). "Across Western Europe, Public News Media Are Widely Used and Trusted Sources of News." Pew Research Center, June 8. www.pewresearch.org/fact-tank/2018/06/08/western-europe-public-news-media-widely-used-and-trusted/

Media Insight Project (2018). "Respondents' Demographics and News Behaviors." Arlington, VA: American Press Institute, February 27. www.americanpressinstitute.org/publications/reports/survey-research/subscribers-appendix-1/

Nelson, Jacob L. (2018). "And Deliver Us to Segmentation." *Journalism Practice*, 12(2), 204–219.

Perrin, Andrew and Maeve Duggan (2015, June 26). *Report: Americans' Internet Access: 2000–2015*. Washington, DC: Pew Research Center.

Pew Research Center (2012). "Demographics and Political Views of News Audiences." In *Changing News Landscape, Even Television is Vulnerable*. www.people-press.org/2012/09/27/section-4-demographics-and-political-views-of-news-audiences/

Prieur, Cécile (2018). "Let's Open the Gates to Paid Content Models: It Is Becoming Urgent to Work on How We Can Expand the Reach of Paid Quality Journalism to Everyone." *Medium*, December 1. https://medium.com/jsk-class-of-2019/lets-open-the-gates-to-paid-content-news-models-e4062c70b7ed

Prior, Markus (2007). *Post-Broadcast News*. Cambridge: Cambridge University Press.

Reinardy, Scott and Chris Bacon (2014). "Feast and Famine? Local Television News Workers Expand the Offerings but Say They Are Hungry for Quality Journalism." *Journal of Media Practice*, 15(2), 133–145.

Satariano, Adam and Elian Peltier (2018, December 13). "In France, School Lessons Ask: Which Twitter Post Should You Trust?" *New York Times*.

Schradie, Jen (2019). *The Revolution That Wasn't*. Cambridge, MA: Harvard University Press.

Scott, David K., Robert H. Gobetz, and Mike Chanslor (2008). "Chain Versus Independent Television Station Ownership: Toward an Investment Model of Commitment to Local News Quality." *Communication Studies*, 59(1), 84–98.

Turner, Fred (2006). *From Counterculture to Cyberculture*. Chicago, IL: University of Chicago Press.

Van Den Bulck, Hilde and Hallvard Moe (2018). "Public Service Media, Universality and Personalization through Algorithms: Mapping Strategies and Exploring Dilemmas." *Media, Culture, and Society*, 40(6), 875–892.

Waterson, Jim (2018, July 24). "Guardian Media Group Digital Revenues Outstrip Print for First Time." *The Guardian*.

Williams, Bruce and Michael X. Delli Carpini (2011). *After Broadcast News*. Cambridge: Cambridge University Press.

8

Afrotechtopolis

How Computing Technology Maintains Racial Order

Charlton McIlwain

On September 6, 2018, *The Intercept* announced a startling revelation. IBM had been, for at least five years, using NYPD surveillance footage to develop automated/artificial intelligence technology that allows police to use skin color as a marker to search for criminal suspects (Joseph and Lipp, 2018). The revelation laid bare a list of vexing concerns: about the close relationship and data flow between law enforcement and private enterprise. Privacy concerns. But most of all, concerns that such a system is destined to ingest and manifest our worst stereotypes, prejudices, and fears about racial Others. Concerns that the so-called usual suspects from communities of color would be unnecessarily and disproportionately targeted, criminalized, incarcerated, and stripped of their civil rights and liberties.

As alarming as *The Intercept*'s revelations were – the fact that IBM and the NYPD collaborated to build such a problematic tool isn't the primary problem here. What should concern us, give us pause, and motivate us to action is that the development of such a tool was utterly predictable. Predictable not just from five years out – but fifty. Here's what's worse. If this precise scenario was foreseeable fifty years ago, it means we also had plenty of time to derail it, but failed to do so.

This failure is encompassed in a concept, a theory, that I call *Afrotechtopolis*. I build the concept on the foundation of Omi and Winant's (1998) racial formation theory, which, among other things, helps to explain how racial orders, systems, and hierarchies develop, persist, and potentially change. Racial formation theory posits that representational systems define and determine racial meaning, and influence our perceptions of racialized people – usually in the form of value. These representational systems shape and are shaped by institutional structures. Together, representational systems and institutional structures distribute power, resources, benefits, and privileges along racial lines and in accordance with the dominant racial group. Representational systems and the institutional structures are self-regulating, but can be influenced through particular racial projects that are used to maintain racial order (equilibrium) or that try to upset that equilibrium.

Outlined in the following text, *Afrotechtopolis* describes the way that the new computer revolution and the civil rights movement developed not in parallel but were set on a collision course at the start of the 1960s. This was the moment that race, racism, and white supremacy developed as part and parcel of the development of new computational systems and networks whose first principles and use cases sought to ameliorate the threat posed by blackness, black people, and black claims to civil rights. This formation resulted in a master–slave relationship to new computational systems in which black people were subject to, rather than agents of this new technology. This relationship, I argue, continues to negatively shape black people's relationship to computing technology up through the present day. Further, I argue that the fact that computer technology's first principles were racially defined by the need to neutralize the criminal threat posed by black people calls into question the degree to which we may actually be able to marshal it today to engineer racial justice.

8.1 REVOLUTION, REVOLUTION, REVOLUTION: OUR STORIES ABOUT RACE AND TECH

By their very nature, revolutions materialize abruptly. Revolutions rupture. Revolutions divide. Revolutions transform old into new. And as the 1960s dawned on the United States, black people were revolutionizing their place within the country's social structure – by hook and crook, through rage and riot, launching protests, demonstrations, and constitutional offensives. But their actions – and the reasons for them – also made black people America's greatest problem. Meanwhile, the scientists, the psychologists, the linguists, the engineers, the would-be titans of industry, heads of state, political power brokers, and bureaucrats – they all mixed and mingled money and ideas. They invented and innovated. Simultaneously independent of, but dependent on black Americans, they began to march the nation fast and forward toward a predictable and seemingly inevitable technological future. But a new generation came of age in the middle of it all. They wanted to imagine a different future, chart a course that they had designed for themselves. These are our revolutionary stories from the 1960s.

Historian Jacqueline Dowd Hall (2005) once said that the stories we tell about this particular moment in our past have serious implications. The political futures and racial projects enabled by the stories we tell are – in some ways – as critical as the historical moments themselves. And we've told ourselves many stories about the revolutions that ran their course throughout the 1960s – the computer revolution, the countercultural revolution, and the civil rights revolution. The books and journals that preserve them bow library shelves. We showcase them on pedestals at warehouse bookstores. They lay side by side on outdoor magazine racks, inviting the casual browser. But three computer and Internet origin stories in particular, told from within this triple revolution moment in the 1960s, illustrate what is fundamentally wrong with the decade's history, as we've come to know it.

In *When Wizards Stay Up Late*, Katie Hafner (1998) leads us on a journey back in time to the Internet's prime visionary – J. C. R. Licklider. Licklider began his scholarly career in psychoacoustics. Over the years, he animated several of MIT's electronics, communications, and computing laboratories. He sparked a number of early computer networking adventures at the MIT-spawned company Bolt, Baranek and Newman (BBN). And, in 1963, before returning to the Corporation, he took the helm of the US Advanced Research Projects Agency (ARPA). There he directed critical funding to projects at MIT, BBN, and other universities and private sector labs. These entities – and more importantly the networks, collaborations, and competition that formed between them – developed critical innovations. These included everything from the packet-switching technologies needed to build computer networks, to the computer operating systems that power large-scale computation, to the graphical user interface, artificial intelligence, and other explorations into human–computer interaction. Hafner's story about the 1960s computer revolution that led to the Internet's creation is a story about invention and individual genius. It is also a story about the explosively creative power formed when the public sector invests in, and private sector capital sustains the application of such inventive genius.

Hafner's is an ivory tower tale that dramatizes the Internet's origins as a networking enterprise sparked and shaped firmly within the 1960s computer revolution. But some passed through those same ivory towers, captured its cybernetic vision, rejected its computerized command and control systems, and then charged out its front doors to evangelize the masses. They launched a quest to radically reimagine human social life. This is the story Fred Turner tells about Stuart Brand, and the attempt within the 1960s counterculture to wrest computing technology away from the warmongers and technocrats. They wanted to harness its connective ethos and technological power to create a culture of connection, a culture of mutuality, and a culture of sharing and peace. This vision of "digital utopianism," described in Turner's *From Counterculture to Cyberculture* (2008), follows computing's sociotechnical development throughout the 1970s, 1980s, and 1990s. That vision, Turner argues, established a "cyberculture" that was already deeply rooted when Tim Berners-Lee's World Wide Web came online in 1992.

Hafner brought us her story in 1998, when the Internet was still – essentially – new. Turner's appears almost a decade later. But it would be five more years still until someone offered a story – at least a glimpse of one – that attempted to connect the 1960s computer and counterculture revolutions to the black revolution playing out across America's cities, ghettos, churches, lunch counters, labor union meetinghouses, college campuses, the halls of Congress, the court, and the Oval Office. In 2011, software historian Tara Mcpherson wrote the lead essay for Lisa Nakamura and Peter A. Chow-White's (2011) collection *Race after the Internet*. There, McPherson chronicles what she describes as two parallel histories germinating in the 1960s. On one side, she describes turmoil within the computing community. At Bell Labs and in similar institutional spaces, computer scientists and their ilk debated the utility of the UNIX versus MULTICS operating systems. On the other, she depicts the civil rights battles being waged by its range of organizations and activists, from the NAACP and Southern Christian Leadership Conference to the emerging Black nationalists and black power movements.

These two stories, however – as McPherson tells them – resemble two invisible ships passing blindly in the night. They share just a single quality: a modular and lenticular logic. "This push toward modularity and the covert in digital computation," McPherson wrote about the UNIX operating system's primary feature, also reflects other changes in the organization of social life in the United States by the 1960s. For instance, if the first half of the twentieth century laid bare its racial logics, from "Whites Only" signage to the brutalities of lynching, the second half increasingly hides its racial "kernel," burying it below a shell of neoliberal pluralism. These covert or lenticular racial logics take hold at the tail end of the Civil Rights Movement at least partially to cut off and contain the more radical logics implicit in the urban uprisings that shook Detroit, Watts, Chicago, and Newark. (2011: 29)

McPherson positions the 1960s computing and 1960s civil rights battles as worlds apart in terms of the everyday concerns that dogged their respective players and the implications each had for the other. However, this version of the story reflects precisely why the familiar narratives told about the computing, counterculture, and civil rights revolutions limit our ability to understand the historical and contemporary relationship between black people, computing, and the Internet. The fact is that the computer, counterculture, and black revolutions are not three separate narratives. Rather, together they comprise a single story.

The computer revolution – popularly described in those days by the terms automation and cybernation – animated the civil rights movements, its activists, its organizations, its platforms, its planning, and its proposed policy resolutions. To say, as McPherson does, that the folks developing software at computing labs had nothing to do with these concerns misses the point. The civil rights revolution played out quite literally on these people's doorsteps. Those cloistered safely in their campus labs decided that the protests, demonstrations, and boycotts happening within earshot of their unbroken windows did not concern them. They chose to tinker with their machines.

Meanwhile, Stewart Brand's counterculturalists embraced the same cybernetic vision that A. Philip Randolph spoke about, standing before the Brotherhood of Sleeping Car Porters:

Inasmuch as technology is a collective creation of the people, the people should share in the fruits of technology and hence the worker should not be displaced by the machine. The community and the government have a responsibility to see to it that the machine does not take bread out of the mouths of the workers. (1962)

But the counterculturalists took their work and vision and slipped off to the countryside and the communes. Those that did not waged a war against the emerging conflict in Vietnam. Though they championed racial justice in principle, their link to black people's fight and fate remained tenuous at best.

Here is the problem. Hafner conjured men and machines that apparently have no politics. Turner's counterculturalists imagined technological futures that black people were not equipped to summon. McPherson describes black people battling oppression at the hands of white men, but does not directly connect that oppression and the supposedly colorblind machine that threated to replace them both. If we are to understand what I call *Afrotechtopolis* – the ways in which America's racial representations and institutional structures inculcated the new computing systems that came to define our new technological and social order – then we need a new story. We need to frame technological innovation, utopianism, and racially marked dystopian futures so that they narrate a single story.

8.2 AFROTECHTOPOLIS

As much as today's digital technology is available, open, and hackable, it – or, maybe more appropriately, we – remains tethered to computer technology's first principles (as a problem-solving tool) and what animated its first uses (to thwart racial revolution). This is to say that the capacity of today's digital would-be revolutionaries is governed and regulated by *Afrotechtopolis*, a history, a politics, as a set of relationships embedded in America's technological and civil rights past, which explains how our preexisting racial order was folded into, taken up, maintained, and extended by a new computational order that began to be developed, in earnest, at the dawn of the 1960s.

Afrotechtopolis is not a place. It is the name I use to describe a theory that explains a uniquely American techno-racial formation. *Afrotechtopolis* developed at the beginning of the 1960s when computing soldered black America's revolution for racial equality onto an emerging technological revolution, commonly labeled "automation" and/or "cybernation." These fused revolutions exposed and exploited a specific set of interests and relationships between key people and institutions connected to them both: higher education, private enterprise, and the combination of federal, state, and local government. This institutional fusion produced *Afrotechtopolis*, a matrix that began to structure and regulate black people's social, economic, and political position and standing within a society increasingly governed by computational thinking. In the following paragraphs, I summarize how *Afrotechtopolis* was built, and how this particular techno-racial formation worked to shape our prevailing technological order in the service of maintaining our prevailing racial order.

8.3 NOT-SO-STRANGE BEDFELLOWS

The nation's "race problem" was the first major social problem computers were asked to solve when they were first being developed in the early 1960s. When President Johnson needed to subdue and contain the 1960s black revolution and urban uprisings throughout the 1960s – from Watts to Newark, Rochester, New York, to Kansas City, Missouri – his government enlisted and incentivized IBM to do the job.

Under the guise, and operating under the authority of Johnson's twin commissions – the 1965 Crime Commission and the 1968 Kerner Commission – IBM used federal, state, and local government crime data, and local police practice protocols to develop the prototype systems (hardware, software, predictive algorithms, and telecommunications systems) used to profile, target, apprehend, and incarcerate criminal suspects based on race – beginning in 1964. IBM personnel (from software designers to salesmen) and systems were part of the vast majority of the more than 900 law enforcement surveillance systems built for police departments across the nation, from 1965 to 1980 and beyond – long after the black, revolutionary "threat" had seemingly subsided.

Having been represented fundamentally as a "problem," race and blackness became uniquely subjected to computing machines' primary utility – problem-solving. Government institutions framed the problem, enjoined their counterparts in private enterprise and higher education to translate the problem into computational form, and then set it loose to do its work.

8.4 WHAT MUST WE DO TO BE SAVED?

> After the computer has defined, on tape, the ideal Holstein, could it then turn its impersonal, unprejudiced magic upon our agonizing race problem? Could it not, after digesting the facts which both whites and blacks have fogged over for so long, give us an outline of our obligations? Instead of being a measure of the Negro's lag, cannot the computer become a guidepost to interracial justice and peace?(Wilkins, 1967)

This was presented as a technical question, asked not by a technologist but by a civil rights leader and activist – in 1967. The question recognized computational power. It recognized that the machine – carrying out human motivations through its programming – was ambivalent, malleable. It recognized that if we just reframed the problem so that the scourge of racism and white supremacy – not black people – was our most prominent national threat – perhaps the computer's great data processing capabilities could calculate a solution for us. If only we were so motivated.

It is hard to tell whether NAACP President Roy Wilkins meant this question to be rhetorical or a call to action. I suspect it was the former, especially given that Wilkins had a seat on Kerner's Commission and at least had the opportunity to witness firsthand the manifold ways that the government, private enterprise (IBM), and elite higher science and engineering institutions (like MIT) colluded to make black people the first targets of new computational systems. However, Wilkins' outlook, upbringing, and conservative-leaning politics suggest the latter. Either way, his question offered us a way forward by proposing that we sit, ask, and contemplate the possibilities of a problem thusly framed and computational power thusly mobilized.

Bayard Rustin – the principal architect with labor leader A. Philip Randolph of the 1963 March on Washington – contemplated the computer and Negro futures differently. Bayard, like Randolph, like Adam Clayton Powell saw what Lyndon Johnson's Labor Secretary saw coming in 1965 – a collision between the black civil rights revolution and the developing computer revolution. "Call it automation, cybernation or age of the robots, the technological revolution is here and here to stay; call it civil rights, or equal opportunity or 'peaceable protest for freedom now', it is equally evident that the Negro revolution is here," stated President Lyndon Johnson's Labor Secretary W. Willard Wirtz:

> There are machines now which can play excellent games of checkers, and they can play pretty good games of chess; they can play a fair hand of bridge; they can interpret books. They are doing in a good many ways skilled as well as unskilled jobs in the economy. They have no hands but they can tabulate checks, and they make no mistakes. They have no eyes and yet they watch over the industrial process without ever blinking. It has taken only thirty years to move from the fantasy of "Rossum's Universal Robot" to the reality of Univac and its brother computers, and today's reality is more fantastic than the fiction of the 1920's. (Wilkins, 1967)

Randolph, Rustin, King, Wirtz, and even Wilkins recognized the writing on the Wall. Alogorithmic decision-making (what those of that era referred to as "cybernation") predestined an outcome of apocalyptic proportions for black people and other people of color in the United States. Predestined because history showed at every turn that America's system of white supremacy always determined how technology would be used – to enrich white men with wealth and power and keep black people in bondage of one form or another.

Still, Rustin (perhaps more than the rest) recognized that our past did not have to be a prologue. He envisioned a detour from our usual path. He could see a way for black women and men to thrive economically, socially, and politically through the computer revolution. His vision required three necessary conditions. First was education – black folks would have greater access to it, particularly math, science, and engineering education and training. Rustin recognized in 1964 that "there is nothing taught in any school in the United States today which is in the direction of preparing people for the fundamental revolution which is taking place in this nation, which is a technological revolution which will change our total way of life and every institution in it, and that is the revolution of Cybernation and Automation."

Second, Rustin's vision required planning. Those in power leading key institutions would, like a computer, have to develop and run an algorithm specifically designed for black people to gain access to what they needed to master their own fates in the new computer society – at scale, and within a particular time period before it was too late to reverse course. "We must have a national response which would include massive planning, revolutionary planning if we are to deal with these problems," Rustin wrote.

Third, Rustin's vision required national will:

The question before us today is whether that alliance can remain intact to deal with much more fundamental questions than the limited public accommodations aspects which the church and others were willing to come into because they came in not as if these were political objectives; they came in in response to what the Negro said he wanted, which was dignity. But in order to truly put Negroes back to work and to tear down slums, in order really to get a decent education there has to be a national response which goes to government and which demands billions and billions and billions of dollars. And the alternative to this is social chaos.

Rustin advocated for a specific racial project that would fundamentally transform black people's relationship to the computer and the developing computational society. Rustin argued that only by restructuring this relationship to computational tools, the institutions that produced them, incentivized their use, and prepared people to use them, could black people imagine a different fate – a fate in which they could master, rather than perpetually be the victims of, computing technology.

8.5 RUSTIN, RANDOLPH, AND WILKINS: THE CALL FIFTY YEARS LATER

Much has changed since that initial confrontation between civil rights and the computer revolution. We live not just in a computer society but a computational age. Not a society that merely uses computers as means to particular ends, but a society organized, structured, and built on computational thinking. Part of this new technological environment, this new media environment is the ability for the masses, in limited ways, to seize the reins of technology for revolutionary (and counter-revolutionary) purposes.

After fifty years, some things have not changed – chiefly the drive to deploy digital technology to target, surveil, apprehend, incarcerate, and incapacitate individuals and communities of color. But we have seen some recent successes marshaling digital technology to thwart these ends. The movement for black lives is perhaps our greatest exemplar and requires that we acknowledge the extraordinary power that today's digital tools provide activists organizing to pursue racial justice.

Think about this. The year 1972 was, until recently, the last year that US citizens heralded racial issues among the nation's most pressing problems. On the heels of the 2016 presidential election, race and racism ranked third on the list of Americans' greatest concerns. Fewer whites today believe America's criminal justice system treats whites and blacks equally, than they did when the Black Lives Matter movement began in Ferguson, Missouri. In the years following Ferguson, Black Lives Matter remains a household phrase.

Black Lives Matter was, and in some ways continues to be, a disruptive movement, reflecting the most visible, persistent, and concentrated demonstration of racial justice activism since the 1960s. In addition to the public opinion and behavioral shifts it ignited, the movement for black lives made a considerable impact on our politics and public policy in real and significant ways. The Democratic Party in 2016 inked in its platform the most lengthy, detailed, and forthright position statement on racial justice, discrimination, and inequality in recent history. For the first time in that same recent memory, the Republican Party actually did the same (though theirs was considerably shorter and predictably less audacious in terms of what should be done to remedy discrimination). For the first time in recent memory, the US Department of Justice investigated, documented, and described in elaborate detail through the Ferguson Report how structural, institutional racism develops and flourishes in twenty-first-century America. Many public outlets – from the *Washington Post* to Mapping Police Violence (Sinyangwe, 2018) – now for the first time track the number of police-involved shootings and other acts of violence where people of color are most frequently victims.

Recognizing these successes, we must also acknowledge that today's racial justice activism didn't explode on the scene spontaneously. It required disruptive technologies and disruptive people to channel that technology toward disruptive ends. It necessitated an information infrastructure that both produced and distributed compelling, consumable, and usable content about race, racial issues, and racial politics. Social media organizing on this scale required a level of comfort with doing identity work, race work, and organizing work in a digitally mediated environment. And, it required the ability to fuse new and old media, and new and old principles of organizing in complementary ways. In this sense, Black Lives Matter was, practically, thirty years in the making.

The necessary conditions for today's increasingly visible, reinvigorated, and technologically driven racial justice movement developed over three decades, through five overlapping phases. In the first, black hobbyists, gossips, tinkerers, and racial uplift advocates hacked early computer networks to form racial interest-based communities. In phases two and three, an emerging digital elite (motivated by educational, political, and entrepreneurial interests) harnessed the Internet's new connective power to produce new markets for racialized and racially targeted content. In phase four, journalists, intellectuals, celebrities, and activists of color leveraged the new forms of social media to create dense networks poised to heighten public attention to the new millennium's most pressing racial issues. In phase five, this network flexed its collective muscle, bringing its power to bear on changing the political and public policy dynamics that continue to structure racial inequality. This is the Black Lives Matter story. This was America's first demonstration that technology, trickled down to the previously excluded masses, could both intellectually (those with expertise to think deeply about how technology works) and practically (those with the creative ingenuity and risk aversion to experiment with technology and thus stimulate action and reaction) leverage technology for limited revolutionary purposes. The question is – is it enough? This is to say, can access to today's digital tools liberate us from a longstanding technological structure that has long been nestled inside an even longer standing racial order (Browne, 2015)?

Today's racial justice movement must transform its relationship with technology. Continuing to rely on corporate, third-party media platforms limits the movement's ability to apply ample pressure to force change. Today's new media vanguard mastered other people's digital tools to accomplish its goals. Tomorrow's must own and control the means of disruption. It is imperative that media and communication scholars work to communicate why we should, what it means, and how we must go about controlling the means of technological and political disruption to our current racial order. But how do we begin to accomplish these objectives and do so at a scale that makes a difference?

As an example, the free software movement – and variations thereof – was once offered as such a revolutionary possibility. In some ways, the free software movement was a fulfillment of Stewart Brand's counterculturalists – a way to radically democratize technology by placing it in the hands of anyone and everyone who wanted to wield its power. According to the Free Software Foundation:

A program is free software if the program's users have the four essential freedoms: The freedom to run the program as you wish, for any purpose (freedom 0); The freedom to study how the program works, and change it so it does your computing as you wish (freedom 1); Access to the source code is a precondition for this; The freedom to redistribute copies so you can help your neighbor (freedom 2); and the freedom to distribute copies of your modified versions to others (freedom 3). (2019)

This form of neoliberal freedom provides maximum agency to individuals rather than governmental or capitalistic institutions. However, it fundamentally disregards the fact that black people and people of color more generally have never been free to act independently of strong state and private institutions that limit their physical, social, economic, and technological mobility and therefore their agency. Software can be as free as it wants to be, but that will not change the fact that our educational institutions only minimally prepare people of color to even use such tools, much less master and control them. And returning to the Black Lives Matter story with which I began this chapter offers a more strident admonition that, for black people, even technological mastery does not equal control. Black Lives Matter proliferated, organized, and transformed itself again on social media platforms like Twitter in part because black people had mastered that digital platform and used it to diffuse into mass visibility or contract into fractured, simultaneous, independent offline protests. But it did not take long before local, state, and national law enforcement had begun to infiltrate Black Lives Matter social media networks to surveil their movements, communications, planning, and actions (Joseph and Hussain, 2018).

I am not prepared to provide a complete answer to my own question: How do we transform our technological order so that black people and people of color are not doomed to a future where we remain its laborers, its caretakers, its data, and its victims? If our technological order is not only tethered to but integrally bound up with our prevailing racial order, then it is that racial order that must change in order for our technologies to work differently for marginalized peoples. I remain pessimistic that that will take place anytime soon.

What I would offer for the moment as a first step toward that change hearkens back to Bayard Rustin's admonition. Transforming our racial order and our technological order begins with a transformational shift in representation. Representation that is not just descriptive in nature (focused on demographics) but substantive. This means we must be represented – in critical mass, at every level, in educational programs that provide the opportunity to access, master, and decide how we will use technological tools to further our own interests. We must be represented – in critical mass, at every level, among the private enterprises that produce our computational systems and determine their design, use cases, development, and distribution. We must be represented – in critical mass, at every level, among the governmental institutions that define national problems, regulate technological use, and distribute resources to carry out its prerogatives. At the very least, we will not begin to transform our racialized technological futures unless this representational work is accomplished. This work alone requires deliberate attention, planning, and, even in the most optimistic of circumstances, at least the timespan of a generation to accomplish.

References

Browne, Simone (2015). *Dark Matters: On the Surveillance of Blackness*. Durham, NC: Duke University Press.

Free Software Foundation (2019). "What Is Free Software?" v. 1.163, March 20. www.gnu.org/philosophy/free-sw.html

Hafner, Katie and Matthew Lyon (1998).*Where Wizards Stay Up Late: The Origins of the Internet*. New York: Simon and Schuster.

Sinyangwe, Samuel (2018). "Mapping Police Violence." https://mappingpolicevio lence.org/

McPherson, Tara (2013). "US Operating Systems at Mid-Century: The Intertwining of Race and UNIX." In L. Nakamura and P. Chow-White (eds.) and A. Nelson (cont.), *Race After the Internet* (pp. 27–43). New York: Routledge.

Joseph, George and Kenneth Lipp (2018, September 6). "IBM Used NYPD Surveillance Footage to Develop Technology That Lets Police Search by Skin Color." *The Intercept.*

Joseph, George and Murtaza Hussain (2018, March 19). "FBI Tracked an Activist Involved with Black Lives Matter as They Travelled Across the U.S., Documents Show." *The Intercept.*

Omi, Michael and Howard Winant (1998). "Racial Formation." In R. Levine (ed.), *Social Class and Stratification: Classic Statements and Theoretical Debates* (pp. 233–242). Lanham, MD: Rowman & Littlefield Publishers.

Randolph, A. Philip (1962, September 9). "Public Labor Education Meeting of the Fourth Triennial Convention and Thirty-Seventh Anniversary of the Brotherhood of Sleeping Car Porters, AFL-CIO/CLC" [transcript]. Montreal, Canada.

Turner, Fred (2010). *From Counterculture to Cyberculture: Stewart Brand, the Whole Earth Network, and the Rise of Digital Utopianism.* Chicago, IL: University of Chicago Press.

Wilkins, Roy (1967, September 11). "Computerize the Race Problem?", *The Los Angeles Times.*

9

Exploiting Subalternity in the Name of Counter-Hegemonic Communication

Turkey's Global Media Outreach Initiatives

Bilge Yesil

In the summer of 2015, President Recep Tayyip Erdogan celebrated the launch of TRT World, Turkey's first English-language news channel, as an opportunity to disrupt the existing international media order. Criticizing "Western" news outlets for turning a blind eye to the plight of "the downtrodden and the oppressed," a reference to world Muslims, Erdogan reminded the audience that "unless the lions write their own stories, we will continue to listen to the hunters' stories." This appeal for new voices thus invoked a global Muslim community in need of a spokesman; indicated the Erdogan government's geo-political economic ambitions to play that role; and decried biased western media coverage of Turkey, which allegedly ignored the country's achievements and "twisted" domestic events to project a negative image of the ruling AKP government (Justice and Development Party) (Turkiye Cumhuriyeti Cumhurbaskanligi, 2016).

In what follows, I contextualize the processes behind this anecdote, revealing a Turkish media ecosystem using antihegemonic rhetoric and claiming to speak on behalf of select subaltern groups (Muslim refugees in Europe, black Muslims in the United States, Palestinians, etc.)

in the global public sphere.[1] I begin with a brief overview of how the AKP and its allies use channels of global communication to manage Turkey's reputation and proceed to analyze in detail a number of Internet and social media projects that are undertaken by Bosphorus Global – a pro-Erdogan group. I then trace Bosphorus Global's political and financial connections to the AKP regime, discuss its instrumentalization of subalternity, and make suggestions for future research concerning political communication in other national contexts.

The place of subalternity at the core of the AKP's global media outreach presents scholars of media and public life with an important question: How can one approach initiatives that are seemingly aimed at advocating for equality, democracy, and human rights on a global level but are intertwined with antidemocratic practices at home? Can one take the self-identified antihegemonic communication projects at face value when they are deployed by politically and economically privileged actors, or should otherwise accurate critiques of xenophobic or illegal behavior by global actors be discounted as merely deflecting attention from domestic oppression?

Much ink has been spilled in recent years on the decline of liberal democracy and the rise of populist strongmen and highly personalized authoritarian regimes. Especially in the wake of the Brexit referendum, Donald Trump's election, and the resurgence of far-right politics in Europe, scholarly inquiries have focused on the articulation of authoritarian populism and right-wing nationalism with economic grievances, low education levels, antielite cultural backlash, and media manipulation in specific national and regional contexts. In this body of research, analyses of media and communication structures and practices have mostly focused on populist politicians' style and discourse (Breeze, 2018; de Vreese et al., 2018; Moffitt, 2016; Wirz et al., 2018), the role of (social) media fragmentation and polarization in the rise of populist movements (Engesser et al., 2017; Enli and Rosenberg, 2018; Gerbaudo, 2018; Postill, 2018), and the manipulative effects of social media on poorly informed masses (Alvares and Dahlgren, 2016; Krämer, 2017; Sheets et al., 2016).

While these studies have much to offer concerning the national and regional contexts they analyze, less attention has been paid to how

[1] I would like to thank Matthew Powers and Adrienne Russell for including me in this project, and Divya McMillin, Ergin Bulut, and David Weil for their helpful comments during different stages of research and writing.

populist politicians, right-wing nationalist actors, and/or authoritarian leaders use certain channels of communication to legitimize themselves and neutralize criticism in the global public sphere. Such an analysis is in order given the constitutive relationships between local and global politics, the ubiquitous instrumentalization of *ressentiment* by authoritarian leaders for domestic and international political gain, and strategic dissemination of information focused only on select subaltern groups at the expense other marginalized communities.

At this point, a brief note about how I use the term "subaltern" in this chapter is in order. Erdogan's purported championship of subaltern groups inevitably evokes the ways in which the term has been used in subaltern and postcolonial studies. Originally introduced by Antonio Gramsci, the term was picked up in the early 1980s by the Subaltern Studies Project as part of the attempts to privilege the experiences of the dispossessed and the marginalized and write "revisionist histories from 'below.'" It has since been used to denote relationships of power and subordination between social groups: those who occupy established political, economic, social, cultural institutions, and those who are cut off from the centers of hegemonic power (Arnold, 2000: 33).[2]

In this chapter, I draw upon Erdogan's and his supporters' own references to Muslim subjects' subordination by the putative West and contextualize these references within anti-western critiques and visions of pan-Islamic solidarity. The AKP's ideological stance, born out of the 1970s Milli Gorus movement (National Outlook), is deeply influenced by the historical legacy of the Ottoman Empire and the Turkish Republic's Westernization and modernization processes. Milli Gorus emphasizes Islam as a marker of Turkish national identity, blames the Westernizing elite for political, economic, and cultural oppression of Muslims, and advocates for pan-Islamic solidarity.[3] In this ideological version of

---

[2] When postcolonial critic and feminist theorist Gayatri Spivak penned her seminal chapter "Can the Subaltern Speak?" in 1988, the term became the subject of considerable theoretical debate in regards the subaltern subject's possibility of speaking and representing herself despite being constituted through the discourse of the dominant groups (Spivak, 1988). For a detailed examination of the concept of subalternity, see Guha (1982), Guha and Spivak (1988), Chattarjee (1993), Lazarus (1994), Chaturvedi (2000), and Spivak (2005).

[3] For a detailed discussion of the anti-Western critique inherent in Milli Gorus and its leader Necmettin Erbakan, who was also Erdogan's political mentor, see Toprak (1984), Sakallioglu (1998), Dai (2005). It is also important to note that anti-Westernism in Turkey is not exclusive to Islamist politics, but is also a key pillar of left-wing nationalist movements.

history, Turkey is also given the role of leading the global Muslim community, which can help us to contextualize the deployment of subalternity by AKP cadres. Erdogan, his government, and supporters draw upon the marginalization of Muslims around the world (real or perceived) and use it to confront the historical legacy of Western colonialism, economic underdevelopment in predominantly Muslim countries, and the more recent rise of Islamophobia around the globe.[4]

9.1 THE AKP'S GLOBAL MEDIA AND COMMUNICATION OUTREACH

Once hailed as a model for Middle Eastern and North African countries by western media and policymakers, Turkey is now depicted as the epitome of a democracy in an authoritarian turn. Beginning with the Gezi Park protests in 2013 and intensifying after the failed coup attempt and the declaration of State of Emergency in 2016, the AKP government has received mounting criticism of its attacks on civil liberties, press freedoms, and human rights (Amnesty International, 2017; Cook, 2016; Human Rights Watch, 2016; Somer, 2016,).[5] To counter such negative portrayals and to promote Turkey as a rising global player, the AKP government has relied on its international broadcasting outlets and broadened the scope of its existing public diplomacy and public relations initiatives.[6] Partisan media outlets contributed to these efforts by launching English-language dailies, while pro-Erdogan organizations

[4] Erdogan's and the AKP's anti-Westernism and pan-Islamism have oscillated throughout the course of their tenure as per structural constraints and shifting political frameworks. Erdogan has pragmatically downplayed the party's right-wing, nationalist, Islamist ideology during its first two terms in office, but resuscitated it once he was faced with domestic and geopolitical challenges beginning with Gezi protests in 2013 and continuing up to present time with revelations about widespread corruption, the unraveling of the Kurdish peace process, and the failed coup. At the present time, faced with a looming economic crisis and frayed relations with the United States and the EU, Erdogan has once again amplified his anti-Western discourse blaming external and internal enemies for Turkey's problems.

[5] The AKP's authoritarian tendencies have been in the making long before the Gezi protests and before western media and policy circles began to pay attention to Erdogan's crackdown on civil liberties and freedoms. See Akca (2014), Yesil (2016), Somer (2016), and Tansel (2018).

[6] Among the entities that focus on public diplomacy and public relations work are the Directorate of Communications of the Presidency, the Office of Public Diplomacy of the Prime Ministry, SETA (Foundation for Political, Economic, and Social Research), TIKA (Turkish Cooperation and Coordination Agency), Turkish Heritage Organization, and Yunus Emre Institute.

and grassroots actors undertook political fact-checking initiatives and social media campaigns to refute critical press coverage in the West. To be sure, these initiatives are composed of a variety of state and nonstate actors and cannot necessarily be viewed either as a homogeneous entity or as components of a unified propaganda effort, but they nevertheless collectively disseminate a pro-AKP narrative to global audiences, and thus demand analysis in terms of this systemic effect.

It should also be noted that the entry of these Turkish voices (broadly defined) into the global public sphere is not a unique phenomenon, but an outcome of the overall restructuring of international media and communication sectors. Aided by technological and political economic changes, the number of non-western media organizations and communicative spaces has grown at a remarkable pace over the past four decades chipping away at the domination of their US and Western European counterparts and expanding the counter-flow of texts, images, and ideas from east to west, global south to north.[7] Advances in satellite technology and deterritorialization of broadcasting as well as deregulation and privatization in national media markets gave rise to various regional and global news outlets, be it state-sponsored, commercial, or in-between (e.g., Al Jazeera English, Russia Today, China Global Television Network, Press TV, Zee News, and TRT World).

The emergence of AKP's global projects is also associated with technological and geopolitical economic transformations of the 1990s and 2000s. For example, digitalization facilitated the growth of alternative communicative spaces, upended existing structures of content production, distribution, and access, and enabled states, corporations, and ordinary users to reach large(r) number of audiences.[8] Meanwhile, world politics and economics shifted in significant ways, including the rise of new centers of power, the eruption of ethnic and nationalist crises, and the weakening of the Western neoliberal dominance. In light of the convergence of these forces, AKP's global media outreach is indicative of a global trend, that is, the strategic targeting of foreign publics for purposes of realizing certain geopolitical economic and promotional goals.[9]

---

[7] For a detailed discussion of these developments, see Thussu (2018), Volkmer (2014), and Cottle and Rai (2008).

[8] See for example Benkler (2006), Napoli (2011), Harsin (2018), and Bennett and Livingston (2018).

[9] For a discussion of Chinese and Russian case studies, see Thussu et al. (2017), Monroe and Dayan (2008), Oates (2017), Lokot (2017), and Weitz (2009).

To go back to the AKP's global outreach projects, first and foremost among these is TRT World, the aforementioned 24/7 English-language news channel. According to its executives, TRT World is an independent public broadcaster; however, one must note that it is run by the TRT (Turkish Radio and Television Corporation), which itself is a state-funded and highly politicized entity. Positioned as a competitor to CNN International, BBC World, and Al Jazeera English, TRT World distinguishes itself by bringing a "humanitarian understanding" to international news; that is, it does not "discuss the effects of an event on the great powers or international institutions," but instead focuses on the "local populace in countries like Afghanistan, Syria and Iraq" (*Daily Sabah*, 2016). The prioritization of countries and peoples that have been on the receiving end of Western intervention is indicative of TRT World's claims to being the "voice of the voiceless" and can be interpreted as an illustration of the postcolonial perspective it seeks to bring to international news (Milliyet, 2019; TRT World Research Center, 2017).

Another entity that seeks to "carry Turkey's voice to the world" and "change the balance" of the global media order is Anadolu Agency (AA), the country's official news agency, founded in 1920 (*Daily Sabah*, 2014). Part joint-stock company and part state venture, Anadolu Agency's heavy reliance on state funding has always cast doubt on its autonomy. During the AKP's tenure, however, its politicization has reached new heights, which can be seen in the partisan composition of its executive board, its recruitment of pro-Erdogan employees, and its slanted editorial line (Irak, 2016). It was also during the AKP era that Anadolu Agency expanded significantly (as per the words of its past Director General, "a globalizing country needs a globalizing news agency"), and it now boasts of thirty-nine offices around the world and provides services in thirteen languages (*Daily Sabah*, 2014).

In addition to these AKP-controlled entities, there are two English-language newspapers, *Yeni Safak English* and *Daily Sabah*, that disseminate pro-Erdogan viewpoints to international readers. Launched in 2012 and 2014 respectively, both are owned by pro-Erdogan media conglomerates that receive a remarkable share of the state advertising purse as well as cheap credit from state banks, privatization deals, and government contracts. They both aim to supplant what they perceive to be duplicitous western media coverage, but in the process use a rather conspiratorial and anti-Western lens (and anti-Semitic in the case of *Yeni Safak English*) (Armstrong, 2014). These publications' broadcasting counterpart is A News, a 24/7 English-language online news channel that similarly takes an openly pro-Erdogan stance and is owned by *Daily Sabah*'s parent conglomerate.

Other tools in the AKP's global media outreach program are English-language (and to a lesser extent French, Arabic, Russian, and Kurdish) digital communication projects. One such project is @TRDiplomacy, which is run by the Ministry of Foreign Affairs. Using infographics, often times jam-packed with information, @TRDiplomacy aims to "bring Turkey's domestic, regional and international diplomatic issues to the attention of...global communities" in seven languages. In addition to covering a wide variety of geopolitical issues that range from Turkey–Russia relations to the AKP's fight against ISIS, @TRDiplomacy also claims to take a critical look at the problems of the West, such as "coups engineered or supported by the US," "French colonialism, invasions and massacres," and the even the alleged role of George Soros in backing "color revolutions."

There are other digital communication projects that seek to manage Turkey's reputation and promote government policies and are run by pro-Erdogan groups. One such project is *The New Turkey*, a "digital platform" that describes itself as independent despite its links to the pro-AKP think tank SETA (Foundation for Political, Economic, and Social Research) (The New Turkey, 2018). The New Turkey publishes op-ed pieces on its website and aims to reach English-speaking audiences through its YouTube, Facebook, Twitter, and Instagram accounts. Similar projects are also undertaken by Bosphorus Global, another pro-Erdogan entity, which I examine in detail in the remainder of this chapter.

9.2 BOSPHORUS GLOBAL

Bosphorus Global is a self-identified NGO founded in 2015 by a pundit in Erdogan's close circle, Hilal Kaplan, and her husband Suheyb Ogut. It undertakes various communication projects online and via social media to rectify western media representations of Turkey and to call out the putative West for violating its own standards of democracy and human rights. Bosphorus Global also carries out a patchwork of public relations events, such as bringing together international journalists and parliamentarians with Erdogan and AKP officials, taking Lindsay Lohan on a tour of Syrian refugee camps in southeast Turkey, and collaborating with an Italian wine estate to publish a calendar that features Istanbul's historic sites (Bosphorus Global News, n.d.).

Bosphorus Global claims that it is an independent entity with a "transparent funding structure," yet it is deeply imbricated with both Erdogan and his son-in-law, Berat Albayrak, the Minister of Treasury and Finance. Hilal Kaplan, the co-founder of Bosphorus Global, has close ties with Erdogan, accompanying him on foreign trips, writing partisan op-ed columns in pro-AKP newspapers, and appearing on television talk shows to defend AKP policies and/or attack opposition figures. Kaplan and her husband are known for the blog they published anonymously in 2016 wherein they vehemently criticized the then prime minister (possibly under Albayrak's direction), eventually paving the way for his resignation and the installation of a more Erdogan-friendly cabinet (Letsch, 2016; Sozeri, 2016).

More importantly, Bosphorus Global was founded by seed money directly provided by Albayrak. As per leaked emails, in September 2015, Ogut requested from Albayrak (then an AKP parliamentarian) 400,000 Turkish lira (approximately $133,000 as per the exchange rate at the time) for the first month of operations, and 120,000 Turkish lira per month thereafter (approximately $40,000) (Sozeri, 2016). Ogut also sent Albayrak the link to the waterfront villa in Istanbul that rented at approximately $6,700 at the time. Today, the villa still serves as the headquarters of Bosphorus Global.

In its mission statement, Bosphorus Global notes that "subaltern groups" have been alienated from the "international public sphere" because their "opinions, requests and representations" have been "stigmatized as subjective and biased" (Bosphorus Global Mission, n.d.). To rectify this situation, it promises to "generate public(ity) [*sic*] for political and social actors" that have been marginalized by "official discourses and institutions" (ibid.). Imposing a simplified center-periphery framework on Turkish and global history, Bosphorus Global directs attention to the "polarity [*sic*] between state institutions and the people" that emerged during the "transition process of the Ottoman Empire to the Turkish Republic [*sic*]" in the early 1920s and has since then resulted in military coups, class elitism, "harsh suppression of Islam," and "cultural representations that blindly imitate the West" (Bosphorus Global Perspective, n.d.). In its uncritical application of the center-periphery cleavage, it identifies the center as the military-bureaucratic establishment, the "Westernizing elite" and their economic allies, and recognizes Erdogan as the one and only "peripheral actor" that successfully fulfilled political and economic reforms and "moved the periphery to the center" (ibid.).

As seen in the quotations above, Bosphorus Global's concern with subalternity manifests in a complex mixture of international and domestic contexts. Despite some focus in its mission statement on redressing perceived imbalances in Turkey's own political history, Bosphorus Global's ongoing activities show a primary focus on creating spaces to enable subaltern subjects to speak out against hegemonic Western news media. That is, Bosphorus Global's performance reveals a statist conception of hegemony that grounds it in an international context, which transforms antihegemony from a principle – by which policies in Turkey could be judged – into a tool for criticizing the AKP's alleged external enemies. In the following section, I highlight three projects undertaken by Bosphorus Global that display this contrast.[10]

9.2.1 Fact-Checking Turkey

Founded in response to representations of Turkey "as yet another dictatorship" in international media, Fact-Checking Turkey (from here on FCT) aims to monitor the "factual accuracy of various news and claims about Turkey" (Bosphorus Global Our Projects, n.d.). As per its website, it focuses on international media coverage of the failed coup, the Kurdish issue, press freedoms, refugees, Turkish economy, and foreign policy. Yet unlike genuine fact-checking initiatives, it relies on AKP officials' or anonymous sources' statements and unverified media reports instead of publicly available and verifiable information (Sozeri, 2017). It also prioritizes extraneous details, skirting the issue at hand. For example, to counter the "factual mistakes" in an article in *The Independent* about the prosecution of Kurdish politicians, FCT used a news clip from the AKP-controlled state broadcaster and cited its own and a sister organization's reports (Fact-Checking Turkey, 2019a). When US and European news media covered the story of Enes Kanter, a basketball player then with the New York Knicks who announced that he could not travel outside the United States for fear of being assassinated by the AKP government (due to his affiliation with Fethullah Gulen, who is Erdogan's arch enemy and is widely believed to be the key figure behind the 2016 coup attempt), FCT wrote on Twitter that "the actual reason was that [Kanter] is not holding a passport, which the UK requires each Turkish national to [present in

---

[10] Bosphorus Global has various other digital projects aimed at domestic audiences, such as Gunun Yalanlari (Daily Lies), Demokrasi Gunlugu (Timeline Turkey), and FETO Gercekleri (FETO Facts).

order to] apply for a visa" (Fact-Checking Turkey, 2019b). Instead of addressing assassination claims directly, FCT shared a tweet in which Kanter employed an anti-Semitic epithet and engaged in what can be better described as a political offensive rather than fact-checking (Fact-Checking Turkey, 2019c).

9.2.2 Chronicles of Shame *and* Crackdown Chronicles

While FCT aims to correct news coverage of Turkey, Bosphorus Global's other digital communication projects are concerned with directing attention to oppressed groups (African Americans, refugees, Muslims in Europe, etc.) and inverting the western gaze. One of these projects is Chronicles of Shame, which mainly focuses on the United States, Europe, Israel, and to a lesser degree Saudi Arabia, the United Arab Emirates, China, and Russia. It publishes abridged versions of news stories from international media outlets on four topics: refugees, Islamophobia, racism, and human rights violations. Additionally, its Twitter and Facebook accounts feature news clips from international outlets in an effort to present an "archive" of various acts of racism and discrimination around the globe.

Whereas Chronicles of Shame highlights the suppression of subaltern groups, Crackdown Chronicles focuses on the "inner political contradictions" of the United States, European countries, Canada, and Australia. "Despite their efforts to present themselves as a consistent democratic whole," Crackdown Chronicles argues, these countries "monitor and censor the media, respond to protests with police violence, arbitrarily designate [people] as terror suspects under extensive terror laws and [violate] their rights" (Crackdown Chronicles, n.d.). Similar to its sister project, it reposts articles from international news media on its website, and uses news clips and amateur videos on its Facebook page and Twitter account.[11]

Despite Bosphorus Global's lofty mission statement and generous funding from the state purse, the popularity and effectiveness of the above-mentioned projects remain questionable. For example, as of this writing in February 2019, Fact-Checking Turkey has 4,099 followers on Twitter, Chronicles of Shame 1,126, and Crackdown Chronicles 792. There is no information available on Bosphorus Global's website about

---

[11] Obviously, there is a high level of redundancy across the two projects since they post the same stories under different categories.

these projects' effectiveness in reaching intended audiences. The only concrete outcomes mentioned in the group's website are the international media coverage of Lindsay Lohan's tour of a Syrian refugee camp in southeast Turkey and the publication of an op-ed piece in the *New York Times* about Turkey's humane treatment of refugees (Bosphorus Global News, n.d.).

9.3 CONCLUSION

Bosphorus Global's communication projects, similar to TRT World and other pro-AKP print and digital initiatives, aim to invert Western narratives about Turkey and interrogate the putative West for violating its own ideals about human rights, democracy, and rule of law. Each employs a strategy of what-aboutism and an instrumentalized postcolonial critique to shed light on "Western hypocrisies" (Bosphorus Global Activities, n.d.). This is also evident in TRT World's editorial policy, which seeks to disrupt the current global order replete with "inequity, human rights violations and exploitation." As per Erdogan's mantra "the world is bigger than five" (a reference to the domination of the UN Security Council by five countries), TRT World programs expose "the [internal] problems of the West; its predicaments, dilemmas and tragedies" and reverse the western media's gaze on "tragedies of the East" (Milliyet, 2019).[12]

These pro-AKP media and communication projects can be interpreted, to varying degrees, as attempts to "provincialize" the West and "analyze it as a local curiosity," to use Deniz Kandiyoti's terminology (2002: 285) and to reorient Turkey and the Muslim world from passive to active, inert to sovereign, represent*ed* to represent*er*. But can one interpret such attempts to disrupt the Western (and Orientalist) gaze as genuinely antihegemonic?[13] In identifying with the oppressed peoples around the world, does Bosphorus Global genuinely undertake a humanist critique of the West? Does it offer a sincere affirmation of universal norms and values as it highlights the perils of rampant Islamophobia and racism? Does its engagement in dialogue with an (imagined) Western public opinion truly

---

[12] "The world is bigger than five" was often repeated by Lindsay Lohan in media interviews about her trip to the Syrian refugee camps in Turkey.

[13] Due to space limitations, I am unable to discuss the AKP's and its allies' anti-Orientalist stance in this chapter. It is, however, a topic I address in detail in *Talking Back to the West?: Turkish Muslim Voices in the Global Public Sphere*, the book manuscript I am currently working on.

serve to be the voice of the voiceless? My answer to these questions is a resounding "no" for the following reasons.

Bosphorus Global seeks to develop voice in the global media arena on behalf of select subaltern groups, but ends up reproducing the ahistorical Self-Other dichotomies it nominally criticizes. It deploys the center-periphery paradigm in such an uncritical manner that it views Turkey, Muslims, and the West as homogeneous entities without any attention to the presence of multilayered, hybrid identities, and experiences that exist in between these monolithic categories. In its direct and indirect descriptions of Turkey as virtuous and of the West as the oppressor, it perpetuates the idea of an East–West divide and resurrects essentialist contrasts in ways almost akin to Samuel Huntington's "clash of the civilizations" thesis.[14]

In addition to the above issues, Bosphorus Global's response to Islamophobia, racism, and human rights violations in the West is transactional rather than morally principled. For example, if Bosphorus Global was genuinely concerned with the oppression of *all* Muslims, why has it not ever denounced China's mistreatment of its Uighur Muslim population? Could it be because Erdogan has long planned to deepen economic cooperation with China? And now that the Turkish Foreign Ministry after a notable period of silence urged China to close Uighur internment camps, will Bosphorus Global, TRT World, and others follow suit?

While Bosphorus Global highlights the plight of Muslim refugees, African Americans, and Palestinians, it ignores the oppression of Kurds, journalists, academics, and activists at the hands of its benefactor. Ignoring the fact that the national and the global are constitutive of each other, it voices (a faux) outrage against human rights violations in the West while it conveniently overlooks the AKP's authoritarian policies at home. No wonder then the "Western hypocrisies" it seeks to expose have to do with the very antidemocratic practices with which the AKP is engaged at home: decline of the rule of law, media censorship, police violence, human rights violations, and crackdown on academics.

Last but not least, Bosphorus Global and Hilal Kaplan have questionable connections to Erdogan's troll army (known as AK Trolls), which engages in phishing, harassment, and intimidation of dissidents, activists, and local and foreign journalists, and uses bot-powered hashtags to praise Erdogan

---

[14] It is not my intention to suggest that Bosphorus Global, Erdogan, Islamists, or Muslims should not be criticizing the West. To the contrary, what I am suggesting is that scholars should take a critical look at entities and discourses that wield subalternity, and ascertain whether their critique of hegemonic centers of power is authentic or not.

and condemn his opponents on social media (Freedom House, 2017; IPI, 2016; Sozeri, 2017). Although the AK Trolls are not a homogeneous entity and their relationship to the AKP has never been formally acknowledged, existing research points to veritable connections between party officials, pro-AKP pundits, and prominent trolls (Bulut and Yoruk, 2018; Karatas and Saka, 2017; Saka, 2018). Indeed, according to Erkan Saka's network analysis, Bosphorus Global emerges as one of the major nodes on Twitter that produce "AK Troll discourse" and Hilal Kaplan's Twitter account is linked to the wider network of AK Trolls (2018: 168, 176). In light of these findings that point to "agitational" practices, can one argue that Bosphorus Global is a "virtuous" voice speaking for the subaltern?[15]

The case of Bosphorus Global and the AKP's global outreach program unlocks a critical path into the inquiry of how subalternity and more broadly victimhood and *ressentiment* are articulated with conservative subjectivities and subsequently instrumentalized by populist, right-wing nationalist, and/or authoritarian actors and movements around the globe. While attention has mostly focused on the convergence of political economic, technological, and media-centric dynamics, it is time to investigate the role of cultural-historical residuals in prompting state and nonstate actors to wield subalternity in the name of disrupting the existing media and political orders – be it national or global. By using this framework, scholars can, for example, make sense of how highly partisan media outlets in the United States (e.g., Breitbart and Fox News) identify themselves as the underdogs of the American media system and advocate for the so-called victims of establishment politics. What vestiges of *ressentiment* do these outlets activate as they accuse the *New York Times*, *Washington Post*, and CNN of elitism? What are the implications of their embrace of white victimhood and the "forgotten men and women" in terms of their coverage of white supremacist, anti-immigrant, anti-Muslim politics – not only in the United States but around the world? What discursive solidarities do they build with similarly positioned media outlets in France, Hungary, Germany, and the United Kingdom where anti-immigrant sentiments are on the rise? Analysis of subalternity and its exploitation can also help scholars contextualize Russian social media campaigns within the country's broader global media outreach, including Russia Today and *Sputnik News*. By looking at the historical roots of anti-Westernism in Russia and more broadly Putin's rekindling of Russian imperialist aspirations, scholars can unbind the analyses of international

---

[15] Here, I am inspired by Nancy Fraser's terminology (1990).

news and social media from the weaponization/propaganda framework that has dominated much of the literature on this topic and instead focus on history and culture.

Additionally, the subalternity framework can be used to reveal the linkages between religion and populism – an area that deserves more critical attention – both in global north and south contexts. For example, scholars can explore how the religious right in Europe and the United States and their allies in media lament the so-called persecution of Christianity and conservative family values and with what implications. They can ask: What kind of alliances do political actors from Viktor Orban to Matteo Salvini forge by decrying the alleged suppression of Judeo-Christian values by global secular elites and the consequent decline of European civilization? On the flip side, there is room for analysis of how political leaders in Muslim-majority countries co-opt politics of Islamophobia for political gain and how minorities (e.g., Shia, Alevite) are potentially rendered invisible when these leaders promote the suffering of select religious groups (e.g., Sunnis).

These are only a few examples of how certain participants in the earlier-mentioned media and political contexts promote a thematic focus on select causes and function to instrumentalize subalternity and antihegemonic communication. I hope scholars working on other national and transnational contexts will find value in thinking with and about some of the questions these examples raise.

References

Akca, Ismet, Ahmet Bekmen, and Baris Ozden (eds.) (2014). *Turkey Reframed: Constituting Neoliberal Hegemony*. London: Pluto Press.

Alvares, Claudia and Peter Dahlgren (2016). "Populism, Extremism and Media: Mapping an Uncertain Terrain." *European Journal of Communication*, 31(1), 46–57.

Amnesty International (2017) "Annual Report: Turkey 2016/2017." www .amnesty.org/en/countries/europe-and-central-asia/turkey/report-turkey/

Armstrong, William (2014). "Army of Spin." *Foreign Policy*, December 9.

Arnold, David (2000). "Gramsci and Peasant Subalternity in India." In Vinayak Chaturvedi (ed.), *Mapping Subaltern Studies and the Postcolonial* (pp. 24–49). London: Verso.

Bakiner, Onur (2018). "A Key to Turkish Politics? The Center–Periphery Framework Revisited." *Turkish Studies*, 19(4), 503–22.

Bayazit, Huseyin Kemal (2016). "Turkey." In Eli Noam and the International Media Concentration Collaboration (eds.), *Who Owns the World's Media* (pp. 387–424). New York: Oxford University Press.

Benkler, Yochai. (2006). *The Wealth of Networks: How Social Production Transforms Markets and Freedom*. New Haven, CT: Yale University Press.

Bennett, William and Steven Livingston. (2018). "The Disinformation Order: Disruptive Communication and the Decline of Democratic Institutions." *European Journal of Communication*, 33(2), 122–139.

Bosphorus Global, n.d. "Activities." http://bosphorusglobal.org/en/activities

Bosphorus Global, n.d. "Mission." http://bosphorusglobal.org/en/mission

Bosphorus Global, n.d. "News." http://bosphorusglobal.org/en/news

Bosphorus Global, n.d. "Our Projects." http://bosphorusglobal.org/en/activities

Bosphorus Global, n.d. "Perspective." http://bosphorusglobal.org/en/perspective

Bulut, Ergin and Erdem Yoruk (2017). "Digital Populism: Trolls and Political Polarization of Twitter in Turkey." *International Journal of Communication*, 11, 4093–4117.

Breeze, Ruth. (2018). "Positioning 'the People' and Its Enemies: Populism and Nationalism in AfD and UKIP." *Javnost-The Public*, 26(1), 1–16.

Chattarjee, Partha. (1993). *The Nation and Its Fragments: Colonial and Postcolonial Histories*. Princeton, NJ: Princeton University Press.

Chaturvedi, Vinayak (ed.) (2000). *Mapping Subaltern Studies and the Postcolonial*, London: Verso.

Cook, Steven A. (2016). "How Erdogan Made Turkey Authoritarian Again." *The Atlantic*, July 21.

Cottle, Simon and Mugdha Rai (2008). "Global 24/7 News Providers: Emissaries of Global Dominance or Global Public Sphere? *Global Media and Communication*, 4(2), 157–181.

Crackdown Chronicles (n.d.) https://crackdownchronicles.com/.

Dai, Hsan D. (2005). "Transformation of Islamic Political Identity in Turkey: Rethinking the West and Westernization." *Turkish Studies*, 6(1), 21–37.

de Vreese, Claes, Frank Esser, Toril Aalberg, Carsten Reinemann, and James Stanyer (2018). "Populism as an Expression of Political Communication Content and Style: A New Perspective." *The International Journal of Press/Politics*, 23(4), 423–438.

Engesser, Sven, Nicole Ernst, Frank Esser, and Florin Büchel (2017). "Populism and Social Media: How Politicians Spread a Fragmented Ideology." *Information, Communication & Society*, 20(8), 1109–1126.

Enli, Gunn and Linda Therese Rosenberg (2018). "Trust in the Age of Social Media: Populist Politicians Seem More Authentic." *Social Media and Society*, 4 (1), 1–11.

Fact-Checking Turkey (2019a). "Independent article makes factual mistakes." http://factcheckingturkey.com/kurdish-issue/independent-article-makes-factual-mistakes-491

Fact-Checking Turkey (2019b). "The actual reason was that he is not holding a passport, which the UK requires each Turkish national to apply for a visa." https://twitter.com/FactCheckingTR/status/1086247235095093248

Fact Checking Turkey (2019c). "He used an anti-Semitic epithet." https://twitter.com/FactCheckingTR/status/1085887594435629056

Fraser, Nancy (1990). "Rethinking the Public Sphere: A Contribution to the Critique of Actually Existing Democracy." *Social Text*, 25(26), 56–80.

Gerbaudo, Paolo (2018). "Social Media and Populism: An Elective Affinity?" *Media, Culture & Society*, 40(5), 745–53.

Guha, Ranajit (ed.) (1982). *Subaltern Studies I: Writings on South Asian History and Society*. New Delhi: Oxford University Press.

Guha, Ranajit and Gayatri Chakravorty Spivak (eds.) (1988). *Selected Subaltern Studies*. New York: Oxford University Press.

Harsin, Jayson (2018). "Post-truth and Critical Communication." In *Oxford Research Encyclopedia of Communication*. http://oxfordre.com/communication/view/10.1093/acrefore/9780190228613.001.0001/acrefore-9780190228613-e-757

Irak, Daghan (2016). "A Close-Knit Bunch: Political Concentration in Turkey's Anadolu Agency through Twitter Interactions." *Turkish Studies*, 17(2), 336–60.

Kandiyoti, Deniz (2002). "Post-colonialism Compared: Potentials and Limitations in the Middle East and Central Asia." *International Journal of Middle East Studies*, 34(2), 279–97.

Karatas, Duygu and Erkan Saka (2017). "Online Political Trolling in the Context of Post-Gezi Social Media in Turkey." *International Journal of Digital Television*, 8(3), 383–401.

Krämer Benjamin (2017). "Populist Online Practices: The Function of the Internet in Right-Wing Populism." *Information, Communication & Society*, 20(9), 1293–1309.

Kismet, Sercan (2019). "Yayınlarımız uluslararasi adaletsizliğe karsi." *Milliyet*, February 7.

Lazarus, Neil (1994). "National Consciousness and the Specificity of (Post)colonial Intellectualism." In Francis Barker, Peter Hulme, and Margaret Iversen (eds.), *Colonial Discourse/Postcolonial Theory* (pp.197–220). Manchester: Manchester University Press.

Letsch, Constance (2016). "Turkish PM Davutoglu Resigns as Erdogan Tightens Grip." *The Guardian*, May 5.

Lokot, Tanya (2017). "Public Networked Discourses in the Ukraine-Russia Conflict: 'Patriotic Hackers' and Digital Populism." *Irish Studies in International Affairs*, 28, 99–116.

Mardin, şerif (1973). "Center-periphery Relations: A Key to Turkish Politics?" *Daedalus*, 102(1), 169–190.

Media Ownership Monitor Turkey. (2019). "Media Ownership Matters." https://turkey.mom-rsf.org/

Moffitt, Benjamin (2016). *The Global Rise of Populism: Performance, Political Style, and Representation*. Stanford, CA: Stanford University Press.

Napoli, Phillip M. (2011). *Audience Evolution: New Technologies and the Transformation of Media Audiences*. New York: Columbia University Press.

Oates, Sarah (2017). "Kompromat Goes Global? Assessing a Russian Media Tool in the United States." *Slavic Review*, 76(1), 57–65.

Postill, John (2018). "Populism and Social Media: A Global Perspective." *Media, Culture & Society*, 40(5), 754–765.

Price, Monroe and Daniel Dayan (eds.) (2008). *Owning the Olympics: Narratives of the New China*. Ann Arbor, MI: University of Michigan Press.

Saka, Erkan (2014). "The AK Party's Social Media Strategy: Controlling the Uncontrollable." *Turkish Review*, 4(4), 418–23.

Saka, Erkan (2018). "Social Media in Turkey as a Space for Political Battles: AKTrolls and Other Politically Motivated Trolling." *Middle East Critique*, 27 (2), 161–77.

Sakallioğlu, Umit Cizre (1998). "Rethinking the Connections between Turkey's 'Western' Identity versus Islam." *Critique: Journal for Critical Studies of the Middle East*, 7(12), 3–18.

Salgado, Susana (2018). "Online Media Impact on Politics: Views on Post-truth Politics and Postmodernism." *International Journal of Media & Cultural Politics*, 14(3), 317–31.

Sheets, Penelope, Linda Bos and Hajo G. Boomgaarden (2016). "Media Cues and Citizen Support for Right-Wing Populist Parties." *International Journal of Public Opinion Research*, 28(3), 307–330.

Somer, Murat (2016). "Understanding Turkey's Democratic Breakdown: Old vs. New and Indigenous vs. Global Authoritarianism." *Southeast European and Black Sea Studies*, 16(4), 481–503.

Sozeri, Efe Kerem (2016). "Pelikan Dernegi: Berat Albayrak, Ahmet Davutoglu'nu Neden Devirdi?" *Medium*, November 3. https://medium.com/ @efekerem/pelikan-derneği-berat-albayrak-ahmet-davutoğlunu-neden-delird i-5fabad6dc7de

Sozeri, Efe Kerem (2017). "These Fake 'Fact-Checkers' are Peddling Lies about Genocide and Censorship in Turkey." *Poynter*, May 31. www.poynter.org/fact-checking/2017/these-fake-fact-checkers-are-peddling-lies-about-genocide-and-censorship-in-turkey/

Spivak, Gayatri Chakravorty (1988). "Can the Subaltern Speak?" In Cary Nelson and Lawrence Grossberg (eds.), *Marxism and the Interpretation of Culture* (pp. 271–313). Urbana-Champaign, IL: University of Illinois Press.

Spivak, Gayatri Chakravorty (2005). "Scattered Speculations on the Subaltern and the Popular." *Postcolonial Studies*, 8(4), 475–86.

Tansel, Cemal Burak (2018). "Authoritarian Neoliberalism and Democratic Backsliding in Turkey: Beyond the Narratives of Progress." *South European Society and Politics*, 23(2), 197–217.

The New Turkey (2018). "About Us." https://thenewturkey.org/pages/about-us

Thussu, Daya, Hugo De Burgh, and Anbin Shi, (eds.) (2017). *China's Media Go Global*. New York: Routledge.

Thussu, Daya (2018). *International Communication: Continuity and Change*. New York: Bloomsbury Publishing.

Toprak, Binnaz (1984). "Politicisation of Islam in a Secular State: The National Salvation Party in Turkey." In Said Amir Arjomand (ed.), *From Nationalism to Revolutionary Islam* (pp. 119–133). London: Palgrave Macmillan.

TRT World Research Center (2017). "Inspiring Change in an Age of Uncertainty." http://researchcentre.trtworld.com/images/files/TRTWorldForu m2017Report.pdf

Turkiye Cumhuriyeti Cumhurbaskanligi (2016, November 15). "TRT World, Kameralarinin Vizörünü Güce ve Güçlüye Degil Mazlumlara, Ezilenlere Odaklamali."

Unal, Ali (2016). "TRT World CEO Ibrahim Eren: We Will Tell the Truth Even If It's Inconvenient or Disturbing." *Daily Sabah*, November 21.

Volkmer, Ingrid (2014). *The Global Public Sphere: Public Communication in the Age of Reflective Interdependence*. Cambridge: Polity Press.

Weise, Zia (2018). "Fact Checker Seeks Grain of Truth in Turkey's Fake News Onslaught." *Politico*, December 21.

Weitz, Richard (2009). "China, Russia, and the Challenge to the Global Commons." *Pacific Focus*, 24(3), 271–297.

Wirz, Dominique S, Martin Wettstein, Anne Schulz, Philipp Müller, Christian Schemer, Nicole Ernst, Frank Esser, and Werner Wirth (2018). "The Effects of Right-Wing Populist Communication on Emotions and Cognitions toward Immigrants." *The International Journal of Press/Politics*, 23(4), 496–516.

Yediyıldız, Elif Merve (2014). "Anadolu Agency: Linking Turkey and the World." *Daily Sabah*, April 14.

Yesil, Bilge (2016). *Media in New Turkey: The Origins of an Authoritarian Neoliberal State*. Urbana-Champaign, IL: University of Illinois Press.

PART IV

ENGAGEMENT WITH AND THROUGH MEDIA

10

Constructive Engagement across Deep Divides

What It Entails and How It Changes Our Role as Communication Scholars

Hartmut Wessler

10.1 INTRODUCTION

Constructive engagement is used here as an umbrella term for mediated and nonmediated forms of communication in which differences can be expressed, respected, and resolved. Much research in the field of communication has focused on problems that lead to an absence of constructive engagement such as increased polarization of opinion, echo chambers, media bias toward conflict, and scandalization or populist communication strategies. While all of this is important, I propose to *reverse* the perspective by engaging in a sustained search for the *positive* sources of constructive engagement in communicative behavior, institutional arrangements, and technological affordances. I also call for investigations into the

precise mechanisms through which these conditions foster constructive engagement.

In my view, such a change in perspective can help overcome the
dichotomy between alarmist (Bennett and Pfetsch, 2018) and
appeasing accounts (Van Aelst et al., 2017) of the current shifts in
the landscape of public communication because it points to potentials for improvement relatively independent of the severity of the
diagnosis. The two divides I am thinking about most in the current
situation comprise the rift between refugees/migrants and majority
populations and the chasm between extreme partisans on the right
and the left. I am interested in these groups not as "troublemakers"
but as important examples of cultural or ideological estrangement,
and of the potential for redressing some of it through communicative engagement. In an even wider perspective, I am interested in the
cultural resources, however scant and subdued, that lie at the heart
of constructive engagement in different national or cultural contexts
(see Katriel, 2004). I see this as part of a "cultural reappropriation"
of deliberation, which reconnects deliberation with the cultural
resources needed for it, and ties cultural analysis back to the formation of considered opinions and to large-scale societal learning
(see Wessler, 2018: 159).

In this chapter, I will use the concept of constructive engagement in
two distinct ways. On the one hand, I use it as a theoretical tool with
the aim to enhance our understanding of public communication. In
particular, I will argue that a focus on positive, self-transcendent emotions (Oliver et al., 2018) and on practices of democratic listening
(Dobson, 2014) can enhance our understanding of mediated exchanges
between deeply divided groups. Such theoretical innovations help
reconstruct and enrich the normative imaginary of how public communication could function in situations of deep division and directs
our imagination toward what can be done. On the other hand, I will
also use the term "constructive engagement" meta-reflexively, to
describe our relation as scholars vis-à-vis people entangled in nonconstructive conflicts. Should we take sides, and if so, whose side should
we take? More concretely, should we intervene in public debate with
particular arguments on behalf of one side, or should we criticize
nonconstructive engagements as such? I will look at these meta-
reflexive questions first and describe what I see as helpful theoretical
innovations in understanding constructive engagement in the second
section of the chapter.

10.2 A "SOCIAL SCIENCE OF THE POSSIBLE": CONSTRUCTIVE ENGAGEMENT FOR COMMUNICATION SCHOLARS

The business model of the technology giants as well as the mediation of communication through algorithmically steered social network sites disrupts the very basis of public communication. Not only the form and content but also the infrastructures and power dynamics of public communication are in turmoil, albeit to different degrees in different countries. A fundamental reconfiguration of societal communication systems is underway, but the contours of the new order are not yet fixed and clearly discernible. This is due in part to the speed of change (see Mark Zuckerberg's motto "Move fast and break things") and in part to countertendencies and emerging legal regulations, however insufficient they may be, that keep the transformation open-ended.

For communication scholars, the present moment is indeed no time for normal science. Instead, we are compelled to rethink and redefine our role in the process. How should we constructively engage with the present situation, particularly in situations of deep conflict? My answer to these questions revolves around the notion of a "social science of the possible" introduced by the sociologist Erik Olin Wright (2013). Researching possible worlds can serve as the mission for constructively engaged communication scholars precisely because it involves both normative and empirical knowledge, and cannot be reduced to mere opinion or blunt partisanship (see Figure 10.1).

When normative questions arise in academic discourses, we often tend to think in terms of a simple dichotomy between the real and an ideal world. Very often, too, the real is pitched against the ideal, which is then presented as a facile idealization that has nothing to do with how things "really work" and that should thus be abandoned. Or, conversely, the ideal is sometimes pitched against the real in the form of simple critical assertions or moral appeals for the better. Both stances represent strong and unnecessary simplifications. Instead, in keeping with the most helpful distinctions presented by Rinke (2017), two shifts in perspective seem warranted. For one, the relation between the Is and the Should in communication scholarship should be formalized in transparent research procedures, in "empirical validation" and "normative assessment," respectively (see Figure 10.1). Secondly, and more importantly, it seems helpful to think about normative inquiry in communication scholarship in terms of a triangle rather than a dichotomy.

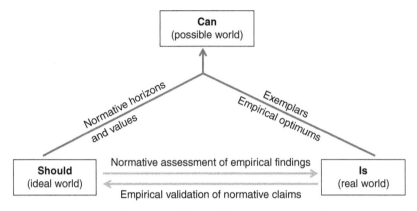

FIGURE 10.1 Researching possible worlds as a mission for constructively engaged communication scholars

At the apex of the triangle sits the Can, an understanding of the world in terms of possible alternatives to the actually existing world informed by theories of desirable worlds (Rinke, 2017; Wright, 2013). I will briefly address the components and edges of the triangle in turn.

Empirical validation is warranted when a specific normative theory includes distinct empirical claims, as most normative theories actually do, that can be tested against reality. One example for this kind of empirical validation would be a test of the expectation that social movement actors close to the lifeworld – actors Habermas (1996) has called autochthone – engage in more deliberative communication than power-holders at the center of the political system. For all we know, this conjecture is indeed wrong. In thinking about the role of social movements more deeply, it appears quite plausible that they specialize more in pointing to problems, demanding change, and mobilizing dissent, than in arguing for specific solutions and engaging in the forging of compromise. Such empirical validation thus induces both progress in our empirical knowledge (of the public role of social movements, in this case) and refinements in our normative theories of public communication (adjusting and specifying our normative expectations, and thus our standard for critique, to what can reasonably be expected).

The ideal and the real also have a reverse relationship that is captured by the procedure of *normative assessment* in which normative criteria are used to assess the performance level in real communication contexts. Althaus (2012) proposes a scheme of four types of normative assessment in order to move the procedure away from simple critical assertions (level 1) toward clearly defined normative judgments based on a rank order of explicit values (level 4). An example for this higher type of normative assessment is presented by Freelon (2015), who shows how different social media platforms have different performance profiles with respect to the diverging values of liberal individualism, communitarianism, and deliberative democracy.

Beyond these improvements "at the bottom" of the triangle, the main benefit of the trilateral model of normativity in communication scholarship lies in bringing the "Can" into focus. Only when thorough normative reflection and hard-nosed empirical knowledge come to mutually inform each other does a "social science of the possible" emerge. Wright (2013) also uses the term "real utopias." A social science of the possible has a utopian element in that it envisions, even thinks up, desirable futures, and it has a realistic element in that it ascertains the conditions under which such desirable states will be likely to emerge. How can communicative engagement between deeply divided groups – for example, refugees and indigenous populations; extreme partisans – be made more constructive, given what we know about the functioning of social media, ingroup–outgroup dynamics, and cognitive confirmation biases, among other things? Finding answers to such questions is no simple task at all. In the words of Erik Olin Wright, "This is a tricky research problem, [...] discussions of possibilities and limits of possibility always involve more speculative and contentious claims about what could be, not just what is." Many academics are not so comfortable with the speculative and contentious, but in my view public engagement for communication scholars cannot be had on completely safe grounds.

Research into possible worlds depends, firstly, on the clarity of a well-developed *normative horizon* (see the left edge of the triangle in Figure 10.1). Not any normative claim qualifies here. Normative values should instead be embedded in larger theories. For example, in political communication, competing normative theories of democracy often constitute an implicit or explicit reference point for normative judgment (Baker, 2002; Ferree et al., 2002; Wessler, 2018). Should democracy be about representing groups and opinions proportionally to their existence in society, as the representative-liberal model would have it? Should it be about empowering the marginalized, as agonistic critics would contend? Or should democracy aim at facilitating respectful dialogue leading to genuine societal learning? Can some of these values and aims be combined in new and hybrid models? If so, which? Answers to questions like these are not self-evident, but rather require good justifications, which in turn require a level of normative theorizing sometimes lacking in communication scholarship. My attempt at clarifying the concept of constructive engagement across deep divides in the second section of this chapter can be understood as an attempt in that direction. I try to be explicit about what we should expect in public communication, and what we do not need to expect? More specifically, I argue against a narrow interpretation of the deliberative tradition as argumentation under ideal speech conditions. Instead, I aim at showing the connections between constructive position-taking and supportive emotions and at complementing the usual focus on acquiring voice in public communication with a new emphasis on listening practices. This is not meant as an ivory-tower pursuit, but as a contribution to identifying possible worlds.

The second element of research into possible worlds, however, must not be neglected. Possible worlds cannot be thought of, let alone brought about, without empirical knowledge on the likely conditions of their realization (see the right edge in Figure 10.1). We need research on *exemplars* of more or less constructive engagement from which we can then infer such conditions. For example, those moments in which young migrants and majority youth do come into contact with each other online tell us not only about how rare such encounters are but also about the conditions under which they do occur, and which emotions and mutual perceptions prevail when they do (Dovidio, Love, Schellhaas, and Hewstone, 2017; Schieferdecker and Wessler, 2017). Similarly, some journalists' efforts at receptively listening to hostile and angry users (Craft and Vos, 2018) might at some point hint at those sources of disenchantment that can actually be remedied by journalists themselves, for example, by admitting mistakes and explaining professional constraints. One more specific outcome of such exemplar analysis is the identification of *empirical optimums*, that is, of instances in which a particular normative value is realized best. Note that this type of analysis is not about the best possible state conceivable (i.e., the theoretical optimum), but, as befits the empirical leg of a "social science of the possible," about the best empirical exemplar that could be found to date (see Wessler and Rinke, 2014, for a study pertaining to television news). In this way, the research I am envisioning is always unfinished because there could always be a new empirical optimum, an improvement in the real world that was not theoretically anticipated.

10.3 THEORIZING CONSTRUCTIVE ENGAGEMENT IN MEDIATED DISCOURSE

I conceptualize constructive engagement using three components that build on each other: expression, acknowledgment, and exchange. Under *expression*, I subsume opportunities for differences to be voiced as clearly and diversely as possible. *Acknowledgment* means that differences should be tolerated and accepted. *Exchange* refers to the demand that differences should be confronted and weighed in public communication. One could speak of "constructive engagement light" when only expression and acknowledgment are present in public communication, and reserve the full meaning of the term for situations in which all three components come together. While these three elements are fairly universal and feature prominently in different accounts of desirable public communication, I propose to draw in fresh concepts and ideas to specify those characteristics of the components that make them conducive to constructive forms of engagement and to point out potential pitfalls that should be avoided.

10.3.1 Expression: Highlighting Self-Transcendent Emotions

For constructive engagement to emerge it is, first of all, necessary that a broad variety of actors can express themselves freely. The expression of grievances and demands by those affected is central to the exercise of democratic voice. The Internet has greatly expanded opportunities for such expressions, often associated with anger and a sense of affective urgency (Papacharissi, 2015). Such emotions are important vehicles for agenda-building and mobilization. But do they also make critical engagements constructive in any way? For constructive engagement, I contend, a different set of emotions is more helpful, namely self-transcendent emotions that are "other-oriented, diminishing one's focus on the self and encouraging greater sensitivity and attunement to others" (Stellar et al., 2017: 2; see also Oliver et al., 2018). Important examples of self-transcendent emotions are not only *compassion* (connected to pity, sympathy, and empathic concern) but also *gratitude* (connected to appreciation) and *awe* (related to admiration, inspiration, and elevation). It is intuitively plausible that constructive engagement is deeply connected to transcending the self because it involves taking into account the needs and perspectives of others. It seems clear that self-transcendent expression involving compassion, gratitude, admiration, and so on will take on a very different flavor than expression revolving around self-centered emotions like fear, anger, sadness, or even amazement, hope, and joy.

Of course, especially the negative self-centered emotions are prone to generating a lot of clicks and likes. For example, Brady et al. (2017) show that moral-emotional words in messages on social media will boost their diffusion throughout the network, with every additional moral-emotional word in a tweet increasing the retweet rate by 20 percent on average. But they are less likely to engender constructive engagement than self-transcending emotions. On the other hand, the role of positive self-centered emotions for constructive engagement is less clear. It could well be that feelings such as amazement and hope can be connected to an opening of discursive space for free expression as well as an expansion of the publicly available repertoire of ideas (Wessler, 2018). Consider sudden positive turns of events like the fall of the Berlin Wall or the beginning of the Arab Spring. But even positive self-centered expressions will be less likely to constructively engage with others than expressions that are empathic with, appreciative of, or reverential toward others.

However, especially the role of empathy in facilitating constructive engagement has also been questioned. Scudder (2016) warns that, because empathy is based on imagination of the feelings of others, it might lead us to project such imagined feelings onto them rather than reflecting or doubling their feelings and perspectives in our experience. In this sense, empathy may be intentionally constructive, but not actually engaging the other. This is a powerful reminder that the benefits of empathy and other self-transcendent emotions unfold best in actual communication, not in merely internal feeling or in monologue. Such emotions should be tested against the thoughts or feelings of the other in actual communicative exchanges. Therefore, constructive engagement requires an additional element beyond free expression, namely acknowledging the other through actual listening.

10.3.2 Acknowledgment: Supplementing Voice with Democratic Listening

Much prior research in communication focuses on problems of voice, particularly on inequalities of voice and on how marginalized actors can make themselves heard in counter-publics or the mainstream public sphere (Fraser, 1992; Mouffe, 2013). With the proliferation of possibilities for voice on the Internet, however, the counterpart, that is, practices of democratic listening, have become the real issue: Who is being listened to, and how can the act of listening do justice to what is being expressed? There is an instructive differentiation in the sparse literature on listening between apophatic listening (aiming at a clear understanding of what the other wants to say) and cataphatic listening (aiming at loading your own ammunition in relation to the other) (Dobson, 2014; Rinke and Moy, 2018). Consequently, people and institutions engaged in apophatic listening try to understand all facets of the issue as well their counterparts' emotions and moods before reacting. Cataphatic listeners, on the other hand, are disruptive in the sense that they either only seek errors in other people's utterances or focus on immediate practical tasks, quickly becoming impatient when others take time to express themselves. It seems clear that apophatic rather than cataphatic listening should be conducive to constructive engagement and should eschew the dangers of projecting one's thoughts or feelings onto others.

When we apply the idea of apophatic listening with its tint of genuine curiosity to the realm of actually existing public communication, however, it becomes clear that not everybody should be listened to in the same way. In relations of unequal power distribution or outright marginalization, it makes sense to posit an obligation for those at the center of power to apophatically listen to those in the periphery, not necessarily the other way round. Critical, error-seeking listening vis-à-vis the powerful can be legitimate, if this is not the only way social actors relate to each other in democratic contestation. Critical listening also seems to be associated with other beneficial political outcomes, such as political information processing and a normative appreciation of political disagreement (Rinke and Moy, 2018), which can be considered an important attitudinal underpinning of constructive engagement.

Finally, beyond power relations and exclusion, I see a third issue in listening practices that might pose a danger to constructive engagement: Communicators might be compelled to cut the burden of listening short by easily accepting and superficially tolerating each other's views without taking each other's underlying concerns seriously. Of course, no one can quarrel about everything. So there are certainly areas in which a posture of benevolent indifference is a viable way to avoid disruptive conflict. But not all conflicts can and should be avoided, and for those that are necessary, deeper forms of apophatic listening on both sides are needed to create genuine communicative exchange.

10.3.3 Exchange: Fostering Integrative Qualities of Conflict

Conflict has often implicitly or explicitly been juxtaposed with social integration, leading to an understanding of integration that hinges on harmony or the absence of conflict. But there is a lineage in social theory from Georg Simmel to Lewis Coser and Helmut Dubiel that highlights the integrative potential of robust but contained conflicts. Dubiel (1999) distinguishes genuine conflict from two other types of dispute: the routinized competition and alignment of diverging interests regulated by well-known, shared settlement rules on the one hand and the logic of civil war that knows no rule but sheer force and in which the enemies deny each other the right to existence on the other. Situated in a broad field between those two extremes, social conflicts are characterized by robust, but contained, forms of dispute. Conflicts in this sense should reflect the deeper concerns of the opponents, but each party's conduct should also be constrained by rules that emerge in the very exchange itself (Dubiel, 1999: 141). In conflicts like these, the opponents (a) know and acknowledge each other, (b) do not see each other as enemies, but as legitimate opponents, and (c) embrace their dispute as necessary (see also Mouffe, 2013).

The point of Dubiel's argument is not that social conflict is better than civil war (of course it is), but that robust and contained conflicts produce an awareness of the shared social and political space in which they take place. At the same time, this shared space is not at all identical to tradition-based value agreement, which tends to evaporate in modern societies, or to substantive consensus achieved through discussion.

Democratic societies are not sustained by conflicting groups sacrificing their particularistic interests and opinions for an imaginary consensus. Instead the normative capital that integrates them develops precisely in the chain of conflicts that are [...] fought "by the rules." If speaking about a collective identity should make any sense at all it is the accumulated experience of dramatic conflicts that have been overcome and that lead to an awareness of a shared social space. (Dubiel, 1999: 138, author translation)

In this way, the process of living through dramatic conflicts for which no preordained mechanisms of interest alignment exist yet creates the symbolic resources that can integrate even radically pluralistic, modern societies.

10.4 FUTURE PERSPECTIVES: PLANNING THE ONLINE CONSTRUCTIVE ENGAGEMENT LAB

In my view, one formidable task that communication scholars face today consists in reformulating and specifying this idea of robust, but contained, symbolically rich, and integrative conflict in terms of concrete communicative practices, institutions, and technologies. One step in this direction might be a conception of constructive engagement that captures self-transcendent forms of self-expression, genuine curiosity in listening to others, and robust exchanges constrained by an awareness that there is no alternative to somehow living in a shared social and political space.

If we take this substantive conception of constructive engagement and pair it with the meta-reflexive idea of a constructively engaged "social science of the possible" sketched above, what vision for future research endeavors emerges? I would like to end this chapter with a concrete idea on how to organize collaborative research on constructive engagement that is itself constructively engaged with the real world and pushes the limits of what seems possible.

Imagine an Online Constructive Engagement Lab: Communication scholars work alongside political theorists and computer scientists to develop practices, institutions, and technologies that help make online communication more constructive.

On the level of *individual participants*, the interdisciplinary group would investigate the emotional underpinnings of constructive engagement and the value of listening. Do self-transcendent emotions like pity, gratitude, or admiration, and does curiosity in listening, have the salutary effects that I have posited above? What are the platform characteristics, group dynamics, and individual traits that best support the surfacing of self-transcendent emotions and episodes of genuine listening in online debate? And how do expressions of such feelings, and signals of acknowledgment and appreciation of disagreement, influence subsequent utterances and the emotional atmosphere of entire discussion threads?

On the level of *institutional performance*, the lab group might investigate what media organizations and journalists do to foster constructiveness beyond the ubiquitous blocking of "problematic" content. Which styles of moderation, and what type of information base, best support constructive behavior by participants? Are publicly funded media better equipped to foster constructiveness, or do they exhibit an elitist bias that inhibits expression of diverse viewpoints and true listening to the underprivileged?

Finally, on the level of *technological affordances*, the lab team works on algorithms and tools that can partly emulate what human discussion moderators would do to foster constructiveness. Can a "DebateEnhancer" software be developed that automatically detects the relative strengths of conflicting positions in online debate, reinserts arguments that have been neglected or sidelined, and reminds participants of the issues that are still open in a particular discussion sequence? Can discussants be technically reminded to listen in an apophatic way?

To be sure, not every problem can be solved with technology, and many problems call for human ingenuity to be tackled. Therefore, research on individual behavior and institutional performance is paramount. On the other hand, those problems caused by the current technological set-up of discussions on the commercial social network sites can in principle be addressed with a different type of technology. Just as Facebook, Google, and Twitter encode their own values and aims into their algorithms – maximizing users' attention, duration of use, and willingness to share private data – these can also be "re-programmed" for democratic ends. As communication scholars we should not shy away from this task even though we may not be trained to do the reprogramming ourselves. Interdisciplinary collaboration is needed, but our disciplinary input is essential. What we need most of all, however, are spaces of institutional independence and intellectual freedom to facilitate thinking about possible alternative forms and platforms of online engagement. In my view, an Online Constructive Engagement Lab could be just such a space. The proposal is somewhat speculative and probably also contentious, as Wright has pointed out. But if we don't try, we will never know.

References

Althaus, Scott L. (2012). "What's Good and Bad in Political Communication Research? Normative Standards for Evaluating Media and Citizen Performance." In H. A. Semetko and M. Scammell (eds.), *Sage Handbook of Political Communication* (pp. 97–145). Thousand Oaks, CA: Sage Publications.

Baker, C. Edwin (2002). *Media, Markets, and Democracy.* New York: Cambridge University Press.

Bennett, W. Lance and Barbara Pfetsch (2018). "Rethinking Political Communication in a Time of Disrupted Public Spheres." *Journal of Communication,* 68, 243–253.

Brady, William J., Julian A. Wills, John T. Jost, et al. (2017). "Emotion Shapes the Diffusion of Moralized Content in Social Networks." *Proceedings of the National Academy of Sciences of the United States of America,* 114(28), 7313–7318.

Craft, Stephanie and Tim P. Vos (2018). "Have You Heard?" *Journalism Practice,* 12(8), 966–975.

Dobson, Andrew (2014). *Listening for Democracy: Recognition, Representation, Reconciliation.* New York: Oxford University Press.

Dovidio, John F., Angelika Love, Fabian M. H. Schellhaas, and Miles Hewstone (2017). "Reducing Intergroup Bias through Intergroup Contact: Twenty Years of Progress and Future Directions." *Group Processes & Intergroup Relations*, 20, 606–620.

Dubiel, Helmut (1999). "Integration durch Konflikt?" In J. Friedrichs and W. Jagodzinski (eds.), *Soziale Integration. Sonderheft 39 der Kölner Zeitschrift für Soziologie und Sozialpsychologie* (pp. 132–143). Opladen, Wiesbaden: Westdeutscher Verlag.

Ferree, Myra Marx, William Anthony Gamson, Dieter Rucht, and Jürgen Gerhards (2002). *Shaping Abortion Discourse: Democracy and the Public Sphere in Germany and the United States*. New York: Cambridge University Press.

Fraser, Nancy (1992). "Rethinking the Public Sphere: A Contribution to the Critique of Actually Existing Democracy." In C. Calhoun (ed.) *Habermas and the Public Sphere* (pp. 109–142). Cambridge, MA: MIT Press.

Freelon, Deen (2015). "Discourse Architecture, Ideology, and Democratic Norms in Online Political Discussion." *New Media & Society*, 17(5), 772–791.

Habermas, Jürgen (1996). *Between Facts and Norms: Contributions to a Discourse Theory of Law and Democracy*. Cambridge, MA: MIT Press.

Katriel, Tamar (2004). *Dialogic Moments: From Soul Talks to Talk Radio in Israeli Culture*. Detroit: Wayne State University Press.

Mouffe, Chantal (2013). *Agonistics: Thinking the World Politically*. London: Verso Press.

Oliver, Mary Beth, Arthur A. Raney, Michael D. Slater, et al. (2018). "Self-Transcendent Media Experiences. Taking Meaningful Media to a Higher Level." *Journal of Communication*, 68, 380–389.

Papacharissi, Zizi (2015). *Affective Publics. Sentiment, Technology, and Politics*. New York: Oxford University Press.

Rinke, Eike Mark (2017). *A Framework for Critical-Empiricist Research in Political Communication*. Paper presented at the annual conference of the International Communication Association (ICA), May 24–28, San Diego. https://osf.io/8u5vb/

Rinke, Eike Mark and Patricia Moy (2018). *Political Correlates of Apophatic and Cataphatic Listening Styles*. Paper presented the annual conference of the American Political Science Association (APSA), August 30–September 2, Boston. https://osf.io/aqk6d/

Schieferdecker, David and Hartmut Wessler (2017). "Bridging Segregation Via Media Exposure? Ingroup Identification, Outgroup Distance and Low Direct Contact Reduce Outgroup Appearance in Media Repertoires." *Journal of Communication*, 67(6), 993–1014.

Scudder, Mary F. (2016). "Beyond Empathy: Strategies and Ideals of Democratic Deliberation." *Polity*, 48(4), 524–50.

Stellar, Jennifer E., Amie M. Gordon, Paul K. Piff, et al. (2017). "Self-Transcendent Emotions and Their Social Functions: Compassion, Gratitude, and Awe Bind Us to Others through Prosociality." *Emotion Review*, 9(3), 1–8.

Van Aelst, Peter, Jesper Strömbäck, Toril Aalberg, et al. (2017). "Political Communication in a High-Choice Media Environment: A Challenge for

Democracy?" *Annals of the International Communication Association,* 41(1), 3–27.

Wessler, Hartmut (2018). *Habermas and the Media.* Cambridge, UK: Polity Press.

Wessler, Hartmut and Eike Mark Rinke (2014). "Deliberative Performance of Television News in Three Types of Democracy: Insights from the U.S., Germany, and Russia." *Journal of Communication,* 64(5), 827–851.

Wright, Erik Olin (2013). "Real Utopias." *Politics & Society,* 41(2), 167–169.

11

Fostering Engagement in an Era of Dissipating Publics

Lynn Schofield Clark

11.1 INTRODUCTION

In this chapter, I ask how it might be possible to open journalistic opportunities that make youthful engagement on matters of public interest not only possible but also constructive. I consider the challenge both theoretically and methodologically. First, how should scholars rethink youthful engagement and the role journalism plays in igniting it, and second, what role might scholars play in exploring and fostering such opportunities in our own work? I want to think about these questions in relation to what I am calling *dissipating publics* – or the kind of publics that the young people I have been studying and working with have in mind when they talk about engagement: publics that come into being and then come apart in real time and in relation to such ephemera as hashtags, memes, gifs, emoji, and online witticisms (Bruns and Burgess, 2011). This kind of public coalesces and then dissipates after a school shooting, when a flurry of online activity documents and laments the tragedy and then gives way to clashes over gun policies before melting away into duck-faced friends and "Simpsons" memes.

This is a very different experience of the public than the one imagined in so much of the Habermasian-influenced research on engagement, where publics gather information and participate in sustained deliberation before arriving at actionable conclusions through the consensus-building processes of a functioning system of governance. Indeed, most of these young people I am referring to are between the ages of 13 and 21, so few of them can vote and fewer still have access to the halls of governmental decision-making. Their dissipating publics come together and come apart rapidly – and the interactions seem less focused on and, in the experience of many of the young people, not very effective at engendering change. I argue that, in considering how journalism might open opportunities for constructive youth engagement, it is necessary to think through not only how young people become informed but also, given their experience of publics as ephemeral, how they may or may not develop a sense of political efficacy, or the belief that public engagement can result in productive change. And in order to embrace political efficacy, young people also need to constitute adults with power into the publics with which they want to speak and work. They need adults to be audiences to their concerns. But how can they bring this about, especially when publics dissipate so quickly?

For more than a decade, I have been studying young people new to the United States and new to politics, looking in particular at how social media serves as a venue through which they become aware of the political activities of their friends as those friends share artifacts online of their political engagement. I have been especially interested in the news practices of young people who have experienced forced displacement due to the disruptions of poverty, war, natural disasters, and other crises. These young people demonstrate creativity and resilience as they approach challenges unique to their situations, drawing upon resources from differing cultural and national contexts, often placing a great deal of hope in and aspirations onto the youngest members of their families. In part due to this sense of hope, I have found that some of these young people may be engaged or engage-able in the kind of civic mobilization understood in the political sense as the "process whereby political actors encourage people to participate in some form of political action" (Vermeersch, 2011). I have sought to learn how these young people develop the capacity to engage in political action, what happens when they do engage in action, and what roles encounters with news and with journalism practices have played in that engagement.

11.2 ENGAGEMENT: THEORETICAL CONCERNS

Several important recent studies have explored the many ways young people today engage with news (Boczkowski, Michelstein, and Matassi, 2017; Edgerly et al., 2016, 2018; Kligler-Vilenchik and Literat, 2018; Thorson, 2014; Thorson et al., 2016; Vraga et al., 2014). I want to contribute to that literature by foregrounding the question of how new forms of engagement with news relate to the formation of youth publics and to youth engagement in political action. I draw on John Dewey's (1954) pragmatic understanding of engagement in relation to democratic civil society. Individuals or groups are engaged, Dewey wrote, when they are actively addressing issues of public concern. As they become informed about and active in addressing themselves to public concerns – voting, organizing, protesting, donating, for example – they can be viewed as members of engaged publics. As they do this with others and experience themselves as collectively and politically agentive, they can be said to be *constructively* engaged. I argue that constructive engagement has several dimensions that involve *recognition*: We recognize issues of concern, and in addressing those concerns through political action, we recognize ourselves as part of a public that is collective and agentive. Journalism plays a role in these processes of bringing us to recognize first issues, and second ourselves, as parts of larger groups of people and organizations who care about and are positioned to address those issues.

Journalism's role in constructive youth engagement thus comes into focus as youths also participate in recognizing themselves and the issues they care about, sometimes in relation to professional journalism and at other times once or twice removed from professional journalism in the form of journalistic stories quoted or referenced in memes, hashtags, TikToks, or other artifacts shared in social media. As journalism addresses its audiences not only directly through professional journalism but also indirectly through these media forms, professional journalism and its referents evoke into being the publics journalism claims to inform. Journalism thus participates in recognition, as Chouliaraki (2013) has pointed out, because it not only provides information but also serves as a source for the definition of reality itself: through journalism, we recognize our world with its concerns and can then formulate how we want to address those concerns through collective action. And recognition, Chouliaraki says, is the "symbolic process by which journalism ascribes a specific identity to an undefined body of viewers, through designating who belongs to this body and who does not" (Chouliaraki, 2013: 268). In this sense, journalism plays a role in constituting political communities of belonging, a process that occurs in relation to affect (Dahlgren, 2009; Papacharissi, 2015). And, for the purposes of my argument, youth citizen reporting of the kind I will detail below is *journalism*, in that it seeks to draw others into the recognition of issues, and seeks to hail into being the publics that can address themselves to those issues. The young people I study want to engage constructively, which means they also want to be recognized by others, and specifically by adult decision-makers. They want youth and adults to be part of the same public that constructively engages in bringing about positive change. They want to tell stories that will help their peers as well as adults to recognize issues, recognize themselves as capable of addressing those issues, and then, as they engage constructively, they want journalism that tells stories that bring into recognition how they have collectively worked toward bringing into being a new reality. I am therefore especially interested in how young people become, and are invited to become, such storytellers for themselves, their friends, and their communities – and how they are received and understood by influential others who may recognize the reality embedded in their stories.

In thinking about how to study constructive engagement in relation to coalescing and dissipating publics, I lean on the work of Paulo Friere (1970), who introduced the concept of *critical consciousness* development as a way to imagine how scholars might help people recognize issues of concern and themselves as members of a public that can address those concerns. For Friere (1970; see also Fals Borda 2006), research is viewed not as an end in itself but as a means to reflect, consider courses of action, and engage in action to create change. Friere's "critical consciousness," or *conscientizacão*, is the practice of "learning to perceive social, political, and economic contradictions and to take action against the oppressive elements of reality" (1970/2000). Inherent in the development of critical consciousness is the ability to recognize one's position and place within a system that is not fixed but instead the result of an "unjust order" that "[one] can transform" (Freire, 2000).

In youth participatory action research (YPAR), a tradition rooted in Friere's thinking, young people partner with adults to discuss issues of social inequity. Together, they collect information about the topic and consider actions that might best disrupt and change the systems that hold those inequities in place (Anyon et al., 2018; Cammarota and Fine, 2010). YPAR can also present an opportunity to do the work of resistance through youthful citizen journalism expression, as young people take up investigative techniques to analyze and respond to oppression. Researching youth journalism opens avenues for scholars to both explore and foster constructive youth engagement. And such efforts may be particularly important in a context in which young people express concern about both how quickly news moves on from their concerns and how quickly publics can coalesce and dissipate.

Friere's experiences with helping Brazilian adults learn to read and write have further implications for thinking about and studying constructive engagement. Too often, traditional educational efforts embrace a "banking model" that treats students as empty vessels to be filled with knowledge. Too often, scholars have conceptualized journalism using the same "banking model," understanding journalism's role in youth political development as one of providing information. Friere argues that learners should instead be approached as "co-creators of knowledge." In a social-media era in which young people think of "news" as the material and information that comes to them via their social-media feeds, we must further examine the journalist–audience dichotomy and the systems of power inherent in it. Approaching people as "co-creators of journalism" challenges this dichotomy, a point made by Jay Rosen (2006) in his reframing of news publics as "the people formerly known as the audience." In seeking to explore the role of journalism and journalists in constructive youth engagement, we need to ask not only what would it mean for the young people formerly known as the audience to become co-creators of journalism but also what would it mean for the people formerly known as journalists, as well as those of us who study journalism, to create spaces for decision-makers to be constituted as audiences? To reconceptualize constructive engagement in this manner would require scholars to consider how decision-makers might be best positioned to listen, what contextual factors shape the practices of their listening, how and when journalism contributes to amplifying the stories that the co-creators of journalism wish to have decision-makers hear, and what conceptual frameworks shape what the listener will hear and understand? In the next section of this chapter, I introduce several of my own experiences designing and implementing media-rich youth-participatory-action research projects that have sought to explore the role of professional journalism and journalists in facilitating constructive youth engagement.

11.3 ENGAGEMENT: METHODOLOGICAL CONCERNS

I have overseen several research efforts that position communication scholars as partners with young people, effectively utilizing Marcuse's idea of *the is and the ought* as a framework for youth to think about what is and what could and should be (Marcuse, 1964; Thevenin, 2017). In this section, I discuss several experiences in which my colleagues and I worked with young people as co-creators of journalism in order to constitute decision-makers as audiences and publics, with an eye to combatting the experience of dissipating publics. Each of the efforts described here drew upon a media-rich youth-participatory-action research framework, as mentioned earlier and described elsewhere, that sought to draw adult decision-makers into youthful publics through the work of youthful citizen journalism activities (see Clark and Marchi, 2017; Clark and Thompson, 2021).

In undergoing the research, I first established the after-school Digital Media Club (DMC) in a Denver public high school that includes a number of students who are recent immigrants to the United States. The intent was to bring YPAR practices into conversation with media and communication studies. The after-school context was important, as research has established that, for a variety of reasons, teachers are less likely to address racism and other oppressions from a critical perspective and that peer social support is an important antecedent for social action (Diemer and Li, 2011). The after-school club's aim was to invite students to "use digital media to make a difference in their community." Students worked with a team of educator/researchers, graduate, and undergraduate students from the nearby University of Denver to develop a project. The communication researchers and graduate students helped identify which decision-makers were best positioned to address the concerns of the young people and leveraged connections with journalists and city and state officials to find ways to bring those groups together into the spaces where they could hear, amplify, and address the young people's concerns.

11.4 KIDS AND COPS: IMPROVING RELATIONS

One group of students seeking to explore law enforcement issues teamed with Denver's Office of the Independent Monitor (OIM), a citizen advocacy organization empowered to moderate relations between citizens and members of the police and fire departments. The OIM regarded the students as a target audience for a program they wished to develop specifically aimed at improving relations between students of color and members of law enforcement. The program would introduce students to their rights and responsibilities when involved in encounters with the police. The OIM staff, therefore, had a set of objectives for the project complementary to those of the students. Amid negative publicity about relations between law enforcement and students of color, officials in law enforcement contacted by the Office of the Independent Monitor about the project participated enthusiastically.

The young people interacted as reporters and recorded interviews with members of the police department over the course of the 2014–15 academic year and decided, in consultation with their adult advisers, that a research brief would be the most effective form in which to present their reporting. In the end, the Office of the Independent Monitor was able to leverage the findings detailed in the brief to effect change. The city created a voluntary training program titled "Bridging the Gap: Kids and Cops" based on the idea grown out of the youth reporting program that the city would benefit from trainings in youth development and cultural bias and in how police and youth interactions could follow a more productive dialogic model.

The OIM had begun its initiative aiming to ensure youth better understood their rights and responsibilities, hoping that such training could lower rates of incarceration as young people learned and practiced de-escalation techniques. Over the course of the pilot year with the club, the OIM moved toward a model of joint training, with both police and youth listening to and learning from each other. The voices of the student participants in the club, as expressed in the co-authored research brief that the OIM circulated widely among their constituents, gave the OIM staff an important source of legitimacy for the *Bridging the Gap* program. The program was successful by many measures. As of 2019, according to its own reports, the program had taught more than 1,700 at-risk Denver youth new skills to make interactions with law enforcement officers safer and more effective. It had educated more than 330 Denver Police Department officers on adolescent development and de-escalation techniques and equipped more than 180 adult and youth community members with the skills necessary to facilitate transformational dialogue at youth–officer forums. The OIM had held more than 39 youth–officer forums in schools and neighborhoods and raised more than $500,000 in grants (Horton, 2019).

This media-rich youth-participatory-action project arguably constituted the OIM as an "audience" for youth voice and the OIM subsequently constituted the Denver Police Department as a secondary "audience" for that voice. The young people who collected video materials as evidence of their interactions and posted them to a curated website saw themselves as initially engaging in practices of youth citizen journalism. Ultimately their work was a form of advocacy journalism in that, as their goals aligned with OIM, they were able to leverage their storytelling toward a particular end. Professional journalists did not tell the story of youth involvement in the OIM's efforts until much later (Campbell, 2018).

The young people involved in the OIM program in Denver had analyzed what is (the real world), what could be (the possible world), and what should be (the ideal world) and saw their efforts joined with the efforts of others to bring about political change. They experienced themselves as participants in a public that had coalesced to bring attention and then widespread change to the issue of school discipline. And even though many of their friends and school peers had participated only marginally or not at all, they too felt themselves part of this coalesced public when following developments and sharing news of the project online.

11.5 DENVER REGIONAL TRANSPORTATION DISTRICT: IMPROVING BUS SERVICE

Another group in the same club sought to address slow and overcrowded bus service to city schools. Following the same youth participatory action framework described earlier, they worked with adults to conduct a survey of student opinions about how well they were being served by Denver's Regional Transportation District (RTD) in order to present the collected findings to members of the RTD staff and the elected officials who represented the school district and who served on the RTD commission. The students decided their pitch would be most effective if it included both a PowerPoint presentation featuring the findings from their survey and a journalistic video that illustrated the problems of crowded and slow buses from the perspective of the students.

Thanks to arrangements made through nonprofit organizations Transportation Solutions and Mile High Connects, the RTD scheduler, and RTD commissioner agreed to meet with the students. The largest community-based newspaper in the area covered the meeting at the invitation of one of the adults advising the student group and gave extensive coverage to the students' concerns, placing its story of the meeting on its front page.

Again, the project enjoyed success. The RTD scheduler and commissioner who attended the meeting immediately agreed to reinstate closed bus lines that had left student commutes long and crowded. The students reported their success to the school population and shared their project video and the news story via their Twitter feeds. Although the effort was spearheaded by a core group of fewer than a dozen young people, peers who had participated minimally, such as by completing the transportation survey, later expressed pride in the fact that "we" in the student body had successfully changed the bus schedule. The student citizen journalism effort had constituted a political community of belonging, and the core group then shepherded the RTD officials toward a new understanding of reality that included a change to bus schedules that would better accommodate the students and their needs. The professional work of the community journalist amplified the student requests, but it was the youth journalism effort that brought into being a public that, in turn, put forward a story that constituted public officials as an audience and evoked a response from them.

11.6 CONSTITUTING DECISION-MAKERS AS AUDIENCES: SCAFFOLDING MATTERS

In the years following the experiences described earlier, I have been involved in additional efforts to consider how best to constitute decision-makers as audiences for youth initiatives. One of the projects was part of an exhibit funded by Denver in which high school participants were asked to take photos and tell stories of how gentrification was playing out in their neighborhoods (DiEnno et al., 2019). In two other projects, young people were invited to contribute their own story narrative or poetic works outlining problems they and their neighborhoods faced or celebrating experiences of resilience in the face of those challenges (Gomez and Zyphers, 2018; Jimenez et al., 2020).

The exhibit featured photos taken by the students and included paragraph descriptions about how the work captured the experience of gentrification in their neighborhood. Another part of the exhibit featured videos of poems spoken aloud by the student authors that explored the educational and environmental problems that affected their everyday lives. The third part of the exhibit featured videos that a group of junior-high students had produced, also focused on environmental and social problems.

The exhibit was held in a government building and attracted attention and some press coverage. Yet many of the young people involved later said they felt "irrelevant" to policymakers who passed through the exhibit. The graduate students involved later offered an academic paper presentation on the experience in which they highlighted the frustrations that the young people expressed and concluded that "feel-good" efforts that bring youth voices into spaces where adults can hear and affirm their experiences may not be enough to support the development of political self-efficacy among young people. They argued that there is a need for scaffolding experiences between youth and policymakers that recognizes and addresses the ways that adultism, and adult systems, can render young people's experiences "irrelevant" to those systems unless they are specifically addressed to problems that the adults recognize (Engle et al., 2019).

None of the youth citizen-journalism efforts in the shared exhibit specifically sought to address a particular problem in the way that either the Denver Police Department or Regional Transportation District projects had. Many of the exhibit works were understood by attendees as personal expressions that did not translate easily into the decisions made in the municipal or nearby state offices. This helped the research team to see that bringing young people and their co-creations into places where it would be convenient for adult decision-makers to see and interact with them failed on its own to fully constitute adults into an audience for youth concerns. The results of this experiment in engineering an experience of constructive youth engagement – one in which young people felt that they were capable of finding an audience for their concerns and thus engaging in actions that could bring about change – were minimal at best.

11.7 DISCUSSION

Not all efforts to involve young people as co-creators of journalism are successful, and it can be difficult to constitute public officials or other relevant decision-makers as audiences for youth concerns (see, e.g., Clark, 2016; Levine, 2008). But each of the experiences outlined earlier, as well as several others my collaborators and I have designed and evaluated, have led my research team to draw some preliminary conclusions about the role of journalism, media production, and storytelling in engendering constructive youth engagement.

Youth engagement can be considered constructive when it meets two criteria: it must contribute to the ongoing development of youthful political efficacy, enabling young people to believe that their political actions can bring about the changes they desire, and it must contribute toward the goals of the broader publics of which they are a part, which, given limited access youth have to decision-makers, means that they need adults to recognize themselves as part of that public. Constructive youth engagement brings recognition into being: recognition on the part of young people that the issues that concern them are shared by others who can be constituted into an audience for their concerns, and recognition that they can act and have acted in ways that bring about change.

I have argued that professional journalism enters into and informs the development of critical consciousness, the development of political efficacy, and engagement in critical action in three different ways, as illustrated in the cases mentioned earlier. First, professional journalism enters into these processes of critical consciousness development when young people are motivated to engage. The motivation to engage is sparked, sometimes directly but more often indirectly, from professional journalistic stories they encounter via social media. Second, professional journalism enters processes of critical consciousness development when young people not only consume but also engage with news content in their relationships with others as they highlight discrepancies between what reality is and what it ought to be. With social media, young people can and do engage in constituting reality by creating, sharing, linking, liking, commenting on, and recommending content. In this sense, they are co-creators of the meanings of news stories, especially among their peers. Third, journalism enters into processes of the critical consciousness tradition when young people create and share reporting of their own.

Our research also demonstrated that when youthful journalistic endeavors aligned with adults' agendas, it was more likely for youth to find that the adults could be constituted into a sympathetic audience, and more likely for adults to find that the co-journalistic efforts of young people could be harnessed to their own political aspirations. This is clear in the example of the Denver Office of the Independent Monitor. The OIM staff gave great access and encouragement to the young people. The staff distributed the research brief to more than thirty-five individuals and representatives of organizations, and was able, basically, to distribute and leverage the young people's findings much more broadly than the youth themselves could have done. Similarly, because the RTD officials were interested in being responsive to their young constituents and the young people provided them with the evidence to support that responsiveness, they were able to respond to the young people's demands for change. Each of these experiences set up a context in which young people could recognize themselves as part of a political effort that contributed to the changes they wished to see and could recognize, constructing an alignment between what both they and adult decision-makers wanted. Participating in these efforts underscored the young people's own sense of political and collective agency, countering experiences of dissipating publics with experience of another kind of public and an enhanced sense that their actions could bring about desired changes. Participation in efforts to bring about political change may be especially important in an era in which publics are perceived to coalesce and dissipate quickly via social media.

The experiences reviewed above also contribute to understanding how journalism researchers can both investigate and play a role in fostering constructive youth engagement. First, adults working with youth citizen journalists can support young people by interpreting for them how decision-makers are best situated to listen and what factors shape their listening. Adults can shed light on instances when antagonism might work well and when it might not and can also help identify topics of shared interest so that youth can see how their interests align with those of key decision-makers. Second, adults can use their connections to broker meetings with government officials and others charged with serving the public in efforts to support government accountability. Third, they can help young citizen journalists make connections with professional journalists at the right time and can participate in shaping stories when appropriate.

11.8 CONCLUSION

This chapter set out to explore how we think about constructive youth engagement and how we as scholars might play a role in fostering it. I have suggested that thinking of young people as co-creators rather than solely as consumers of journalism is an important place to start, not least for providing a means through which young people might experience constructive engagement. The student projects outlined earlier saw participants working with adults committed to connecting community concerns to political action. The student work enabled them to draw a connection between their own stories and concerns and those of people throughout their communities. Through their involvement in these journalistic efforts that incorporated both grassroots work among their peers and work with advocacy organizations, the students came to see themselves as engaged in a much broader effort of reform, efforts attempting to bring to life "what ought to be" in the realms of public school, law enforcement, and city transportation.

We may need programs that bring people together online to hash out disagreements in a deliberative fashion. But what I argue we also need are data literacy programs grounded in caring and in critical consciousness development that are media-rich in their application and that will give young people a chance to practice voicing and addressing issues of injustice in local ways that matter to them, and in a manner that finds partners, as well as audiences, for their ideas and their work. My work has taught me that we need to move beyond thinking solely of how young people produce particular kinds of content, how they mobilize themselves apart from adults, or even how they interact with those whose views and lived experiences differ from their own. Young people may have heightened skills in the online environment, but evidence suggests that they also value constructive interactions with those they know and with those they don't know but who share their commitments.

In the episodic context of today's social media environment, we must seek a contextually rendered theory of how publics coalesce and dissipate to provide insights into how we might build bridges and find productive ways forward. What this chapter has argued, ultimately, is that youth engagement might be well fostered by devoting time and resources to taking into account the nature of experience in an era of dissipating publics and embracing the role adults can play in fostering the productive engagement of young people.

References

Anyon, Yolanda, Kimberly Bender, Heather Kennedy, and Jonah Dechants (2018). "A Systematic Review of Youth Participatory Action Research (YPAR) in the United States: Methodologies, Youth Outcomes, and Future Directions." *Health Education & Behavior*, 45(6), 865–78.

Boczkowski, Pablo, Eugenia Michelstein, and Mora Matassi (2017). "Incidental News: How Young People Consume News on Social Media." Paper presented at the 50th Hawaii International Conference on System Sciences, University of Hawaii at Manoa.

Bruns, Axel and Jean E. Burgess (2011). "The Use of Twitter Hashtags in the Formation of Ad Hoc Publics." In *Proceedings of the 6th European Consortium for Political Research (ECPR) General Conference 2011*. University of Iceland, Reykjavik. www.ecprnet.eu/conferences/general_conference/reykjavik

Cammarota, Julio and Michelle Fine (2010). *Revolutionizing Education: Youth Participatory Action Research in Motion*. London: Routledge.

Campbell, Ana (2018). "Independent Monitor Nick Mitchell Polices the Police." *Westword*. www.westword.com/news/nick-mitchell-independent-monitor-in-denver-polices-the-police-10601350

Chouliaraki, Lilie (2013). "Re-mediation, Inter-mediation, Trans-mediation." *Journalism Studies*, 14(2), 267–283.

Clark, Lynn Schofield (2016). "Participant or Zombie? Exploring the Limits of the Participatory Politics Framework through a Failed Media-Rich Youth

Participatory Action Research (YPAR) Project." *The Information Society*, 32 (5), 343–353.

Clark, Lynn Schofield and Regina Marchi (2017). *Young People and the Future of News*. New York: Cambridge University Press.

Clark, Lynn Schofield and Margaret Thompson (2021). "Media-Rich Participatory Action Research: Employing Media Research to Foster Youth Voice." In *Handbook of Media and Communication*, 2nd ed.

Dahlgren, Peter (2009). *Media and Political Engagement: Citizens, Communication and Democracy*. New York: Cambridge University Press.

Dewey, John (1954). *The Public and Its Problems*. Athens: Swallow Press.

Diemer, Matthew A. and Cheng-Hsien Li. (2011). "Critical Consciousness Development and Political Participation among Marginalized Youth." *Child Development*, 82(6), 1815–1833.

Edgerly, Stephanie, Kjerstin Thorson, Leila Bighash, and Mark Hannah (2016). "Posting about Politics: Media as Resources for Political Expression on Facebook." *Journal of Information Technology & Politics*, 13(2), 108–125.

Edgerly, Stephanie, Emily K. Vraga, Leticia Bode, Kjerstin Thorson, and Esther Thorson (2018). "New Media, New Relationship to Participation? A Closer Look at Youth News Repertoires and Political Participation." *Journalism & Mass Communication Quarterly*, 95(1), 192–212.

Engle, Corey, Stephanie Nisle, Heather Kennedy, Carlos Jimenez, and Lynn Schofield Clark (2019). "Bringing Youth Voice to Policy: A Review of Bridge Project Youth and Interactions with Denver Decision-Makers." Paper presented at the University of Denver Graduate Research Symposium.

Fals Borda, Orlando (2006). "Participatory (Action) Research in Social Theory: Origins and Challenges." In Peter Reason and Hilary Bradbury (eds.), *Handbook of Action Research: Concise Paperback Edition*. Thousand Oaks, CA: SAGE, 27–37.

France-Presse, Agence (2019). "'The Climate Doesn't Need Awards': Greta Thunberg Declines Environmental Prize." *The Guardian*, October 29, 2019.

Friere, Paulo (1970). *Pedagogy of the Oppressed*. New York: Herder and Herder.

Gomez, Esteban and Tribal Zyphers (2018). *This Is My Denver*. www.du.edu/iri se/ourinitiatives/artinsociety.html

Horton, Gianina (2019). "Annual Report, Office of the Independent Monitor." Denver: UNESCO Child and Family Research Centre, National University of Ireland Galway.

Jimenez, Carlos, Lynn Schofield Clark, Corey Engle, and Heather Kennedy (forthcoming). "The Art of Youthful Restraint: How Young People Take Control of Their Digital Story."

Kligler-Vilenchik, Neta and Ioana Literat (2018). "Distributed Creativity as Political Expression: Youth Responses to the 2016 U.S. Presidential Election in Online Affinity Networks." *Journal of Communication*, 68(1), 75–97.

Levine, Peter (2008). "A Public Voice for Youth: The Audience Problem in Digital Media and Civic Education." In Lance Bennett (ed.), *Civic Life Online: Learning How Digital Media Can Engage Youth* (pp. 119–38). Cambridge, MA: MIT Press.

Marcuse, Herbert (1964). *One-Dimensional Man: Studies in the Ideology of Advanced Industrial Society*. New York: Beacon Press.

Papacharissi, Zizi (2015). *Affective Publics: Sentiment, Technology, and Politics.* New York: Oxford University Press.
Rosen, Jay (2006). "The People Formerly Known as the Audience." *HuffPost.* www.huffpost.com/entry/the-people-formerly-known_1_b_24113.
Thevenin, Benjamin (2017). "Remix Politics: Political Remix as an Analytic Framework for Critical Media Literacy." In Belinha S. De Abreu, Paul Mihailidis, Alice Y.L. Lee, Jad Melki, and Julian McDougall (eds.), *International Handbook of Media Literacy Education.* New York: Routledge, 174–192.
Thorson, Kjerstin (2014). "Facing an Uncertain Reception: Young Citizens and Political Interaction on Facebook." *Information, Communication & Society,* 17(2), 203–216.
Thorson, Kjerstin, Stephanie Edgerly, Neta Kligler-Vilenchik, Yu Xu, and Luping Wang (2016). "Seeking Visibility in a Big Tent: Digital Communication and the People's Climate March." *International Journal of Communication,* 10, 23.
Vermeersch, Peter. (2011). "Mobilization, Political." In George T. Kurlan (ed.), *The Encyclopedia of Political Science* (pp. 1048–1048). Washington DC: CQ Press.
Vraga, Emily K., Leticia Bode, Chris Wells, Kevin Driscoll, and Kjerstin Thorson (2014). "The Rules of Engagement: Comparing Two Social Protest Movements on YouTube." *Cyberpsychology, Behavior, and Social Networking,* 17 (3), 133–140.

.

PART V

THE ROLE OF SCHOLARS

12

What Is Communication Research For? Wrestling with the Relevance of What We Do

Seth C. Lewis

Life, it seems, has never been more mediated. From the smartphones that rarely leave our hands or stray far from our bedsides, to the seemingly insatiable appetite for social media, binge-watching, video games, and always-on connectivity – life in the developed world is saturated with screens and the mediated experiences they provide (Couldry and Hepp, 2018; Deuze, 2011). As more and more of human sociality becomes explored through and manifest in mediated expressions, what we study – mainly, mediated communication and its implications for public life – should be more relevant than ever. In a sense, a growing number of contemporary research questions across the social sciences and humanities are, at bottom, media and communication research questions, or have elements that may be contextualized within what we know about human communication and its expression via media technologies. And, beyond the academy, there has never been a more obvious moment for the study of media, communication, and technology to go mainstream – to become more explainable, interesting, and ultimately informative for the policy-maker and the every-person alike. So, why isn't this happening?

In this chapter, I explore the conundrum of communication's two-way struggle for relevance: how it gets lost among the disciplines internally, and how it fails to connect with publics externally. The first half of the puzzle – communication's poor reception in the academy – is easier to explain and yet harder to resolve in the short run, given the inertia of higher education and the path dependency of institutionalized government funding streams, which, compared to the mainline disciplines and particularly in the United States, have largely ignored communication as a fundable area of research. After discussing that first challenge, I will focus on the timely second half of the problem: communication's disconnection from people and their particular concerns. For example, at a time when democratic liberalism is seemingly in retreat in many parts of the world (Luce, 2017), there is a pressing need to understand how, why, and with what effect our research has failed to speak to the lived experiences of more people.

Of course, I'm not the first to raise these questions, nor am I oblivious to the many good things happening in communication as a research domain – its overall quality, remarkable growth in recent years, and growing diversity in concepts and methods.[1] Rather, following Rasmus Kleis Nielsen's challenge to his political communication peers that "no one cares what we know" (Nielsen, 2018: 145), my purpose is to similarly provoke reflection for the wider body of media and communication studies: What is our research for? Or, just as well, *who* is it for? My central argument is that, at least in some cases, communication research is not demonstrably answering legitimate questions that many people may have about media. For the most part, this is not a problem about our rigor, whether in scientific inquiries, critical questions, or humanistic concerns; rather, our challenge is a more fundamental misreading of the context and consequences related to our modes of exploration and exposition. This is evident in the questions we're asking (or not), the populations we're studying (or not), and the way we share and discuss our findings (or not). My hope is to stimulate a self-reflective conversation about our concepts, methods, and, indeed, our own communication *about* communication research.

12.1 THE PROBLEM OF COMMUNICATION RESEARCH IN THE DISCIPLINES

Thus far, it may appear that I am referring to communication as if it were a single entity, like a well-kept house in a leafy neighborhood of academic

---

[1] See, for example, Christian Fuchs and Jack Linchuan Qiu (2018).

disciplines – all the lawns manicured, with fences clearly outlining the spheres of each discipline's domain. But, of course, in the scrum of intellectual exchange that is academia, borders are not necessarily easy to identify or sustain in practice – and, in any case, perhaps no property on the block is so complex and chaotic as the one called "communication," if it's presumed to have ownership in the neighborhood at all. As a research enterprise, communication is nothing if not beautifully and confoundingly complicated. Administratively, it resembles a real discipline, with an "institutional architecture" of academic units, professional organizations, and journals; intellectually, however, it's "omnivorous, porous, multi-faceted, [and] protean" (Waisbord, 2019a: 123). It is, as Silvio Waisbord goes on to say, "a muddle of a field, with no theoretical or analytical center that could give intellectual coherence to a vast scholarly territory" (121), its researchers avoiding larger ontological debates about communication and preferring, instead, to incorporate multiple theories and directions from other fields and disciplines in developing a range of hyper-specialized areas under an ever-expanding umbrella – from health communication to game studies to organizational communication to cultural industries.

Communication, Waisbord argues, is better understood as a "post-discipline," like other post-disciplines such as sustainability, race, health, environment, development, and criminology – each of them focused on social phenomena that transcend a single discipline's theories and methods and require the integration of multiple orientations and understandings. "Post-disciplines," he writes, "are interdisciplinary meeting points that represent academic trespassing – a growing and productive trend across universities. They are concerned with addressing specific social questions through research and pedagogy rather than with strictly disciplinary matters" (2019a: 9). The problem-driven approach of post-disciplinarity is a theme that I'll return to later on. For now, a comprehensive treatment of communication's historical development is beyond the scope of this chapter, so it suffices to say that communication nevertheless *is* a recognizable container on campuses, at conferences, and in journals, even if it's also, simultaneously, an intellectual bricolage of assumptions, commitments, and concerns that defy tidy description.[2] Any statement about "communication" as a domain worth improving is thus going to look different depending on the relative perspective of the person making the claim and the positions of those interpreting it (Lewis,

---

[2] Cf. Matt Carlson, Sue Robinson, Seth C. Lewis, and Daniel A. Berkowitz (2018).

2020; full disclosure: my primary field is journalism studies, and within that a particular emphasis on *digital* journalism studies).[3]

Regardless of one's background, however, any discussion of the relevance of communication research in the wider world must begin by reconciling its long-standing reputational problem within the academy. That is, before we can worry about why "no one cares" in lay society, it's worth wrestling with the reality that too few seem to care even on our own campuses. Jeff Pooley, a noted historian of media and communication research, captures the conundrum:

> The problem with communication research is not its unbearable lightness. The quality gap between media and communication scholarship and the mainline social sciences – once a plain and embarrassing fact – has largely closed. The work that goes under the "communication" label, taken as a whole, is more heterogeneous and spread about than a tightly disciplined field like economics. But it is not worse. The problem with communication research is, instead, its reputation. The field's marginal status – a product of its peculiar institutional history – means that our work is not read by scholars from other disciplines. The issue is not so much quality as it is prestige. (2016: 621)

The problem, he argues, is that communication research historically has been bound, in a kind of Faustian pact, with the skills training of undergraduates in journalism, advertising, and public relations, particularly in the United States and other countries that have followed its model. This vocational dilemma creates dissonance within communication departments: "A mere classroom wall...separates the lesson on how to write a press-release lead from a lecture on the damage to democracy wrought by public relations" (2016: 622). Worse still, he suggests, the vocational bind exacts a reputational price, exiling communication research to the outer edges of university esteem, cut off from the mainline disciplines. "Ideas flow in, but – like the Hotel California – they can never leave," Pooley (2016: 622) writes: "Exiled to the professional-school margins of the university, communication scholars toil away in well-heeled obscurity." The upshot, Pooley says, is that if John Durham Peters (1986) once likened (US) communication research to being an academic Taiwan (i.e., a small island laying claim to a vast territory), perhaps a more fitting geographic analogy is that of the Galapagos Islands: isolated from the mainland.

This struggle for academic respect is especially apparent in the United States, where, by one measure of academic deans, communication was

---

[3] See Sue Robinson, Seth C. Lewis, and Matt Carlson (2019).

judged to have the lowest prestige among twenty-five disciplines surveyed and where communication research is often left out of reputation studies altogether (Pooley, 2016: 623). And yet, as media and technology become an increasingly central issue for many disciplines (note how many classes with "media" in the title are popping up all over college campuses), now is the moment for our field to find a larger audience in the academy – even becoming, as Pooley suggests, a vibrant "trading zone" for cross-cutting, cross-citing interdisciplinary research (2016: 622). Indeed, as Waisbord argues, the emergent "post-disciplinary" moment is one in which communication scholars, if they manage to bridge both among their multi-layered specializations and across to outside fields and disciplines, should be particularly well-positioned to have a greater voice on public challenges such as media literacy, racism, sexism, digital dystopias, and social inequality (Waisbord, 2019a). This is especially true in light of the difficulties posed by the Covid-19 global pandemic, from the "infodemic" of misinformation spread about coronavirus to the many social and economic challenges that may strain our work as scholars and yet will also benefit from our more earnest interdisciplinary involvement (Lewis, 2020).

Communication research is thus vastly improved and potentially on a path toward greater impact and recognition within the academy. We should be pleased. But if an enhanced reputation translates mostly into improved grant-funding opportunities or more citations to our work, is that all there is to this? Does that satisfactorily answer the question, what is communication research for? What if, in fact, the related but far larger problem is that communication research is all too often marginal to broader public understanding, beyond the academy – even and especially on topics where we have something meaningful to say?

Consider Nielsen's (2018) bracing critique of political communication, one of the largest fields within the communication domain. From the Brexit referendum to the Trump election to ongoing concerns surrounding political advertising and malfeasance on social media, political communication as an "object of analysis" perhaps has never been more front-and-center in policy discussion as well as popular debate. And yet, "political communication research has been at the margins" of such conversations, otherwise dominated by think tanks, hybrid institutions straddling the academic–professional divide, and individual researchers in law, economics, and political science. "Us not engaging does not stop others from doing so," Nielsen argues. As a consequence, "substantially important public (and policy) discussions of issues at the core of our field are dumber than they could have been, in part due to our absence, an absence that is in turn in part due to *the ways in which we as a field do our work"* (2018: 146, emphasis added). It's this field-level mode of working, with its taken-for-granted norms, that deserves our special attention and reflection.

12.2 COMMUNICATION'S MODE OF WORKING: WHAT WE ASK, HOW, AND WHY

While focused on the shortcomings of political communication, Nielsen could well be diagnosing a broader challenge for the communication post-discipline as a whole: What if our ways of working are actually getting in the way, limiting the public reach and relevance of our research?

Consider two modes of scientific work that he describes – both modes committed to peer review and quality scholarship, but bearing differences in orientation and output. Mode 1, Nielsen says, conjures up an older model of science, one "driven by academically exclusive, investigator-initiated, and discipline-based forms of knowledge production that tend to privilege ever more precise answers to inherited questions" – in other words, good science, but internally oriented science (2018: 147). By contrast, Mode 2 emphasizes "context-driven, problem-focused, and interdisciplinary forms of knowledge production," as we see in the likes of medicine, engineering, and computer science today (ibid). These modes reflect the incentive structures of their communities – that is, what their respective institutions revere and reward, formally and informally. In Mode 1, public engagement is nice but unnecessary. In Mode 2, multiple stakeholders and partners are involved in formulating questions and carrying out research, and findings are communicated with multiple communities and audiences in mind – making engagement not some bolted-on feature at the end but a central element throughout.

These modes are not mutually exclusive, and both may yield resplendent or third-rate research alike. What matters for this discussion is how differently these modes take seriously the opportunities (and challenges, too) of external engagement, shaping the ultimate extent to which various actors and communities (including academics in other disciplines, policymakers, funders, industry partners, and citizens) get to have a stake in what communication research ends up reflecting and reinforcing.

In our discipline, the disconnect between what we study and the lived experience of media, I would argue, can be scrutinized according to three dimensions: (1) *what* we study, (2) *how* we do it, and (3) *why*. First, the *what* is about our concepts, or the framing devices and topical reference points that shape what we ask in the first step of research: What assumptions, worldviews, and theories drive our approaches? How do these lead to some questions being asked and not others? Second, the *how* points to our methods, both the tools we use and the populations we choose to study: How are data gathered in general and about certain groups of people in particular? What makes some types of processes and people more interesting and worth studying than others? And, third, the *why* gestures to the ultimate outputs and outcomes of our work, including, in a meta fashion, how we communicate *about* communication research: For whom, precisely, are we doing this in the first place, and why might it matter to them (or not)? Why are we communicating our research aims and findings in certain ways and not others? How often do we spend even a tiny portion of our time on broader public communication and engagement connected with our research? "If your answer is 'I don't have time,'" Nielsen points out for political communication (and, by extension, the rest of us), "it is worth asking what institutions shaped that answer and whether they are conducive for what we want to be as a field" (Nielson, 2018: 147).

These are questions for introspection, not prescriptions with one-size-fits-everyone solutions. If the normative underpinning here is the fabled "so what?" question – a perennial favorite of educators everywhere, pushing their students to more clearly articulate importance and impact in what they write – the answers that emerge for our concepts, methods, and communications may be as unique as the people who ask them. I don't pretend to have it all figured out. But we can briefly discuss one salient example, illustrating potential blind spots in a Mode 1 style of communication research.

12.3 MEDIA BIAS AS AN ILLUSTRATION

Consider, for example, the problem of "media bias," or our field's inability, I would argue, to provide a more satisfactory answer to a perennial and polarizing question about the press. I use scare quotes deliberately because "media bias" is the kind of phrase that elicits eyerolls from many academics, who generally find it to be overly reductive at best and grossly misleading at worst. The influence of corporate control or the disciplining nature of occupational routines, news values, episodic story frames, and taken-for-granted stereotypes or ideologies – those forces, scholars might say, are the "real" forms of bias to be concerned about and critiqued, more so than complaints from conservatives about the "liberal media" favoring one side versus another in news coverage.[4] Perhaps communication researchers prefer different terms, such as framing, that allow for

---

[4] See discussion in Pamela Shoemaker and Stephen Reese (2014).

greater nuance and complexity. Or, maybe we would simply rather leave *bias* alone because the term itself has problems, suggesting that "media deviate in some measurable way from a desirable standard that can be independently known" – a perfectly objective representation of reality that, even post-positivists would acknowledge, is complicated because human beings perceive reality differently (Shoemaker and Reese, 2014: 3). In this sense, it's as if communication researchers are throwing up their hands and saying, "Look, *of course* the media are biased – we all are to a certain degree, right? Let's move on to more interesting things to talk about."

Still, I would argue that communication research, as practiced in Mode 1, has been too inwardly facing and otherwise dismissive about media bias. We have set aside a question that is, for most people, one of the most important issues in media and society, and therefore hardly something to be ignored. Around the world, there is a gnawing distrust, even a loathing, of the news media (Newman, Fletcher, Kalogeropoulos, et al., 2018). People find the news dispiriting and depressing, overly complicated and overly negative, and, yes, biased and belittling. Why do people hate the press? Where does all this animus come from? There is a long, multi-faceted history of disdain for news and journalists, one that defies any simple explanation.[5] But in the present moment, among people who distrust the news media across many countries, the single biggest factor is perceiving problems of bias, spin, and agendas, as Newman and Fletcher show: "Simply put, a significant proportion of the public feels that powerful people are using the media to push their own political or economic interests, rather than represent ordinary readers or viewers" (Newman and Fletcher, 2017: 5).

It's not that communication research does not study bias at all.[6] Instead, our problem, collectively speaking, is that we don't take seriously enough the experiences of media audiences when it comes to bias. We generally prefer to make sense of media bias on our terms, using concepts and measures that sit within familiar paradigms. We prefer a top-down rather than bottom-up approach. In the process, we're missing an alternative way of looking at this problem, one that would begin not with eyerolls about plebeian persistence on this issue but instead with a more organic, people-centric assessment of everyday news users: how they perceive bias, make sense of it, and respond to it – even (and perhaps

---

[5] For a broader historical discussion of why people hate the news media, particularly in the US context, see Jonathan M. Ladd (2011).

[6] For example, see Natalie Jomini Stroud, Ashley Muddiman, and Jae Kook Lee (2014).

especially) if the terms they use or the assumptions they make strike our ears as discordant and ill-informed. This is not to say that we uncritically accept and parrot what people believe about the news media – far from it. Rather, it's about inductively exploring this social problem, and its interrelations with other social problems such as media literacy and misinformation, with the humility that will be required to learn something new and revealing about the phenomenology of news – and with the openness that will be required to co-construct such knowledge alongside other problem-driven scholars joining us from beyond communication.

In this way, we can improve our concepts and methods in making sense of media bias. And, in the process, we can develop better ways of communicating about these issues: more forthrightly explaining the (contested) nature of objectivity in journalism as in science, more clearly articulating what good press performance actually looks like, and more emphatically connecting with people who feel marginalized or misjudged in news coverage. Altogether, this means rethinking what we study (i.e., the questions deemed worthy for research), how we conduct such work (i.e., the methods developed and populations studied), and how we talk about it with a wider set of stakeholders (i.e., the sharing of findings and initiating of conversations with greater public engagement in mind).

Indeed, we already have a good model to follow in Newman and Fletcher's report, "Bias, Bullshit and Lies: Audience Perspectives on Low Trust in the Media" (2017). Based on data collected by Oxford University's Reuters Institute for the Study of Journalism – one of those industry-academy hybrid institutions that exemplifies Mode 2 style of research[7] – the report analyzes thousands of open-ended responses from the 2017 Reuters Institute Digital News Report. The format allowed people to articulate, in their own words, why they distrust the media, thereby serving up a cross-national perspective on an enduring challenge for journalism. Open-ended replies on surveys can only tell us so much, of course; in-person engagement with news users offers greater depth – and here, again, the Reuters Institute presents a useful model. A Reuters Institute Fact Sheet on Fake News, based on focus groups in four countries, shows from a bottom-up perspective that audiences and academics define "fake news" rather differently – that regular news users see the

---

[7] In full disclosure, I was a 2019–2020 Visiting Fellow at the Reuters Institute for the Study of Journalism, though I wrote this essay before receiving the appointment. My interest in joining the Reuters Institute was, in part, to explore the possibilities (and challenges) of a Mode 2 style of scholarship.

difference between "real news" and "fake news" as one of degree rather than kind, and that poor journalism and some advertising, among other things, can be seen as fake news (Nielsen and Graves, 2017). Importantly, both of these reports start from the point of reference of news users and take seriously what they have to say; they assess these issues with methodological creativity, seeking to reach people where they are at; and they are publicly available online – written with the express interest of being easily understood, shared, and relevant. Newman and Fletcher capture the essence of this Mode 2 form of engagement in summing up their research: "These findings should be a wake-up call for journalists, platforms and regulators. Rebuilding trust will require *all interested parties to work together*" (Newman and Fletcher, 2017, emphasis added).

A similar message could apply to communication research. Simply working together won't solve our problems or magically improve our public reach and social relevance, but failing to consider whether a Mode 1 style of work is the right path for our discipline would be a missed opportunity at a time when our insights about media and communication should be more visible than ever before. We can start by simply asking: What is our research for?

12.4 TWO CAUTIONS IN CONCLUSION

I have thus far advocated for communication researchers to at least entertain, and perhaps embrace, a Mode 2 form of working that is problem-focused at its core, post-disciplinary in its trespassing of traditional academic boundaries, and ultimately publicly engaged by making research more relevant to and conversant with various publics. This is not about doing "applied" research without theory; on the contrary, it's about reimagining what theory and scholarship could accomplish in the service of broader concerns. Nevertheless, any effort to alter our research questions, outputs, and orientations carries with it significant risks that cannot be overlooked. The nature and severity of these risks will depend, of course, on the relative capital (social and material) of the person attempting a transition from Mode 1 to Mode 2 style of scholarship. Junior scholars seeking to convince dissertation and hiring committees (and eventually tenure committees) that a retooled way of organizing and articulating research is better than what has come before face a very different calculus than do senior professors with status and security. However, regardless of where one comes from in approaching a Mode 2 style of research, there are at least two cautions to consider.

First, if communication – as a field, discipline, or post-discipline – is truly as intellectually incoherent and widely disrespected as Waisbord and Pooley have described, then shouldn't we be more concerned with strengthening its core and improving its reputation – in effect, resolving these problems rather than running from them? Mode 1 scholarship is designed for discipline-building, emphasizing a traditional mode of scholarly inquiry: investigators building knowledge within a domain, iterating on foundational theories, and publishing for a primarily internal audience. Are we, in a sense, abandoning the possibilities of developing communication as a discipline at precisely the time when it has an opportunity to grow into its own? Because of its rapidly expanding footprint on many campuses and because communication is uniquely suited to address media-centric concerns that are cropping up across the disciplines, communication as an academic enterprise should be having its moment. Will Mode 2 accelerate or actually undermine this progression toward scholarly acceptance and institutionalization?

Being vigilant about communication's place on campus is not a trivial concern; our opportunities to continue doing research depend on having an "academic home" in which to do it and students to instruct. It's true that emerging elements of Mode 2 scholarship apparently haven't undercut the intellectual strength of engineering or computer science, but those disciplines also have a far more established base from which to build and branch out. Communication, by contrast, is a fragmented and fledgling intellectual enterprise, always threatened by the possibility of being swallowed by larger academic units on account of budgetary stress or a provost's whim. Moreover, there is a danger that Mode 2 scholarship too easily slips into consulting for industry and becomes "administrative research," potentially at the expense of academic autonomy,[8] or that it becomes distracted by promotion and publicity in a social media era of self-branding (Duffy and Pooley, 2017). At the very least, Mode 2 should be approached with a clear-eyed sense of how it matches up individually with communication researchers and their goals and institutionally with communication and its way forward in the academy.

If Mode 2 is ultimately about public engagement, then the second caution is about the vagueness associated with that classification. What exactly counts as being "public" and "engaged," and how are such efforts recognized and rewarded? As Nielsen (2018) notes, Mode 2 only succeeds when it is adequately incentivized at the levels of

---

[8] See related discussion in Natalie Jomini Stroud (2017).

department, campus, and discipline. Making the case for a revised set of incentive structures is a politically fraught exercise in the academy, as anyone knows who has tried to make a "blended" case for promotion and tenure through a combination of traditional scholarship (Mode 1) and publicly oriented work (Mode 2). Developing better ways of incentivizing public engagement requires defining what it constitutes and when and how it succeeds. To that end, Silvio Waisbord, in *The Communication Manifesto* (2019b), makes the case for "public scholarship" – not simply public intellectualism or scholar-activism, as conventionally defined, but rather a far larger conception of connecting with publics in and through research goals and activities. Public scholarship, in this sense, "seeks publicity for different reasons: to bring issues to public attention, to persuade policy-makers and citizens, to conduct situation diagnosis, to identify solutions to social problems, to promote social change, and to spread ideas." In this broader framing of public-facing work, every decision about research is ultimately a political one, "signal[ing] our choices about how we want to intervene in public" – whether to spread knowledge, give voice to marginalized communities, help families cope with problems, foster civic practices, facilitate organizational decision-making, and so forth. Public engagement, in this view, is less about one-off appendages to one's research but a holistic appraisal of what communication research is for in the first place – which brings us back to the title of this chapter. Communication research indeed has the potential to discover such purpose; whether and how it accomplishes that, and through which modes of scholarship, is yet to be determined.

References

Carlson, Matt, Sue Robinson, Seth C. Lewis, and Daniel A. Berkowitz (2018). "Journalism Studies and its Core Commitments: The Making of a Communication Field." *The Journal of Communication*, 68(1), 6–25.

Couldry, Nick and Andreas Hepp (2018). *The Mediated Construction of Reality*. Hoboken, NJ: John Wiley & Sons.

Deuze, Mark (2011). "Media Life." *Media Culture & Society*, 33(1), 137–148.

Duffy, Brooke, Erin, and Jefferson D. Pooley (2017). "Facebook for Academics: The Convergence of Self-Branding and Social Media Logic on Academia.edu." *Social Media + Society*, 3(1).

Fuchs, Christian and Jack Linchuan Qiu (2018). "Ferments in the Field: Introductory Reflections on the Past, Present and Future of Communication Studies." *The Journal of Communication*, 68(2), 219–232.

Ladd, J. M. (2011). *Why Americans Hate the Media and How It Matters*. Princeton, NJ: Princeton University Press.

Luce, Edward (2017). *The Retreat of Western Liberalism*. New York: Atlantic Monthly Press.

Lewis, Seth C. (2020). "The Objects and Objectives of Journalism Research During the Coronavirus Pandemic and Beyond." *Digital Journalism*. https://doi.org/10.1080/21670811.2020.1773292

Newman, Nic and Richard Fletcher (2017, December 1). "Bias, Bullshit and Lies: Audience Perspectives on Low Trust in the Media." https://ssrn.com/abstract=3173579.

Newman, Nic, Richard Fletcher, Antonis Kalogeropoulos, et al. (2018, June 14). Reuters Institute Digital News Report. https://papers.ssrn.com/sol3/papers.cfm?abstract_id=3245355.

Nielsen, Rasmus Kleis (2018). "No One Cares What We Know: Three Responses to the Irrelevance of Political Communication Research." *Political Communication*, 35(1), 145–149.

Nielsen, Rasmus Kleis, and Lucas Graves (2017). *'News You Don't Believe: Audience Perspectives on Fake News*. Oxford: Reuters Institute for the Study of Journalism.

Peters, John Durham (1986). "Institutional Sources of Intellectual Poverty in Communication Research." *Communication Research*, 13(4), 527–559.

Pooley, Jefferson D. (2016). "The Field, Fermented: Prestige and the Vocational Bind in Communication Research." *International Communication Gazette*, 78(7), 621–626.

Robinson, Sue, Seth C. Lewis, and Matt Carlson (2019). "Locating the 'Digital' in Digital Journalism Studies: Transformations in Research." *Digital Journalism*, 7(3), 368–377.

Shoemaker, Pamela J. and Stephen D. Reese (2014). *Mediating the Message in the 21st Century: A Media Sociology Perspective*. New York: Routledge.

Stroud, Natalie Jomini (2017). "Helping Newsrooms Work Toward Their Democratic and Business Objectives." In P. J. Boczkowski and C. W. Anderson (eds.) *Remaking the News: Essays on the Future of Journalism Scholarship in the Digital Age* (pp. 157–176), Cambridge, MA: MIT Press.

Stroud, Natalie Jomini, Ashley Muddiman, and Jae Kook Lee (2014). "Seeing Media as Group Members: An Evaluation of Partisan Bias Perceptions." *The Journal of Communication*, 64(5), 874–894.

Waisbord, Silvio (2019a). *Communication: A Post-discipline*. Cambridge, UK: Polity Books.

Waisbord, Silvio (2019b). *The Communication Manifesto*. Cambridge, UK: Polity Books.

13

Communication as Translation

Notes toward a New Conceptualization of Communication

Guobin Yang

13.1 POLARIZATION

For scholars of journalism and communication committed to understanding and changing society, it is crucial to stress that we live in a polarized world. We live in a world of dramatic development in communication technologies that supposedly enhance our connectivity. But the reality is that we are probably connected more by conflict and polarization than by a sense of shared humanity. In this conflict-ridden world, we need to affirm and celebrate more than ever the values of difference and diversity.

Our current institutions do not serve our students or the public well. In most institutions of higher learning in the United States, our student body and faculty do not reflect the diversity of our populations. In elite public and private universities, underprivileged social and ethnic groups are seriously underrepresented. The students already in our programs often do not feel empowered in the learning process. They are hard-working, but anxious and uncertain of their future. Mental health has become a serious problem among the student body.

Despite efforts by some noted scholars and professional associations (such as the American Sociological Association) to promote the public relevance of academic research, much of the scholarship produced in the academia is produced for itself, manifesting a kind of academic narcissism. It is beyond the reach of the public and of little relevance to society. The norms and systems of performance evaluation in the academia continue to encourage the kind of methodologism and theoreticism long critiqued by scholars like C. Wright Mills, E. P. Thompson, and Pierre Bourdieu.[1] They discourage scholars from spending time on communicating our research to the public. Academic publications oriented to the public may even be viewed as unscholarly.

One example is the hierarchy of genres of academic writing. Edited volumes often provide analyses of a set of problems from different angles by a group of researchers. Important edited volumes can create or redefine a whole field of study. Yet in many universities around the world, chapters published in these volumes do not count much when it comes to hiring, tenure, and promotion. In many programs of journalism and communication in China, for example, if you have twenty book chapters and one journal article, that one journal article carries more weight than the twenty book chapters, because in the metrics of institutional performance evaluation, a book chapter counts as o contribution.

Many of us enjoy reading blogs and op-eds, listening to podcasts, or watching documentary films. Making media is a vital research practice and a form of engaged scholarship. It can intervene directly in public debates about issues of social justice. Unlike many academic articles or books, these media genres actually reach a broader public. And yet they rarely count as scholarly output in the current system of academic evaluation.

By retreating into scholasticism, academic research sometimes conveys the message that it is purely about the pursuit of knowledge or that it is a scientific endeavor for the sole purpose of scientific advancement. Fateful questions of ethics, value, and unintended consequences are ignored if not deliberately hidden. Rarely asked are questions of knowledge for whom and for what.

What is to be done? In my view, the most pressing question is how to transform our own institutions of knowledge production, including our own approaches to knowledge and knowledge production. There are no

---

[1] C. Wright Mills (2000: 57) criticizes the "methodological inhibition" that results from the adherence to "The Scientific Method." For E. P. Thompson's critique of theoretical abstraction, see his *The Poverty of Theory* (1978/1995). On "methodologism" and "theoreticism," see Pierre Bourdieu and Loic J. D. Wacquant, *An Invitation to Reflexive Sociology* (1992: 26–35).

easy answers and many structural barriers to institutional change. But there are things we can do and I will start with just one – with the central concept of our field.

13.2 TRANSMISSION

The transmission view of communication has been much criticized, and for good reason. On this view, communication is a one-way street. Typically it implies a top-down process of message delivery, where the recipients are viewed as passive, the faceless "masses." And yet as Raymond Williams wrote, "There are in fact no masses; there are only ways of seeing people as masses" (1960: 319). He argues forcefully that "Communication is not only transmission; it is also reception and response" (1960: 332). He further proposes that genuine communication involving active reception and living response depend on "an effective community of experience.... The inequalities of many kinds which still divide our community make effective communication difficult or impossible" (1960: 336). Thus for Williams, "...any real theory of communication is a theory of community" (1960: 332).

Raymond Williams' critique of the concept of mass-communication recognizes inequality as a key barrier to genuine communication. Yet although he emphasizes that his notion of equality is the "equality of being," his discussion of inequality is largely about inequality within the same national and ethnic community, and not across different national communities. In the wake of feminist and postmodernist onslaughts against the exclusionary and totalizing tendencies in the idealized notions of community,[2] it becomes difficult to hold on to a theory of communication as community, despite Williams' recognition of community's internal differences and of the need for mutual respect. Recognizing this problem, Couldry (2000) proposes the concept of "community without closure," by which he means "a community of incomplete, uncertain selves, working through dialogue to transform one another – a community without closure" (140). Writing in 2000, Couldry proposes the concept in a book-length study devoted to reimagining the method of Cultural Studies. It is an insightful response to a thorny concept, but given the concept's heavy baggage, it is unclear whether opening it up can resolve the issue. It is worth trying to find new conceptual foundations that can put difference,

---

[2] See especially Jean-Luc Nancy (1991) and Iris Marion Young (1986: 1–26).

not commonality, squarely at the center of our understanding of communication.

Like Raymond Williams, James Carey develops his cultural view of communication on the basis of a critique of communication as transmission. He proposes that more attention should be paid to communication as ritual. In his ritual view of communication,

communication is linked to terms such as "sharing," "participation," "associations," "fellowship," and "the possession of a common faith." This definition exploits the ancient identity and common roots of the terms "commonness," "communion," "community," and "communication." A ritual view of communication is directed not toward the extension of messages in space but toward the maintenance of society in time; not the act of imparting information but the representation of shared beliefs. (1992: 15)

Again, the emphasis on communion and commonality in the ritual view presumes identity, not difference. The idea that ritual represents shared beliefs precludes scenarios of what may happen when people with different religious beliefs come together. Carey does insightfully consider the ritual view of communication as a model of dramatic action: "Under a ritual view, then, news is not information but drama. It does not describe the world but portrays an arena of dramatic forces and actions" (17). Yet writing at a similar historical moment as Dayan and Katz, his view of ritual is as Durkheimian as Dayan and Katz's view of media events (1994). They put premium on the values of solidarity and commonality, not difference.

13.3 TRANSLATION

A metaphor that puts difference, and not commonality, at the center of communication is translation. Translation begins with difference. Anyone who wants to translate from or into a foreign language would have to start by learning the foreign language. What is the experience of learning a foreign language like? It is about immersion and absorption, about listening, reading, and experiencing. It presumes an attitude of complete openness and receptiveness toward the foreign other and a pedagogy of practice, revision, adjustment, and attunement. Every little detail requires the most intensive and sustained attention, and many things have to be learned not through explanation or understanding, and more by acceptance and habit. For example, one simply accepts a particular way a preposition is used in the English language. If we take a Wittgensteinian view of language, then learning a new language is really about learning the ways of life and habits associated with that language. That would mean an attitude of openness and receptive to new experiences, new values, and new ways of doing things. This linguistic hospitality is at the center of what Paul Ricoeur refers to as a "translation ethos," which he argued should provide a model for reimagining the future of Europe "for the integration of identity and alterity" (1995: 4).

Translation occurs not just across cultures and language systems, but within the same social group, between friends, and between family members. According to Mikhail Bakhtin's philosophy of language, no two utterances are the same even within the same language (Emerson, 1984). Every utterance has its specific context and therefore a specific meaning. If no two utterances are the same, then the encounter of any two utterances is an act of translation. The essence of all human communication is translation.[3]

Bakhtin's view of language also implies that translation is an open-ended process. Not only does the original text mean different things to different translators in different times, but each translation itself opens up a new conversation through its interpretation of the text. Thus translation is never perfect or complete. It has the attribute of what Bakhtin would have called "unfinalizability." For Bakhtin, linguistic equivalence in translation is an impossible idea.

This does not mean translators do not have to think about consequences. Quite the contrary. To Gregory Rabassa, the well-known English translator of Latin American Spanish literature, a translator is like a prisoner:

he must always be aware that in a very deep sense he is the prisoner of his author, convicted on any number of counts. But at the same time he must be a model prisoner, a trusty, willingly at the mercy of the text he is rendering and of all the turns it might take. If not, he had best return to the original urge of writing something of his own inspiration and bust out. (1971/1987: 81)

---

[3] This view of translation as the essence of all human communication is widely accepted by translation scholars. George Steiner (1998, xii) states in his preface to the second edition of *After Babel*:

After Babel postulates that translation is formally and pragmatically implicit in every act of communication, in the emission and reception of each and every mode of meaning, be it in the widest semiotic sense or in more specifically verbal exchanges. To understand is to decipher. To hear significance is to translate. Thus the essential structural and executive means and problems of the act of translation are fully present in acts of speech, of writing, of pictorial encoding inside any given language. Translation between different languages is a particular application of a configuration and model fundamental to human speech even where it is monoglot.

The potentially infinite number of interpretations of the original text and equally infinite possibilities of translating the original text is a source of profound anxiety for the translators. If translators are creators or re-creators, their creativity is ethically bound to an original, to which they are answerable. To Rabassa, a good translator must be a good listener: "in translation the one doing the writing must be both listener and speaker, and he could go astray in either direction. He must have a good ear for what his author is saying and he must have a good ear for what he is saying himself" (1971/1987: 85).

The result of a translation is never an equivalent of the original, nor is it a derivative. For Walter Benjamin (1968), every translation is an afterlife and therefore an extension and transformation of its original. It transforms the original by letting the light of the original shine forth and by letting the light of other languages shine upon the original. For the same reason, every translation also shines upon the translator's mother tongue, becomes part of it, and contributes to its renewal. Translation is an ongoing conversation of learning, listening, and revision. It is dialogic and self-reflexive. Communicators often want to inform and enlighten others; translators must be prepared for self-enlightenment.

Not surprisingly, the person who wrote about the translator in this way also wrote about the storyteller in the same spirit. In his 1936 essay "The Storyteller," Benjamin lamented that "the art of storytelling is coming to an end" (1968: 83). To Benjamin, storytelling is about the exchange of experiences. An obvious reason for the demise of the art of storytelling was that "experience has fallen in value" (1968: 83–84). What has risen instead is information, and yet "The value of information does not survive the moment in which it was new" (1968: 90). According to Benjamin, what was also being lost with the art of storytelling was the gift of listening, for the continuation of the art of storytelling is inseparable from the art of listening. "The storyteller takes what he tells from experience – his own or that reported by others. And he in turn makes it the experience of those who are listening to his tale" (1968: 87). A good listener retains the story, integrates it into his own experience, and sooner or later repeats it to someone else. A good listener is "self-forgetful": "The more self-forgetful the listener is, the more deeply is what he listens to impressed upon his memory. When the rhythm of work has seized him, he listens to the tales in such a way that the gift of retelling them comes to him all by itself" (1968: 91). This image of the self-forgetful listener has an affinity with Rabassa's notion of the translator as a "prisoner of the author." In essence, it emphasizes the will and capacity to be attentive to the other.

In sum, a view of communication as translation, as opposed to a view of communication as transmission, community, or ritual, is premised on the recognition of difference, dialogue, receptivity, mutual change, and self-transformation. This view of communication as translation has important ethical and practical implications for the practice of communication research, indeed, for any practices of knowledge production.

13.4 IMPLICATIONS

Like translators, communication researchers can never overemphasize the ethos of openness and receptiveness to difference and the pedagogies of listening, learning, and attunement. Communication research is not a one-way street. We translate the experiences of those we study into a language for other researchers so that it can be evaluated by our peers. But if our goal is to better understand the world and its peoples, then our research ought also to articulate the experiences of our human subjects for themselves and their fellow beings, and not just for the academic communities. More importantly, we should cultivate methodological orientations and sensibilities which let human subjects teach us about their experiences, rather than we explaining to them in academic jargon about their own experiences.

That would mean changing our philosophies and methods of knowledge production in several ways. First, it is essential to embrace alternative epistemologies. Patricia Collins points out in her *Feminist Black Thought* that dominant knowledge frameworks – their theories and concepts – do not reflect the experiences of African American women. The majority of African American women have historically been subject to the domination of the matrix of patriarchy, race, and class. To produce knowledge for and about themselves, African American women would have to turn to alternative epistemologies. The first principle of a black feminist epistemology is therefore to use their own lived experiences as the criteria of knowledge (Collins, 1990/2008). First published in 1990, the book remains ever more relevant today with its profound pathos and insights. When I read this book with students in my graduate seminar last year, it was still the book students were most excited about. And yet at the same time, there was a palpable feeling of helplessness among the students that the critical visions for a new epistemology so powerfully articulated in Collins' book are nowhere closer to realization than when she first published her book almost thirty years ago. If anything, the "mainstream" social sciences may have deviated further from her visions.

Second, as a corollary of embracing alternative epistemologies, it is essential to diversify the topics, people, and places we study. We tend to study people and places we are familiar with, and there is nothing wrong with that. Understandably, it is harder to study people who are different from us, who hold different political or religious views, who live in foreign countries. But such tendencies are not conducive to understanding and learning from the wealth and breadth of human experiences. Over time, they may even reinforce biases and prejudices. Like translators, communication researchers might venture more into zones of foreign difference. One case in point is the selection of research topics. The nature of the field of media and communication is such that scholars necessarily have to pay close attention to the dominant media systems, institutions, and the individuals who in one way or another exert great social, cultural, and political influences. And yet intentionally or unintentionally, our scholarship may help to amplify the voices of those who already monopolize public attention. Thus, while it is important to study these institutions and individuals, more attention should be given to marginalized social groups who are excluded from the centers of power and who lack a voice in the public sphere. These include peoples in other parts of the world, not just our own.

One way of promoting research on marginalized social groups is through institutional support. In recent years, the National Communication Association and the International Communication Association have established new divisions or interest groups in the areas of communication and social justice, LGBTQ studies, and so forth. Although limited, there have been faculty hires in the areas of media activism and social justice. This is not to say that these areas are neglected in the past, but to establish new divisions or interest groups in professional associations and to set up faculty positions in these areas are strong institutional statements about the central importance of these issues to the field.

Third, embracing alternative epistemologies also means diversifying our research methods and theoretical orientations. The black feminist epistemologies developed by Patricia Collins are an invitation to humanistic approaches, even in social science fields. By attaching special meaning to human experiences, humanistic approaches are especially relevant to contemporary societies where, as Walter Benjamin saw it already almost a century ago, the value of experience has given place to information.

Current scholarship in the field of media and communication is not particularly good at telling stories of human experiences. There is a poverty of action and the human touch. Even in studies of social movements and protests, it is not easy to see real human action, hear human voices, or feel human feelings when more efforts seem to be expended on producing colorful visualizations of online social networks. New methodologies such as data visualization have their advantages, but they are not a substitute for the power of story-telling.

Exemplary works do appear, and they are superb translations of human experiences. One example is Jeffrey Lane's 2018 book *The Digital Street*. Inspired by sociologist Elijah Anderson's classic study *The Code of the Street*, Lane's study moves from Anderson's inner city world of the 1990s to the social media age of the 2010s. If the inner city youth in Anderson's study wanted street respect at the risk of one's life, Lane finds that the youth in Harlem also want education, work, and a steadier adulthood. Social media interactions among them provide opportunities to mitigate violence even as they expose the youth to new forms of control and surveillance. One of the many fascinating stories Lane tells is about Tiana's "retirement" from fighting. When the author met Tiana in 2010, she was fifteen years old and would fight several times a week. In 2012, Tiana announced on her Facebook page that she had "officially retired" from fighting. One day in late January 2012, however, she was involved in a fight with Gabriella. When Gabriella claimed she had won the fight, Tiana announced on Facebook that she would fight Gabriella again to show she was the real winner. Within about an hour, however, Tiana had deleted her Facebook post. Lane found that it was because Tiana's friends and aunt had persuaded her not to fight again. As Lane argues, on the digital street, "With an audience of concerned and trusted adults and peers, Tiana initiated and took an out from fighting that saved face by showcasing her maturity without negating her toughness" (Lane, 2018: 83).

Another example is Jessa Lingel's study of digital countercultures and communities of alterity. Examining several cases of countercultural communities, Lingel finds rich evidence of social groups such as drag queens building identities and communities through creative appropriations of mainstream social media platforms such as Facebook and Tumblr. Her narrative comes to life with the many voices of her interviewees, such as this drag queen who talks about her commitment to maintaining a separate Facebook account for her drag persona:

> It's claiming a presence a little bit, connecting, mostly having some place where people can go because you meet people out in the nightlife. But the second you leave that bar, [my drag persona is] done. She actually gets washed down the drain, and I go to bed. But in the morning, people are still going to remember [her because of Facebook]. (2017: 109)

With experiences such as these, these social groups produce an Internet of alterity.

Why are there not more works of this kind? Partly it may be due to the persistent problem of methodologism and theoreticism in the social sciences, where methods and theoretical abstraction are reified and take on a life of their own at the expense of the experiences of the people. From the perspective of communication as translation, communication scholars could be better "listeners" and "storytellers" when they develop theory. Any theory about the people we study ought to fully incorporate the views and experiences of those people. Klaus Krippendorf puts it well in his argument for an ethical imperative "to prevent communication scholars from privileging their logic over that of others and relying on a monologic that portrays scholars as rational and superior to those they observe, describe, and theorize" (2009: 28).

Communication scholars could also make our own research output, our "translations," more meaningful to the general public and to those people and communities we study by diversifying our genres and styles of writing. If lay persons prefer reading stories to abstract theories, then researchers may want to incorporate more story-telling into their research and writing. If podcasting and documentary films are more effective media of communicating research to the public, shouldn't our academic gate-keepers consider how to incorporate them into the process of academic evaluation? Indeed, shouldn't researchers seriously consider whether story-telling, filming-making, and podcasting might not be more effective means of giving voice and humanity to marginalized and disadvantaged populations?

We need a broader conversation to radically rethink the tasks of communication and social science research. A view of communication as translation could serve as a small step in this endeavor. The practice of translation highlights the values of openness, receptivity, dialogue, exertion, and self-change. These values cannot be overemphasized in the academia and in today's world.

References

Benjamin, Walter (1968). "The Task of the Translator." In W. Benjamin (ed.), H. Zohn (trans.) and H. Arendt (intro.), *Illuminations*. New York: Schocken Books.

Bourdieu, Pierre and Loic J. D. Wacquant (1992). *An Invitation to Reflexive Sociology*. Chicago: University of Chicago Press.

Carey, James (1992). *Communication as Culture*. London: Routledge.

Collins, Patricia Hill (1990/2008). *Black Feminist Thought: Knowledge, Consciousness, and the Politics of Empowerment*. London: Routledge.

Couldry, Nick (2000). *Inside Culture: Reimagining the Method of Cultural Studies*. London: Sage.

Dayan, Daniel and Elihu Katz (1994). *Media Events: The Live Broadcasting of History*. Cambridge, MA: Harvard University Press.

Emerson, Caryl (1984). "Editor's Preface." In M. Bakhtin (ed.) and C. Emerson (trans.) *Problems in Dostoevsky's Poetics* (pp. xxix–iliii). Minneapolis: University of Minnesota Press.

Krippendorff, Klaus (2009). *On Communicating: Otherness, Meaning, and Information*. F. Bermejo (ed.) New York: Routledge.

Lane, Jeffrey (2018). *The Digital Street*. New York: Oxford University Press.

Lingel, Jessa (2017). *Digital Countercultures and the Struggle for Community*. Cambridge, MA: MIT Press.

Mills, C. Wright (2000). *The Sociological Imagination*. New York: Oxford University Press.

Nancy, Jean-Luc (1991). *The Inoperative Community*. P. Connor (ed.) and P. Connor et. al. (trans.). Minneapolis: University of Minnesota Press.

Rabassa, Gregory (1971/1987). "The Ear in Translation." *In The World in Translation*. New York: PEN American Center.

Ricoeur, Paul (1995). "Reflections on a New Ethos for Europe." *Philosophy and Social Criticism*, 5/6 (21), 3–13.

Steiner, George (1998). *After Babel: Aspects of Language and Translation*. New York: Open Road.

Thompson, E. P. P. (1978/1995). *The Poverty of Theory*. London: Merlin Press.

Williams, Raymond (1960). *Culture and Society: 1780–1950*. Garden City, NY: Anchor Books.

Young, Iris Marion (1986, Spring). "The Ideal of Community and the Politics of Difference." *Social Theory and Practice*, 12(1), 1–26.

14

What Are We Fighting For? Academia or the Humility of Knowledge

Nabil Echchaibi

In his impassioned BBC Reith lectures on what it means to be an intellectual, Edward Said (1993) contrasts two visions of the identity and responsibilities of intellectual work: Italian philosopher Antonio Gramsci's horizontal concept of the "organic intellectual," a large group of social agents and informal educators who operate within civil society to serve or challenge dominant ideology, and French philosopher Julien Benda's vertical image of the intellectual who belongs to a "tiny band of super-gifted and morally endowed philosopher-kings who constitute the conscience of mankind" (1993: 4–5).

At the heart of Said's distinction is a gnawing question of whether intellectuals constitute a large group or a small coterie of thinkers, a wide circle of intimately engaged agents of influence or a highly selective group of autonomous and uncompromised scholars who are permanently opposed to the status quo. Said is sympathetic to Gramsci's more lateral definition of the intellectual, but he fears their easy cooptation in the service of special interests and practical gratifications. Instead, Said is under the spell of Benda's conviction that intellectuals are a special elite who alone have the capacity to raise difficult questions and confront the lulling effects of dogma and orthodoxy. Ideal figures of this portrait of the intellectual are Socrates, Voltaire, and Spinoza for Benda and Jean Paul Sartre and Bertrand Russell for Said. Such are the "real" thinkers whose function in society is to speak truth to power and to the public. But both Benda and Said remain acutely silent about whether the public can talk back to intellectuals, to inform, question, and improve their knowledge and practices.

I start with Said's important plea to re-state the function and place of intellectuals in modern society to underscore the need for our own generation of scholars to spell out clearly the nature of our social and public commitment and identify the difficult reasons behind our persistent irrelevance and isolation. I remain in awe of Said's courage as an outspoken public intellectual whose work was animated by unwavering principles of dissent and engaged critique, but I find his definition of intellectuals as a privileged minority exclusively equipped with special capacities and laboring alone from above arrogantly elitist and counter-productive then and now.

There is no doubt that the university today is under even more strenuous pressure than at the time Said delivered his comments about intellectuals. Universities face alarming funding cuts and this retreat in support is frequently justified by a necessity to prove the instrumental relevance of academic work in economic and political life. In our rush to respond to these ominous calls, we have produced a new set of propositions that academics must make their work accessible to different publics, that their intellectual "aloofness" is a handicap to an informed society, and that our desperate times demand engaged public intellectuals who can simply insert the value of context and reason in our reckless conversations.

At the heart of these propositions is an apparent conceit that we in academia possess the deeper knowledge, the higher wisdom, and the better questions. Insisting that if only our work could circulate more and if only the larger public could become curious about what we do prevents us from confronting the core issue plaguing us today: Why does our work remain inaudible to others?

Of course, the answer to this pressing question is not simple, but our inaudibility will not be eased simply by the instrumental logic of circulation and dissemination, which mirrors the hierarchical oppressions of the same metric models used in assessing academic work today. Our issue cannot be only about the "additive feature" of our scholarly contributions, to borrow Jodi Dean's phrase (2009) in her critique of what she calls "communicative capitalism," a form of communication that underscores the continuous circulation of messages rather than the substance of their content. Nor can our answers be limited to denouncing the anti-intellectualism of the public and the devalorization of deep thinking.

In her nostalgic defense of the role of the humanities in the university, Judith Butler (2014) asks a relevant question: "what can those whose language is consigned to oblivion do?" Her answer: "They can reenter the fray, open up the space between the language that has become obvious or self-evident and the enormous loss it has already accomplished and still portends." Butler is right to point out the injuries the humanities face at the hand of neoliberal managers and their instrumentalist logics, but what is striking about her answer is her conviction that the case of the humanities must simply be made again without engaging in any conversation about the need to also reform how we teach the values of the liberal arts, who we teach them to, and how we can make them relatable to those who need them the most.

Connecting with other publics and stating the value of our work, as Said and Butler insist, is absolutely imperative, but the question is not only how we connect but why. Have we seriously grappled with the fact that the inaudibility of our work may not merely be an issue of whether our articles and theories trickle down, but that various publics simply do not see themselves in them?

14.1 ACADEMIC HUMILITY AND VULNERABILITY

Humility in the sense implied here is a fostering of a spirit of generosity that leverages the public not as a recipient of our wisdom or a bearer of a "pedestrian" perspective but as a partner to read with, to listen with, to think with, to critique with, and to problem-solve with around issues of pressing concern. To be humble is also to acknowledge a degree of epistemic vulnerability, to recognize that our ways of problematizing, historicizing, and knowing might not be enough. This recognition does not assume that our intellectual work is irrelevant when it does not involve publics or that we lack a distinctive identity as scholars. It is primarily a reminder that knowledge production can also benefit from an awareness of vulnerability, that is, as Erinn Gilson (2011) argues, a sensibility that helps us to avoid engaging in a willful epistemic ignorance that can lead to foreclosure of the very possibility of knowledge. "As potential," she writes, "vulnerability is a condition of openness, openness to being affected and affecting in turn" (2011: 310).

Humility understood as vulnerability can be unsettling for it presumes an engagement with other styles of knowing and learning which can be ontologically different, and in some cases, perceived as less rational and excessively subjective. Willfully ignoring these styles based on these perceptions can amount to a form of indifference or isolating reductionism that prevents us from seeing those who are implicated in dealing with the same issues and asking the same questions. A concern with preserving the distinctiveness of our work is not enough to let us off the hook when the issues we face today are of critical urgency and utmost relevance.

Lack of humility can also engender a false dichotomy between the researcher who looks at society and the researched who lives in society, as if the position of the academic is exempt from socioeconomic, political, or cultural realities. It is safe to say that many of our theories over the years, despite the best intentions, have also demonstrated a great deal of ignorance and invulnerability, many of which had to be checked against the sobering wisdom of everyday reality. Gilson's definition of epistemic vulnerability is instructive in this regard:

If invulnerability is, first and foremost, closure (not wanting to know), then epistemic vulnerability begins with being open to not knowing, which is the precondition of learning. Second, it is an openness to being wrong and venturing one's ideas, beliefs, and feelings nonetheless. To refrain from interaction, to abstain from dialogue because one fears that one does not know is simply another way of closing oneself off. Third, epistemic vulnerability entails the ability to put oneself in and learn from situations in which one is the unknowing, foreign, and perhaps uncomfortable party...Without an acceptance of the genuine value of discomfort and the real necessity of immersing oneself in situations in which one does not normally find oneself, learning does not happen. (2011: 325)

The form of humble engagement with publics I outline here implies a productive awareness of these limitations and an endorsement of an hospitable attitude Kathleen Fitzpatrick (2019) calls "generous thinking," a disposition to treat public engagement projects as seriously as we think of scholarly work without engaging in a futile process of hierarchical ordering. She writes,

A mode of generous thinking is a task that is simultaneously extremely difficult and easily dismissible. We are accustomed to a mode of thought that rebuts, that questions, that complicates, and the kinds of listening and openness for which I am here advocating may well be taken as acceding to a form of cultural naïveté at best, or worse, a politically regressive knuckling-under to the pressures of neoliberal ideologies and institutions. (2018: 37–38)

Taking down these boundaries is indeed laced with deep anxieties about denigrating the academic profession and selling out our expertise to respond to immediate concerns that do not always correspond to our scholarly interests. I do not take these anxieties lightly, nor do I intend to argue that the risks of weakening higher education and invalidating the role of the liberal arts are not real. But my argument about humility does not call for aligning our priorities with those of politicians, corporate managers, or the public for that matter. Theodor Adorno was adamant on preserving the autonomy of critical theory and dismissed this kind of capitulation as a form of resignation to the "tyranny of action." Adorno was deeply concerned that the constraints of action would simply maintain the status quo. "Within absolutized praxis," he wrote, "only reaction is possible and for this reason the reaction is false" (1978: 167). Humility or vulnerability of academic work is not a reaction to the public demands of practicality, nor is it a simple act of translating scholarship into actionable political applications. It is an attitude that reclaims the multiplicity of sites of critical thinking. Humility is an invitation, perhaps an imperative, to reimagine our process of knowledge production as an open source of collaboration and deliberation across a diverse set of expertise and genres. We must embrace the obliqueness of knowledge with the hope of producing an "other" form of knowledge, one that opens up the archives beyond the intellectual boundaries and epistemic and linguistic limitations still dominant in our work.

The decolonial turn in academia has something to teach us in this regard. As an intellectual movement, it has sought to expose the arrogance and ignorance of provincial Eurocentric thinking and vindicate those who for long have been told to sit permanently in the "waiting room of history," as Dipesh Chakrabarty (2000) so incisively reminds us. Decoloniality is an exercise in humility because it invites us to question the narrowness of our curricula in the canons of academia and acknowledge the fact that there is no epistemic privilege; only a co-production of knowledge that reaches deep into forgotten histories and wide into other experiences of seeing and dwelling in the world. Far from being a form of relativism or a mere postcolonial vengeance, decoloniality is primarily a form of historical exactitude meant to expand the sources of our thinking so we don't repeat the blunders of yesterday and the epistemicides of past generations (Grosfoguel, 2015).

But it bears repeating that decoloniality is not only an invitation to epistemic disobedience (Mignolo, 2009). It is first and foremost a call to action that spills beyond the walls of the university to address new publics in the global south and include them in dismantling persistent legacies of knowledge production that reproduce power relations and sharp inequalities locally and globally. It is not a conventional intellectual program that limits itself, as important as that can be, to an internal critical discourse of epistemic structures and power struggles. In this regard, Argentinian-Mexican historian Enrique Dussel (2003) argues in favor of an alternative intellectual style that includes those who have "a perspective of the center from the periphery" because "these are the ones who have a clear mind for pondering reality." Decoloniality haunts our present by introducing unsettling queries invoked from the periphery: What if our questions were wrong? What if our data were misguided? And what if our conclusions have been misleading all along?

How we confront the challenges with the publicness of our work will have to incorporate a similar decolonial sensibility and honesty when it comes to thinking about who our publics are and how we converse with them. In an increasingly more lateral information economy and flows, our view of the public is dangerously arrogant and myopic. Instead of thinking only about publics who need our knowledge, why don't we start by identifying knowledgeable publics we can learn from? Various institutions (journalism, music industry, publishing, etc.) also cling to a similar hierarchical stubbornness at their own peril.

In his plea for more public sociologies, Michael Burawoy (2005) argues in favor of adopting a more capacious view of knowledgeable publics:

> There is, however, another type of public sociology – organic public sociology in which the sociologist works in close connection with a visible, thick, active, local and often counterpublic. The bulk of public sociology is indeed of an organic kind – sociologists working with a labor movement, neighborhood associations, communities of faith, immigrant rights groups, human rights organizations. Between the organic public sociologist and a public is a dialogue, a process of mutual education. The project of such public sociologies is to make visible the invisible, to make the private public, to validate these organic connections as part of our sociological life. (2005: 7–8)

It is this kind of vital commitment Antonio Gramsci recognized in the energy of the "organic intellectual" as a way to provide a counterbalance to dominant hegemonic formations. Our role as intellectuals is not simply to labor alone in the isolation of our institutions and the privileges of our research circles. Recently, I started working with a critical performance group in Boulder, Colorado, that focuses on questions of border, race, and undocumented immigration. I initially thought of this project as research involving a community group to help make the point about the growing militarization and securitization of the border unleashed by sophisticated technologies and algorithms of surveillance.

My research is focused on a disturbing precariousness of empathy that seeks to conceal and banalize the trauma of crossing frontiers. A close relationship with the members of this performance group, however, and an appreciation of the ways in which they articulated and performed their own narratives of belonging and displacement have forced me to reconsider not only the questions I was asking but also how I think of the undocumented immigrants I was interacting with. They ceased to be the subjects of my research and quickly became a public I could dialogue with, deliberate with, and direct communication of my reflections and findings to. Such a shift has centered for me some fundamental questions about what knowledge we produce, how we produce it, why, and for whom we produce it. The imagination and difficult optimism of these performance artists have opened up a series of questions about the moral promise of our borders away from their degeneration into pits of death and dehumanization. My work in this sense is no longer just about demonstrating how existing borders function as brutal agents of power and a paranoid proposition of territory, but also about how to weave together a new imaginary of what the border could be: a new poetics of the frontier, of existence that restores mobility and movement as a human right. This is not a form of fugitive theorizing in the sense that it seeks refuge in the comfort of the future. Working with artists and activists forces me out of my mental habits and academic privilege to realize that there is no pure thought or disengaged safety.

Infusing our work with humility and vulnerability means to reject the status quo of our disengagement and the isolating impulses of our academic practices and structures. As a scholar and chair of a department at a major public university, I find it extremely difficult to reconcile this status quo with the aspirations and intellectual convictions of a new generation of scholars who are much more willing to engage publicly and value other sites of knowledge. Yet we meet the rigor of their humility with archaic systems of evaluation that place no value in their public outreach and their desire to cross epistemic bridges. Our tenure and promotion system, despite its internal utility, remains an antisocial process that socializes scholars to labor alone, to value the sound of their own voice, and to dismiss the expertise of nonacademics as lacking rigor. Faced with an estranged culture of aloof evaluation guidelines, we are already losing strong scholars and students who are turned off by the false binaries we still enforce between academia and public engagement. To those who stay, it will always appear counterproductive to do public outreach, even when they are convinced it is the right thing to do, when they know that their peers, disciplines, and institutions will look at their work as insufficiently academic and critically lacking. If we truly value the importance of community engagement and public outreach, we must also work hard to rewrite our curricula to reflect the connections between what we teach and the larger world outside our classrooms. In 2015, when students at the University of Cape Town contested the display of a statue of the nineteenth-century imperialist Cecil John Rhodes on their campus, for example, they were revolting against the persistence of a colonial legacy in their coursework, the texts they were reading, and the Eurocentric model of their university. The successful #RhodesMustFall campaign not only led to the removal of the statue, but it has also spawned a national conversation in South Africa about intellectual dependency and forced administrators and educators to re-examine university curricula and change its fee policies. Examples like these underscore the importance of collective action and the need for scholars to accompany these interventions and help spur similar conversations. Scholars in Africa, Asia, and South America have written extensively about decolonizing knowledge and freeing universities in the global South of the alienating traces of coloniality, but the student activism in South Africa under the hashtag of #RhodesMustFall and #FeesMustFall should have strong implications for academics, students, and other publics alike as they collectively foreground critical issues of value, access, and self-worth.

Many of the problems facing academia are beyond our control, but others are of our own making. Universities, for instance, have long conceived of publics as those who populate their classrooms, students who pay a premium to gain access to higher education. As that access is threatened for many because of rising tuition and waning public support, shouldn't our public outreach become a moral obligation? As one of the sites of knowledge production, shouldn't we seek partners in debates, stage inclusive conversations, and leverage policy change in the most urgent challenges facing us all today such as climate change, environmental justice, immigration, racism, nativism, surveillance, global health, and poverty? Shouldn't we extend the space of the university to reach those who remain in the margins of our politics and on the sidelines of our cloistered discussions?

This institutional challenge is compounded today by deep ideological polarization and the increasing cultural tensions facing our societies. Learning how to avoid the creation of supremacies of expertise that valorize some publics and castigate others, or the building of artificial walls that provide a false sense of independence, is the only viable way forward. In addition to listening to ourselves in academic settings, we must listen to the world speaking, clamoring for attention, and craving for participation in larger conversations. We have seen this in national and global movements such as #RhodesMustFall, Standing Rock, Idle No More, Undocumented and Unafraid, #Whyismycurriculumsowhite, Arab Uprisings, Black Lives Matter, and #MeToo, among others. Our role in academia is not to respond to these grievances or guide them but to join them as theoretical and empirical provocations anxiously awaiting our collaboration.

In order to address this disconnect, some scholars and institutions have embraced public scholarship as a solution and a guiding principle in their work. While insisting on a more public-facing mission of the university is a laudable development, much of what is produced under the label "public scholarship" still subscribes to a view of the public scholar as one who is merely capable of popularizing their research and simplifying their findings for a wider public eager to listen. Public engagement under this logic means primarily expanding one's reach through press publications, television appearances, and other venues of wide circulation. These are significant examples of public outreach, but they are not enough to enact the spirit of humility I've outlined in this chapter. Public engagement is first and foremost a critical pedagogy, an act of thinking that shifts the gaze deeply enough to retrieve voices, cosmologies, temporalities, memories, and knowledge worlds long eclipsed and devalued in conventional spaces of knowledge production, whether it be the university, the art gallery, or the museum. Public scholarship is not merely an extension of research and public discourse outside these spaces, nor is it an empty metaphor. As a praxis, it must amount to an insurgency that forces us to reconceive the world by modeling a spirit of epistemic freedom. As its best, public engagement as a pedagogy is a collective effort to disrupt the historical coherence of disciplinary logics, the deep hierarchies of knowledge production, and the closed sources of learning we have inherited as a given. It is a significant move to reimagine the university beyond its existing limitations and expand its mission to include an ethical obligation to assemble and reconnect publics.

These are to me the most pressing questions we must confront before we address other practical dimensions of how we make our work more public. I invite us to collectively think about a distributed model of academic work whereby the university is only one location of knowledge intimately dependent on multiple nonacademic networks, connections, infrastructures, and institutions to create new forms and levels of knowledge about the world. Perhaps we need a poet's understanding of knowledge to free it from the ominous resignation that it is forever and already suspect and imbricated with power. Publics are not awaiting our ivory-towered thinkers to bestow their wisdom on them. Publics yearn for engagement, partnership, and critical solidarity. Otherwise, we fall back to our lazy instincts and we run the risk of confirming the biting disappointment in the question of Congolese postcolonial poet and writer, Alain Mabanckou: "What if my writing is merely a rewriting?"

References

Adorno, Theodor (1978). "Resignation." *Telos*, 35, 165–168.

Burawoy, Michael (2004). "For Public Sociology." *American Sociological Review*, 70, 4–28.

Butler, Judith (2014). "Ordinary, Incredulous." In P. Brooks and H. Jewett (eds.), *The Humanities in Public Life* (pp 15–40). New York: Fordham University Press.

Chakrabarty, Dipesh (2000). *Provincializing Europe: Postcolonial Thought and Historical Difference*. Princeton, NJ: Princeton University Press.

Dean, Jodi (2009). *Democracy and Other Neoliberal Fantasies: Communicative Capitalism and Left Politics*. Durham: Duke University Press.

Dussel, Enrique (2003). *Philosophy of Liberation*. Eugene, OR: Wipf and Stock Publishers.

Fitzpatrick, Kathleen (2019). *Generous Thinking: A Radical Approach to Saving the University*. Baltimore, MD: Johns Hopkins University Press.

Gilson, Erinn (2011). "Vulnerability, Ignorance, and Oppression." *Hypatia*, 26 (2), 308–332.

Grosfoguel, Ramón (2015). "Epistemic Racism/Sexism, Westernized Universities and the Four Genocides/Epistemicides of the Long Sixteenth Century." In M. Araújo and S. Rodriguez Maeso (eds.) *Eurocentrism, Racism and Knowledge* (pp. 23–46). London: Palgrave Macmillan.

Mignolo, Walter (2009). "Epistemic Disobedience, Independent Thought and De-Colonial Freedom." *Theory, Culture & Society*, 26(7–8), 1–23.

Said, Edward (1994). *Representations of the Intellectual: The 1993 Reith Lectures*. New York: Pantheon Books.

Epilogue

What Media for What Public Life?

Silvio Waisbord

Producing a comprehensive examination of the contemporary challenges for media and public life is an enormous task. Sketching out an agenda of priorities and actions for addressing those challenges is difficult, too. Neither the media nor the state of public life is similar across countries and regions around the globe. Any diagnosis of problems needs to be sensitive to local and national aspects of media and public life. Multiple differences in media systems and public life make it impossible to produce a concise and comprehensive survey of problems and solutions. Media performance and conditions are not comparable in different media and political systems. Media systems with higher levels of pluralism in terms of ownership and content provide quite different conditions for the expression of a range of views. Problems such as limited media diversity, the depletion of public affairs news, citizen surveillance, and hate speech are threats around the world, but the particularities are different given political contexts, media systems and legislation, available media resources, and other factors.

Also, the fact that "the media" are a set of shapeshifting institutions has expanded the ways they intersect with public life and the way we think about the nexus between them. Just as societies continue to wrestle with old problems, such as state repression of critical media and collusion between media and political powers, they are experiencing a host of challenges brought about by the digital revolution.

What makes questions about media and public life pressing matters? The choice of specific problems is predicated upon normative assumptions about the expected contributions of the media to public life. What defines a problem is grounded in premises about the nexus between media and good society – what media are needed for what kind of public life. Do the media fail to provide a diverse information supply? Threaten citizens' privacy? Reproduce social inequalities? Sustain power? Reflect anti-democratic values? Promote hatred?

Specific aspects of the media are problematic for public life insofar as they are contrary to key conditions of public life in democracy. Certainly, the specific aspects of a healthy public life have been a longstanding matter of discussion in communication and media studies and other disciplines. In my mind, public life should feature institutional conditions as well as citizens' values and dispositions that are supportive of democratic politics and social justice, namely, a combination of equal opportunities for public expression and prosocial, other-oriented dispositions – that is, structural conditions and collective skills. Media pluralism in terms of ownership, funding, and conten is needed to provide opportunities for the expression of diverse voices and perspectives (Picard, 2017). Limitations and inequalities in public expression are contrary to democracy. Without media pluralism, a whole slew of issues are neglected, and voices are made invisible. Limited resources deplete the supply of public information and cut down opportunities for citizens to become informed about public matters. Also, public communication needs to be grounded in social attitudes and skills that value public reason and pro-social affect. Values such as dialogue, engagement with difference, tolerance, solidarity, empathy, critical rationality, and facticity are necessary, too.

Certainly, these are ambitious conditions, not unlike any vision of a better social order. One can reasonably argue that no public life in modern society has ever displayed such conditions and, optimists beware, perhaps never will. It is not a case of insufferable pessimism to state that reality inevitably falls short from these expectations. Yet outlining desirable elements of media and public life is necessary to clarify the analytical benchmarks that help us discern contemporary problems and outline possible solutions.

Government censorship is a problem because it violates fundamental citizens' rights to expression. Corporate control of public speech trumps public interest and demands. Media misrepresentation of social groups disempowers populations, feeds distorted beliefs, skews public debates, and shapes wrong public priorities. Echo chambers are a problem insofar as they limit citizens' exposure to and engagement with others who think differently. Hate speech eviscerates the humanity of fellow citizens. Tolerance and acceptability of difference are necessary for viable political and communicative orders. So, even if they are utopian, certain conditions of media and public life provide a set of (elusive) endpoints that anchor the analysis and inspire practical directions.

From this perspective, I believe this book helps us understand important contemporary communication problems.

Some contributors call attention to the funding and the performance of the news media. Benson argues that US news organizations are skewed to producing content for better-off readers. Amid persistent economic difficulties in the news industry, those readers have increasingly become critical sources of financial support. Consequently, news disproportionately reflects the interests of a small slice of the population. Powers and Vera-Zambrano argue that although journalists are bound by different expectations in France and the United States, they similarly contribute to the maintenance of the dominant order. These trends reinforce long-standing patterns of news-rich and news-poor populations in the context of the commercial press in capitalist societies.

Another problem, as Aronczyk and Couldry convincingly show in their chapters, is the further encroachment of marketing practices and data capitalism into every corner of everyday life. Digital platforms have become central intermediaries of public communication with plenty of power and discretion. They control enormously popular, global platforms that mediate public interaction for billions of people. Hyper-commercialized speech is central to the consolidation of surveillance practice in digital capitalism (Zuboff, 2019).

Altogether, the authors describe conditions that deepen social inequalities in public communication brought about by the unprecedented power of a few companies in the global digital society.

Certainly, old and new problems should be added to these concerns about media and public life.

Limited pluralism in the legacy media remains a huge challenge across the world (Guerrero and Márquez-Ramírez, 2014; Valcke, Sukosd, and Picard, 2015). Digital developments have disrupted the old media order, but they have neither resolved nor reduced long-standing, structural problems in media systems, such as governmental control of public expression and the collusion between media–industrial corporations and the state. It is paradoxical that, even as the Internet revolution opened new avenues for information and public speech, overall conditions for freedom of expression have worsened in recent years around the world, especially in the global South. High levels of media concentration coupled with regulatory frameworks unduly influenced by powerful economic and political interests shut off a diversity of voices and perspectives. More opportunities for online public expression have not completely over-turned inequalities in public expression. Also, the financial evisceration and the political manipulation of public media deplete a potential source of quality, public-oriented news. The absence of legal frameworks and economic support for alternative media undercuts the possibility of diver-sifying content. Government discretionary control of public resources for building favorable media environments and suppressing critical media remains a common practice throughout the world.

Also, attacks against reporters and media and social activists have increased in recent years (Council of Europe, 2018; Stremlau, Gagliardone, and Price, 2018). Rising authoritarianism in established democracies has become a threat to public expression. Governments use legal instruments, political pressures, and verbal attacks to crack down on critical voices. Also, they use a variety of digital platforms to spy, silence, and harass dissident journalists. The spiraling crisis of journalism and the news industry around the world is a troubling trend, too, raising questions about the supply of quality news. The crisis of the commercial, advertis-ing-funded model raises questions about the supply of original news in public life, especially quality news about important issues that demand extensive resources. Current trends such as thinner newsrooms, closed-down news organizations, and widespread labor precarity attest to the severity of the crisis. Furthermore, the growing concentration of digital advertising and audiences in a few companies drains potential funding away from news organizations and foreshadows even rougher times ahead. Uncertainty about viable models of news funding makes the situa-tion particularly dire, especially in countries where potential revenue sources such as philanthropy and strong subscription base are limited or non-existent.

Also, the persistence of the digital divide along lines of class, geogra-phy, and gender remains a barrier to access to information and commu-nication, especially in countries in the global South (van Dijk, 2017).

Disinformation poses another significant challenge for public life. Certainly, mass propaganda has been a fixture of liberal democracy and authoritarian regimes for over a century. Yet recent transformations in news and information gatekeeping coupled with sophisticated forms of mass deception have facilitated new forms of large-scale misinformation (Benkler, Faris, and Roberts, 2018). Political, corporate, military, and intelligence actors have used a growing arsenal of tools to poison the public well of information, distort truth-telling efforts, and mobilize publics behind lies. Furthermore, propaganda is no longer a top-down affair of information cascades, created and sustained by pyramidal and centralized structures controlled by powerful actors. Ordinary citizens also participate in the diffusion of propaganda by (un)willingly spreading lies on digital platforms and formats. The relative flattening of the structures and the dynamics of information dissemination make it possible to propagate falsehoods beyond the traditional operations funded and controlled by governments and corporations.

Rising levels of hate speech is another challenge for the communication commons. The Internet has opened new forms of hateful discourse. It also provides possibilities for hate groups to connect, organize, and spread their message. The rise in attacks against racial and ethnic minorities, women, immigrants and temporary workers, and LGBTQI people reflects a political-cultural backlash against advances in human rights in the past decades around the world. We are barely starting to understand the consequences of hate speech in digital societies and to assess the suitability and the consequences of appropriate actions grounded in the principle of democracy and freedom of speech.

The ascent of racism, chauvinism, xenophobia, sexism, and misogyny in digital platforms complicates the argument that lower barriers to public expression would result in virtuous democratic discourse. Classic liberalism expected that "the marketplace of ideas" (Peters, 2004) would foster public goods in the form of better arguments, collective reason, and truth-telling. In the words of Oliver Wendell Holmes (Blasi, 2004), "the ultimate good desired is better reached by free trade in ideas ... the best test of truth is the power of the thought to get itself accepted in the competition of the market." Yet it is hard to find conclusive evidence that uninhibited public discourse inevitably leads to informed public opinion, collective rationality, undeniable truths, or wiser policies in the service of the majority. For every virtuous example, one finds plenty of anti-social speech, more concerned with dehumanizing others, reinforcing prejudice, and asserting factless ideas than cultivating the public good. No need to resort to the dark Web to find hateful discourse flatly opposed to core values of public life: dialogue, understanding, tolerance, sympathy, and solidarity, the everyday web is full of this sort of rancor.

The current debate on the dystopian consequences of digital speech, as well as on the meaning of press freedom as Hallin discussed in Chapter 4, reflects a growing interest in examining both the consequences of more speech as well as suitable regulatory frameworks. Whether hate speech can be effectively governed and regulated remains a key question (Ganesh, 2018). None of the solutions often bandied about seem enough to combat speech that encroaches on the rights and the humanity of numerous groups (Citron, 2014). Free speech advocates reject government regulation and believe that more speech in the form of non-censorial interventions is needed to respond to hate (Strossen, 2018). Recent debates over the effectiveness of legal options, corporate decisions to ban offenders from their platforms, renewed enthusiasm about news literacy, and the role of social norms in fostering tolerance and rebutting hate reflect disagreements over appropriate interventions.

In summary, these problems add up a list of intractable problems related to media and public life.

REASSESSING DIGITAL ACTIVISM AND PUBLIC LIFE

Is everything so bleak? It depends where one looks. Just as troubling trends abound, there are bright spots of public communication in the networked public sphere (Friedland, Hove, and Rojas, 2006). The glass is both half-full and half-empty. The literature brings hopeful studies grounded in cases of collective action inspired by ideals of democracy and social justice, as well as pessimistic assessments of the runaway power of governments and corporations over citizens.

We are past the time of wide-eyed, politically innocent analysis about the impact of digital technologies on public life, peddled by Silicon Valley and repeated by a choir of sycophants. After the tidal wave of bad news and scandals in recent years, the mood is different. Notably, revelations about partnerships between governments and digital corporations to monitor citizens, corporate consent to using their social media platforms for propaganda and privacy invasion, and the cooperation of companies such as Google and Netflix with authoritarian regimes reveals why digital capitalism and democracy are not exactly on good terms. Even the mainstream media and political leaders cast a suspicious eye on corporate promises about digital democracy. Progressives who rhapsodized the power of digitally-enabled actions until a few years ago now produce more sober and skeptical surveys of the current situation. The notion that digital technologies inevitably usher in democratic goods, community, and world peace has been shattered.

Yet, there are forms of mediated action, infused with democratic dispositions, across the Internet (Meikle, 2018). To mention a few examples: Despite the crisis, several news platforms manage to produce original reporting that holds power accountable, bring out silenced stories, and promote public awareness about social problems. Mobilized publics use digital platforms to promote understanding and tolerance, organize against corporate wrongdoing and government corruption, protest state violence, offer opportunities for victims of abuses to tell their stories, monitor human rights conditions (Margetts, John, Hale, and Yasseri, 2015). The proliferation of digital counterpublics attest to the enormous opportunities for challenging dominant media narratives and power (Jackson and Foucault-Welles, 2015). Undoubtedly, these are important developments for they strengthen diversity in media and public life, as McIlwain argues in his chapter.

However, initiatives that comfort the afflicted and hold the powerful accountable flow into the digital flotsam. They are easily lost in the glut of information and misinformation and the relentless churn of news cycles. Journalism's relentless appetite for the new and the news-making power of political and economic elites displace valuable information. Flashes of media attention on important social problems quickly fade as mainstream media and social media turn attention to other subjects.

Getting broad visibility (Dalhberg, 2018) under the new conditions of digital publicity is challenging. In their chapters, Craft and Christensen remind us that journalism constantly emits noise, and Clark argues that public attention quickly dissipates. Concentrated economies of attention (Hindman, 2018) tilt the balance in favor of a few media companies. Therefore, valuable media interventions are thrown into the same media mix with all sorts of negative developments. Community journalism coexists with information inequalities, media-enabled empowerment and tolerance coexists with hate speech, collective action enabled by digital platforms coexists with the growing, virtually unchecked power of social media corporations. Just as antidemocratic content has a robust audience, in this fractured media landscape virtually any positive contribution to public life may find a receptive public – hashtag rights-based activism, public-oriented journalism, movements for digital equality.

So, virtuous forms of media and collective action are not absent from public life. The problem is that efforts to improve media narratives, reduce hate, protect citizens' privacy, promote information access, confront the negative consequences of hate speech, empower people, strengthen media pluralism, support quality journalism, cultivate dialogue across difference are often lost in the sea of noise. We need studies that not only document the presence of media citizenship committed to human rights, but that also examine their connections to sustainable forms of social change.

WHAT MEDIA FOR WHAT PUBLIC LIFE?

It is in this context that the politics of media and public life needs to be discussed. What emerges from this book is a multilayered set of problems, as "the media" have become more fragmented and pervasive in everyday life in the digital society. Growing differentiation and complexity of media infrastructures represent the proliferation of spaces where public life happens.

In line with other authors (Bennett and Pfetsch, 2018; Blumler and Coleman, 2015; Fenton, 2018; Kaiser, Fähnrich, Rhomberg, and Filzmaier, 2017; Pfestch, 2018), I believe it is necessary to revisit the analytical scaffolding and normative arguments about media and public life given unprecedented transformations in public communication.

In my mind, three issues need to be revisited: the existence of integrated mediated spaces, virtuous communicative practices, and epistemological consensus.

First, key notions such as "public sphere" and "public opinion" ring of unified polities and integrated communicative spaces. They are embedded in a time of information scarcity, limited media availability, and relatively unified national media spaces. The contemporary state of public communication is quite different. It is characterized by information chaos, hybrid media, diversified media ecologies, multiple media publics, echo chambers, polarized publics, partisan/ideological media, and broken-up audiences. Although spaces for individual and collective expression are plenty, it is not obvious that common media spaces are equally vibrant or that they bring together different publics around common interests.

Today's public life is rich with spaces to express voice and reaffirm identities. Political collectives that define key contemporary disputes are sorted out in separate spheres for building claims, discussing common interests, reinforcing beliefs, and bringing in new members. Climate change deniers and environmentalists, human rights activists and reactionaries, advocates of science and anti-science groups, cosmopolitans and xenophobes, advocates for minority rights and white supremacists are dispersed in endless media platforms. However, it is not obvious that overarching, integrated media spaces for the formation of common opinion, common will, or common citizenship are equally vibrant. Media fragmentation sets in conditions that favor values and behaviors that reinforce beliefs rather than promote common communicative practices, norms, and ideals. So, the challenge is not only to understand how democracies develop communication systems to support citizens' knowledge and experiences, as several authors in the volume rightly ask, but also how mediated communication effectively promotes common spaces and collective will across multiple differences.

Regardless whether one laments or celebrates the proliferation and the reordering of mediated spaces, this situation raises important questions. What kind of public life is viable when media infrastructures are divided into relatively separate publics according to corporate goals and issue-oriented politics? How are common spaces built and cultivated? Where does collective discourse among groups divided by identities, interests, and politics happen? What media cultivate "the public" as a common actor? What does the public sphere as a common space for the formation of democratic will look like today?

Second, it is necessary to revisit the issue of communicative practices for public life that the media (and other institutions) should stimulate. The ideal of the "public sphere" characterized by public deliberation and collective reasoning is narrow and insufficient to capture the diversity of communicative practices with emancipatory potential and achievements. The Habermasian model of the public sphere, which remains foundational in discussions about public life, envisions specific conditions, namely, bracketing off social differentiations and the force of the best argument. These conditions do not characterize multiple communicative and political practices in the networked public sphere. Just as there are cases that display dispositions that fit that ideal – deliberation, rationality, civility, tolerance, accommodation, compromise, and consensus-building – other examples show the vigor of different values and practices, such as in situations of intractable conflict, citizens' opposition to vicious dictatorships, mob discourse, and hostility to human rights.

It is not obvious that emancipatory politics only necessitates rational-critical debates. Critical citizenship includes a wider set of dispositions and values. Actors who pursue democratic rights and social justice use a toolkit of communicative actions to make their voices heard, influence opinion, and advocate for change. Plenty of emancipatory energy in support of human rights and social justice takes shape through multiple discursive forms (Tumber and Waisbord, 2017). Emotionally sterile actions may not be an option in situations of oppression. Calm exchanges may not be an option under oppression. Rage and incivility may be natural to challenge dominant opinion and structural inequalities, reaffirm identity, and build community. Rowdy, chaotic forms of communication push for changes. Collective rationality as a dialectical, interactive process, may not be an option when other parties are unwilling to engage in dialogue.

It is misguided to expect that only a limited set of communicative practices would foster democracy and social justice, especially when public life is fragmented and polarized. This expectation disregards the vibrancy of multiple media spaces, and the fact that every conceivable type of discourse exists in legacy and digital media. A public sphere characterized by Habermasian conditions is forever elusive. At best, it is one option among virtuous and toxic forms of public communication. Specific forms of communication, such as expression, acknowledgement, and exchange, as proposed by Wessler, are part of a growing menu of diversified options.

Finally, contemporary populism and so-called post-truth politics reflect deep epistemological divides that challenge the notion of public life as a common, collective project. These are not purely political or ideological divides – matters of different interpretation of facts according to personal and collective convictions and loyalties. Rather, they reflect profound disagreements over fundamental matters that undergird public life: the formation of knowledge, the expression and the deliberation of ideas, the definition of news and information, and the deployment of rationalities to assess the veracity of claims. When citizens disagree on basic matters about the production of knowledgeable reality and collective identities negate the humanity and the rights of others, truth is not a collective pursuit in public life, but rather a matter of imposing political will to defeat the enemy.

In sum, the vision of public life organized around common media spaces, animated by virtuous citizens' dispositions, and grounded on a minimal consensus over epistemology clashes with today's fragmented media ecologies, heterogeneous public engagement, and fractured public knowledge.

If public life mainly driven by collective reasoning is, at best, one option, it is worth considering what forms of public life are viable.

One could argue that current trends favor irrational politics. Fractured media do not promote the kind of shared epistemologies necessary to pursue truth as a common good. Instead, they produce discourse that constantly blurs the lines between truths and lies. Particular truths, anchored by tailor-made facts and stubborn dogmas, comfortably live in selected media. Any truth can be neatly squared with any facts, real or imagined. Irrationalism festers when the borderline between reality and fiction is erased, as Theodore Adorno observed. Political entrepreneurs are able to exploit group-based truths through "us versus them" appeals and exacerbate the adversarial dimension of politics. Whipping up group fear, prejudice, and hate are easier when publics prefer relatively homogeneous media networks and are hostile to media that questions their convictions. Populism has recently come to political prominence and power, partially riding these communicative conditions around the world (Waisbord, 2018).

One could also argue that fragmented media landscapes also favor politics that supports the expression of difference and the aggregation of particular demands. The proliferation of media platforms makes it possible to channel a range of ideas. Fractured media offer opportunities for asserting claims, building collective identities, and mobilizing public expression. An array of citizen news brings up a diverse set of voices and perspectives. They produce valuable stories and reflect collective uses of platforms and content that contest news narratives. Subaltern voices use social media to tell their own stories and provide a counterweight to the version of reality produced by mainstream media. Just as victims denounce sexual predators and institutions that condone abuses, other groups question those claims. Just as environmentalists document ecocides, demand justice, and sound alarm bells, climate change deniers reaffirm their stands. So, publics and counterpublics on any public issue take shape. Public life displays the constant mobilization of organized citizens engaged in communicative and political battles.

What remains unclear is the viability of politics informed by dialogue across difference, collective reason, and common facts. When fractured media foster incendiary speech, inflamed passions, and resentment, how do the media contribute to building common ground? How are rational, critical, and civil visions of public life possible when baseless, vicious vitriol finds plenty of room in public communication? How are compassion, solidarity, empathy, tolerance, and mutual understanding possible when citizens find narcissistic media rewarding? While we have inspiring ideas, we do not have a rich body of data to provide solid answers to these questions.

A PUSH FOR PUBLIC SCHOLARSHIP

This brings me to a final theme discussed by several authors: the contributions of academic scholarship to public life.

Lewis interrogates the purpose of communication scholarship and challenges us to think beyond questions that are of interest primarily to academics. We need to study issues that resonate with citizens. This is important, I add, at a time of increased anxieties about the prospects of higher education, changing public support, and significant cuts in public universities under pro-market governments. Echchaibi discusses the idea of scholarship as mutual education with fellow citizens and activists. Embracing this notion is necessary to question assumptions and research directions and adjust scholarly priorities to social needs and demands. Yang invites us to diversify the subjects of study and the way we present ideas. We occupy, he reminds us, a valuable position as translators of academic research about critical social problems. To be effective in that role, communication studies need to diversify the subjects of study and find ways to engage closely with citizens. McIlwain states that communication scholars need to investigate how citizens harness digital technologies and mobilize to upend the dominant racial order. Yesil urges communication scholars to unmask instrumental, shrewd attempts by power to use subaltern tropes to obtain legitimacy.

Together, these chapters both reflect and illustrate a growing sense in communication studies that scholarship should be reoriented to address real-world problems and to engage with publics fighting for social change in multiple ways. We should not only be interested in studying challenges. We should also produce practical, evidence-based knowledge that offers valuable insights for action (Waisbord, 2019).

This book sets us on the right track to explore problems further and outline viable courses of action to build more democratic and just societies. It is important to examine pressing problems and possible solutions by taking comparative perspectives that examine how communities confront similar problems such as privacy invasion, hate speech, collective attention deficit, and the crisis of the news industry.

References

Benkler, Yochai, Robert Faris, and Hal Roberts (2018). *Network Propaganda: Manipulation, Disinformation, and Radicalization in American Politics.* New York: Oxford University Press.

Blasi, Vincent (2004). "Holmes and the Marketplace of Ideas." *The Supreme Court Review*, 2004, 1–46.

Blumler, Jay G. and Stephen Coleman (2015). "Democracy and the Media – Revisited." *Javnost – The Public*, 22(2), 111–128.

Bennett, W. Lance and Barbara Pfetsch (2018). "Rethinking Political Communication in a Time of Disrupted Public Spheres." *Journal of Communication*, 68(2), 243–253.

Citron, Danielle (2014). *Hate Crimes in Cyberspace.* Cambridge, MA: Harvard University Press.

Council of Europe (2018). *Democracy at Risk: Threats and Attacks against Media Freedom in Europe.* Annual Report by the partner organizations to the Council of Europe platform to promote the protection of journalism and the safety of journalists.

Dahlberg, Lincoln (2018). "Visibility and the Public Sphere: A Normative Conceptualisation." *Javnost – The Public*, 25(1–2), 35–42.

Fenton, Natalie (2018). "Fake Democracy: The Limits of Public Sphere Theory." *Javnost – The Public*, 25(1–2), 28–34.

Friedland, Lewis A., Thomas Hove, and Hernando Rojas (2006). "The Networked Public Sphere." *Javnost – The Public*, 13(4), 5–26.

Ganesh, Bharath (2018). "The Ungovernability of Digital Hate Culture." *Journal of International Affairs*, 71(2), 30–49.

Guerrero, Manuel and Mireya Márquez-Ramírez (eds.) (2014). *Media Systems and Communication Policies in Latin America.* London: Palgrave Macmillan UK.

Hindman, Matthew (2018). *The Internet Trap: How the Digital Economy Builds Monopolies and Undermines Democracy.* Princeton, NJ: Princeton University Press.

Jackson, Sarah J. and Brooke Foucault Welles (2015). "Hijacking# myNYPD: Social Media Dissent and Networked Counterpublics." *Journal of Communication*, 65(6), 932–952.

Kaiser, Jonas, Birte Fähnrich, Markus Rhomberg, and Peter Filzmaier (2017). "What Happened to the Public Sphere? The Networked Public Sphere and Public Opinion Formation." In E. G. Carayannis, D. F. J. Campbell, and M. P. Efthymiopoulos (eds.), *Handbook of Cyber-development, Cyber-democracy, and Cyber-defense* (pp. 1–28). Cham: Springer International Publishing.

Margetts, Helen, Peter John, Scott Hale, and Taha Yasseri (2015). *Political Turbulence: How Social Media Shape Collective Action.* Princeton, NJ: Princeton University Press.

Meikle, Graham (ed.) (2018). *The Routledge Companion to Media and Activism.* London: Routledge.

Pfetsch, Barbara (2018). "Dissonant and Disconnected Public Spheres as Challenge for Political Communication Research." *Javnost – The Public*, 25 (1–2), 59–65.

Peters, John Durham (2004). "The 'Marketplace of Ideas': A History of the Concept." In A. Calabrese and C. Sparks (eds.), *Toward a Political Economy of Culture: Capitalism and Communication in the Twenty-First Century* (pp. 65–82). New York, NY: Rowman & Littlefield.

Picard, Robert G. (2017). "The Sisyphean Pursuit of Media Pluralism: European Efforts to Establish Policy and Measurable Evidence." *Communication Law and Policy*, 22(3), 255–273.

Stremlau, Nicole, Iginio Gagliardone, and Monroe Price (eds.) (2018). *World Trends in Freedom of Expression and Media Development 2018*. Paris: United Nations Educational, Scientific and Cultural Organization.

Strossen, Nadine (2018). *HATE: Why We Should Resist It with Free Speech, Not Censorship*. New York: Oxford University Press.

Tumber, Howard and Silvio Waisbord (eds.) (2017). *Routledge Companion to Media and Human Rights*. London: Routledge.

Valcke, Peggy, Miklos Sukosd, and Robert Picard (eds.). (2015). *Media Pluralism and Diversity: Concepts, Risks and Global Trends*. New York: Palgrave Macmillan.

Van Dijk, Jan A. (2017). "Digital Divide: Impact of Access." In P. Rössler (ed.), *The International Encyclopedia of Media Effects* (pp. 1–11). London: John Wiley & Sons.

Waisbord, Silvio (2018). "Why Populism is Troubling for Democratic Communication." *Communication Culture & Critique*, 11(1), 21–34.

Waisbord, Silvio (2019). *The Communication Manifesto*. Cambridge: Polity.

Zuboff, Shishana (2019). *The Age of Surveillance Capitalism: The Fight for a Human Future at the New Frontier of Power*. New York, NY: Public Affairs.

Other Books in the Series (*continued from page ii*)

Richard Gunther and Anthony Mughan, eds., *Democracy and the Media: A Comparative Perspective*

Daniel C. Hallin and Paolo Mancini, *Comparing Media Systems: Three Models of Media and Politics*

Daniel C. Hallin and Paolo Mancini, eds., *Comparing Media Systems beyond the Western World*

Roderick P. Hart, *Civic Hope: How Ordinary Citizens Keep Democracy Alive*

Roderick P. Hart, *Trump and Us: What He Says and Why People Listen*

Robert B. Horwitz, *Communication and Democratic Reform in South Africa*

Philip N. Howard, *New Media Campaigns and the Managed Citizen*

Ruud Koopmans and Paul Statham, eds., *The Making of a European Public Sphere: Media Discourse and Political Contention*

Marwan M. Kraidy, *Reality Television and Arab Politics: Contention in Public Life*

L. Sandy Maisel, Darrell M. West, and Brett M. Clifton, *Evaluating Campaign Quality: Can the Electoral Process Be Improved?*

Douglas M. McLeod and Dhavan V. Shah, *News Frames and National Security*

Sabina Mihelj and Simon Huxtable, *From Media Systems to Media Cultures*

Pippa Norris, *Digital Divide: Civic Engagement, Information Poverty, and the Internet Worldwide*

Pippa Norris, *A Virtuous Circle: Political Communications in Postindustrial Society*

Pippa Norris and Ronald Inglehart, *Cosmopolitan Communications: Cultural Diversity in a Globalized World*

Reece Peck, *Fox Populism: Branding Conservatism as Working Class*

Victor Pickard, *America's Battle for Media Democracy: The Triumph of Corporate Libertarianism and the Future of Media Reform*

Sue Robinson, *Networked News, Racial Divides: How Power and Privilege Shape Public Discourse in Progressive Communities*

Margaret Scammell, *Consumer Democracy: The Marketing of Politics*

Patrick Sellers, *Cycles of Spin, Strategic Communication in the U.S. Congress*

Adam F. Simon, *The Winning Message: Candidate Behavior, Campaign Discourse*

Daniela Stockmann, *Media Commercialization and Authoritarian Rule in China*

Bruce A. Williams and Michael X. Delli Carpini, *After Broadcast News: Media Regimes, Democracy, and the New Information Environment*

Gadi Wolfsfeld, *Media and the Path to Peace*

For EU product safety concerns, contact us at Calle de José Abascal, 56–1°,
28003 Madrid, Spain or eugpsr@cambridge.org.

www.ingramcontent.com/pod-product-compliance
Ingram Content Group UK Ltd.
Pitfield, Milton Keynes, MK11 3LW, UK
UKHW010250140625
459647UK00013BA/1779